OTHER TITLES FROM
FRAN McMANUS & WENDY RICKARD

Eating Fresh from the Organic Garden State

Cooking Fresh from the Bay Area

D1451117

COOKING
FRESH

from the

MID·ATLANTIC

Tantalizing Recipes, Celebrated Chefs,
and Conversations on the Essential Nature
of Small-Scale Organic Farming

Foreword by James Howard Kunstler

Introductions by Nora Pouillon *&* Ann Harvey Yonkers

Compiled *&* Edited by Fran McManus *&* Wendy Rickard

EATING FRESH
PUBLICATIONS

*Dedicated
to Hattie,
Florence,
Frances, and
Lorna Crute
for nurturing
in me a
love of life,
a commitment
to family, and
pride in my
Virginia roots.*

—F.M.

*And to the
Mid-Atlantic's
intrepid
farmers, who
keep watch over
the land.*

—W.R.

About EATING FRESH[SM]

Eating Fresh seeks to connect consumers to local agriculture and to demonstrate the taste, health, and community benefits of eating local, seasonal, organic food. Through regional cookbooks and by other means, Eating Fresh works to help build local food systems and to spark a national campaign for transforming the way we shop for, cook, and think about food.

Eating Fresh[SM] • 16 Seminary Avenue • Hopewell, NJ 08525
609-466-1700 • www.eatingfresh.com

Cooking Fresh from the Mid-Atlantic

Published by Eating Fresh[SM] Publications
Copyright ©2002 by Fran McManus and Wendy Rickard

Excerpt from *Canneries of the Eastern Shore* reprinted with permission from Tidewater Publishers. "Creecy Greens" reprinted from *Mountain Fireflies* (Yosemite, Calif.: Poetic Matrix Press, 2000) with permission from Jeff Mann. *Saving Seeds: The Growing Threat to Our Agricultural Biodiversity* ©2002 by Peter Jaret.

Cover concept: Diana Howard
Cover photograph: Grant Peterson
Cover illustration: Aaron Kobilis
Cover production: Michelle Speckler and Palmer Uhl
Recipe editor: Gerry Gould
Recipe consultant: Linda Twining
Copy editor: Paula Plantier
All recipes in this book have been tested for home preparation.

Printed in the United States on recycled paper.

First Edition

ISBN: 0-9673670-1-8
Library of Congress Control Number: 2002091591

CONTENTS

CHEFS & RECIPES

No region of the United States has been immune from the fiasco of suburbia, but it was especially hard on the Mid-Atlantic states. Some of the very best farmland in the world lay in New York, New Jersey, Pennsylvania, Maryland, and Delaware— between the great industrial cities. Before World War II, that farmland supplied most of the fresh food those cities received—in season. Farms and cities existed in a mutually reinforcing, integral relationship that was as much cultural as economic. Just the idea that there was a hinterland of plants and animals called *the country* as well as the idea that it was a thing distinct from the awesome man-made artifact called *the city* still mattered in the popular imagination. New Jersey was the Garden State, and Long Island—in F. Scott Fitzgerald's words—was a "fresh green breast of the New World." In Lancaster County, Pennsylvania, Amish farmers with horses still outproduced the budding agritechnocrats of the Midwest, acre for acre. Today we mourn places like these: the paved-over green fields of Parking Lot Nation.

My friends arch their eyebrows when I declare that the great convulsion of suburb building is near its end. They point out that the guys in the yellow hard hats with their grunting front-end loaders still seem to find virgin melon fields to desecrate with new, curvy cul-de-sac streets for the depressing ranks of 4,000-square-foot chipboard-and-vinyl McMansions. The extravagant orgy of destruction still seems to go on with the expectation, apparently, that the denizens of those new housing pods will get along just fine, thank you, on New Zealand lamb, peaches from North Africa, and Caesar salads grown in Mexico to fortify them for their 50-mile commutes to the office park. But I maintain that those remaining suburban housing starts represent the brain-dead twitchings of a soon-to-be-bygone way of life.

The 21st century is hard upon us, and the future is telling us loudly that America is about to change—and pretty drastically so. The cheap-oil fiesta is about over. The drive-in utopia will go with it. The key to understanding what that means to normal life is that all parts of a given system do not have to fail in order for a system as a whole to find itself in deep trouble. We're not going to run out of petroleum overnight, but the oil markets are going to be stressed, strained, and destabilized and so will our dependency on them. Our access to oil in the Mideast may be compromised at any moment by the brutal politics of the region. The stark fact is that most of the crude oil reserves in the world are controlled by people who don't like us. I could go on in this geopolitical vein, but the bottom line is simply this: Forget about living in a drive-in utopia much longer. That phase of American history is drawing to a close—which to me implies that many of its accessory operations may be nearing an end, too, and that includes industrial-style agriculture based on huge, petroleum-based "inputs" producing standardized, sanitized, industrialized "outputs" (crops) that are extravagantly processed and denatured at fantastic economies of scale and transported vast distances to colossal megasupermarkets serving a mass car-dependent base of "consumers." (The sheer inane technobabble of our political lexicon saps the meaning out of the word *economy*, which derives from the Greek *oikonomikos*—of or pertaining to the care of one's particular home on this earth. The salient characteristic of suburbia is that it is composed of places obviously not worth caring about.)

We are going to have to take local farming seriously again. In the future, the remaining open land in the east will have to be valued for more than its potential as McMansion "estates." The production of food is apt to become more rather than less labor-intensive. Those changes, which I can only sketch here, may entail considerable social convulsion. There will be a battle to preserve the suburban status quo, and there will be a fight over the table scraps of economic history when the futility of that battle becomes manifest.

Meanwhile, a whole *culture*, specifically an *agriculture*, is waiting to be recovered from the dumpster of American civilization. We've begun to see it, I think, in the birth of Community Supported Agriculture (CSA) projects—that is, local farms producing food for a local subscriber base. We belong to a CSA here in New York State. CSAs produce everything from arugula to zucchini and sell to local restaurants as well as subscription customers. For one thing, the CSA movement has challenged the common idea that the only sort of farming possible in New York State is dairying. We had, in fact, a much more diverse farming scene here before the invention of the electric milking machine and the refrigerated tank truck, and we will have such an agriculture again.

It fascinates me that American eating habits today are simultaneously better and worse now than they have ever been. Fine ingredients that couldn't be found on our parents' tables combined with higher culinary standards have certainly improved eating aesthetics at the higher end. But any trip to the supermarket reveals classes of poorer Americans who seem to subsist wholly on a diet of soda pop and industrially extruded, salt-laden party snacks. And the results are visible everywhere in unprecedented mass obesity and related illnesses. Since the snack industry is a phenomenon of agribusiness, mass production, and long-range transport, the future localization of agriculture might result in better diets for greater numbers of citizens—including the poor, who have been systematically preyed upon by the minions of Cheez Doodles and Pepsi-Cola. Health should be democratic, a matter of the common good.

Here, in *Cooking Fresh from the Mid-Atlantic*, is an excellent operating manual for this coming restoration of local farming and fresh eating. Here's to finer tables and a better landscape! Bring on the Chincoteague oysters roasted with New Jersey baby spinach and Chester County cream. Let the soil speak and the seasons ring.

James Howard Kunstler
Saratoga Springs, New York
March 2002

COOKING FRESH FROM THE MID-ATLANTIC

Eating is more than a biological need. It's a pleasure. It's an adventure. Sometimes it's a comfort. We sit around a table with friends and loved ones and we eat. We put food out and we taste and we talk. We meet friends at cafés. We take first dates to fine restaurants. We celebrate anniversaries the same way. And we mourn the passing of a loved one over a buffet. In my house, we eat one meal while talking about another.

In every way imaginable, human beings have a love affair with food. Culture is most often expressed through language, the arts, and cuisine. Each culture has its own flavors, and we visit that culture every time we taste its food. Good cooking is more than just technique; it's an expression of our creativity. Who doesn't want to be thought of as a good cook? Whose most vivid memories of childhood don't in some respect include food?

Spoken in those terms, our relationship with food is a happy, healthy, and joyous experience. But that isn't always the case. In many segments of the U.S. population, malnutrition and obesity are health hazards that threaten hundreds of thousands of lives. From the anorexic teenager to the diabetic schoolchild, food has devolved into an unhappy, chaotic obsession. Fresh food has either lost its appeal, become unavailable, or—for a new generation—become a mystery. Fast food is a diet staple for many Americans. But while it's possible to purchase a cheeseburger, French fries, and a large soda for roughly $2, the actual costs of a fast-food-obsessed nation are unbelievably high. According to the surgeon general, some 300,000 Americans die annually from illnesses caused or worsened by obesity. In fact, according to the surgeon general's office, obesity may soon overtake tobacco as the chief cause of preventable death. And that doesn't even begin to address the social, economic, and environmental costs.

So what's going on?

What's happening is that we've lost our connection to the source of our food. Our fast-paced lifestyles have ignited a processed-food industry—both conventional and organic—eager to satisfy our desire to eat lean, mean, and on the go. Because processing strips food of its nutritional content, certain vitamins and minerals must be artificially replaced. And manufacturers' promises of improved memories and higher energy levels are equally artificial. Sadly, that same industry would have us believe that fresh foods—fruits and vegetables from small-scale, sustainable, and organic farms—are unnecessary, if not downright dangerous. And even if we don't believe that, we resign ourselves to the notion that small-scale farms are quaint relics of a bygone era; that they're not the future of farming; that they're not going to feed the world.

The facts, however, say otherwise. Small-scale, sustainable, and organic farming is not only feasible; many experts say it is also the only viable form of farming. And it is the only model that offers any hope of sustaining us in the future. Small-scale farms—the same ones that dot the landscape of the Mid-Atlantic from the Chesapeake Bay to the Shenandoah Valley—are where you'll find the highest-quality, freshest, and most flavorful foods. And while it may be difficult—if not impossible—to create a diet that is entirely local, eating locally has a number of culinary, social, economic, and environmental advantages, many of which are described in these pages.

Cooking Fresh from the Mid-Atlantic is based on an old idea that is taking hold again. It is born out of the belief held by great chefs that foods grown and raised on small-scale sustainable and organic farms are the freshest, most delicious foods possible. From those chefs' point of view, ingredients that travel short distances from farm to table—and that are raised by skilled farmers who grow for flavor and not volume—make them look good.

The social, economic, and environmental benefits are equally compelling. Small-scale farms and the farmers who run them give more to their communities in taxes than they require in services, the farms beautify the landscape and communicate the heritage of a region, and the farmers serve as stewards of the land. Most important, small-scale farms offer a measure of food security to a region by minimizing the region's dependence on food shipped from other parts of the country—or even other parts of the world.

Cooking Fresh from the Mid-Atlantic is not a diet book. It's a book about what it means to connect with your region: to taste its flavors, to smell its soil, and to be invested in its future. It brings together great chefs and remarkable farmers, many of whom have been growing and raising food in the region for generations. It's not about encouraging you to buy their products in order to artificially prop up their businesses. It's about buying their products because they're better than any others you can buy.

Spend some time with *Cooking Fresh from the Mid-Atlantic,* and then spend some time getting to know your local farmers.

Eat fresh. Eat local.

Fran McManus
Wendy Rickard
Hopewell, New Jersey
October 2002

*We would like to extend endless thanks
and deep gratitude...*

ACKNOWLEDGMENTS

...to the chefs, farmers, and authors who contributed so graciously to this book. Your generosity and enthusiasm helped us define—and realize—our vision.

...to Gerry Gould, Grant Peterson, Paula Plantier, and D. Teddy Diggs. Your individual and collective talents, skills, and expertise challenged us to go further than we imagined possible. We look forward to many future collaborations.

...to all of you who led us to great Mid-Atlantic chefs and farmers and who took the time to share your knowledge, experience, and opinions on local foods, community canneries, and small-scale farming. To Eugenia Anderson-Ellis, Cathy Belcher, T. Robins Buck, Ruth Burnette, Aubrey Davis, Shirley Estes, Tony Evans, Charlie Franks, Chris Fullerton, Jeanne Nye Harris, Otis Hawker, Aileen C. Martin, Larry McPeters, Herman Melton, Dr. Orson K. Miller Jr., Henry Mitchell, Trish Murphey, John Parker, Bernie Prince, Bill Russell, Dave Robishaw, Joel Salatin, Cinda Sebastian, Clifton Slade, Emmett Snead, Herb Stiles, Greg Stoner, and Ann Harvey Yonkers. And to Docia Pillow, Annie Lynskey Lovell, and everyone down at the Brosville Community Cannery for being so generous with their time, their recipes, their homegrown foods, and their tales of community life built around community canneries.

...to the friends and family who gave us access and insight into the Mid-Atlantic. To Richard Batiuk for pointing us toward the experts on the forces that shape the health of Chesapeake Bay. To Bill and Cheryl Estes for sharing in some great road trips and fabulous meals. To Tim and Carol Anne Kernodle for making sure we didn't miss Southside Virginia's community canneries or their delicious cantaloupes. To Margaret Scott for a firsthand experience with a true country ham. To Martha and Philip Stafford for sharing their connections to Virginia small-farm products and the chefs who use them. And to George Swingler for being so generous with his time, his knowledge, and his incredible home cooking.

...and to coworkers, friends, and family at home, whose time, energy, and support made this project happen. To Palmer Uhl for cheerfully answering our many cries for technical and culinary aid. To Ed Batejan of Nassau Street Seafood for advice and troubleshooting tips. To Linda Twining for sharing her cooking secrets. To Roger Bollentin and Laurent Chapuis for their wine expertise. To Coby Green-Rifkin for keeping us together and making us look so good. To Ira Greenberg for making sure we always remember how important the work is and for helping us move ahead. And to Herb and Ian Mertz for their loving companionship during the many culinary, roadside, and barnyard adventures that led to the creation of this book.

WHY CHEFS CARE ABOUT SUSTAINABLE AGRICULTURE

"The earth does not belong to man; man belongs to the earth. (All things are connected like the blood that unites us all.) Man did not weave the web of life; he is merely a strand in it. Whatever he does to the web, he does to himself."

—CHIEF SEATTLE

by Nora Pouillon

Chef/Owner of Restaurant Nora and Asia Nora, Washington, D.C.

Today a chef is more than someone who runs a restaurant and puts food in front of customers. Chefs have become role models, setting an example for consumers. People look to chefs to guide them in making food choices not only in the restaurant but also at home. The majority of people don't spend a great deal of time cooking or gardening anymore. They've become distanced from their land and food supply. People rely on chefs to restore that connection and to convey the concept that food isn't grown in a supermarket; it's grown by a farmer.

We chefs need to ensure that our animal and plant products stay preserved; after all, they are the natural resources with which we earn our living. We need to make the decision not to squander our resources but to use them intelligently, so that we have enough left over for the next generation. As a chef, I understand that I have a considerable amount of power and that with that comes a moral obligation to wield that power in a knowledgeable and responsible fashion.

American food is often served in an unhealthy manner—oversized portions, all-you-can-eat buffets, deep-fried, and saturated-fat laden—all of which have contributed to some of the overwhelming health problems that are evident in the United States. Now chefs are thinking about the impact they make, from the origin of the food they serve to the portion size and balance of a dish, to the fate of the leftovers.

There are questions that need to be raised about our food supply: Why is there such a prevalence of health problems among livestock, such as foot-and-mouth disease and mad cow disease? What will the impact of genetically modified foods be on the health of humans and the environment? If chefs want to be recognized and leave their mark on society, they will have to make an effort to guide consumers, many of whom are becoming wary of the food they eat and many of whom find themselves relying on culinary professionals to provide safe, nutritionally sound food for them.

I work with local farmers who raise certified organic foods for me. In return, I pay them what they need to survive. It's a mutually fulfilling and respectful relationship. Those farmers and I share the same philosophy, and we understand each other's needs and challenges. Fostering good relationships with farmers and paying them what they deserve ensure that chefs will have good, wholesome products that haven't drained the earth of its resources.

I believe we must do what we can to take care of the earth and its resources. By doing so, we will leave it to the next generation so they too can enjoy the natural richness that this planet provides. Supporting a sustainable agriculture system will not only help us achieve that goal; it will also help us serve up delicious culinary creations for years to come. ▪

FARMING IN THE CHESAPEAKE WATERSHED

Maryland. Virginia. West Virginia. Delaware. Pennsylvania. The region stretches from the Atlantic beaches past the prodigious shore of the Chesapeake Bay, through the fertile and rolling Piedmont to the soft rounded shoulders of the Appalachian Mountains, over the blue and green beauty of the Shenandoah Valley to one mountain range short of the Ohio and Mississippi river drainage. Although John Smith saw only the coastline of the Chesapeake Bay, he glimpsed the possibilities of the whole Mid-Atlantic region when he wrote, "Heaven and earth never agreed better to frame a place for man's habitation."

These lands supported permanent and thriving communities of Native Americans, who fished with weirs in the rivers and bays, burned clearings in the forests where they hunted the abundant game, and planted the sustaining trinity of corn, beans, and squash. These were the beginnings of American agriculture.

The new chapter of agriculture began when the Europeans, who initially huddled in primitive settlements along the coastlines, moved out into the landscape, cleared forests with fire and ax, and plowed and planted not only to feed themselves but also to trade with the mother country, England. America's first commercial agricultural crop was tobacco, and the African slaves, imported to work the vast waterside plantations, became the bitter human hostages to that crop. Agriculture was already shaping the new America.

In the 18th and early 19th centuries, when more than 90 percent of American citizens were engaged in agriculture, the patterns of settlement mapped their close relationship to—and reliance on—the land. Cities and towns located themselves on rivers and streams surrounded by farmland that fed and clothed the growing population. For the early settlers, living in the Mid-Atlantic meant "eating your landscape": living off and depending on the nearby landscape. Even today, when we have cut through and paved over too many of these fertile fields and dammed too many of its rivers, the land that remains still marks the turn of the seasons providing sustenance and the pleasure and reassurance of a working landscape.

In early spring, when the chill is barely gone from the air, the athletic, iridescent shad swim upstream to spawn in quiet inland creeks, and the serviceberry bush, called the shad bush by the locals, puts out white blossoms on bare branches signaling this annual migration from the land. The full moon of May usually means the first big harvest of soft-shell crabs as Atlantic blue crabs emerge from the muddy depths of Chesapeake Bay to search out eelgrass in which to shed their shells. Summer means plump ears of sweet corn boiled, buttered, and on the cob and fat slices of the pinkish and deeply flavorful Brandywine tomato named for and prized by the

by Ann Harvey Yonkers
Manager of FRESHFARM Markets, Washington, D.C.

citizens of the valley of the same name in Pennsylvania. Pears from the foothills of the Appalachian Mountains announce fall. Most of them bear foreign names and pedigrees, except the early-ripening Bartlett—named for Yankee Enoch Bartlett, who brought them from England—and the diminutive Seckel, whose lovely green-to-russet-tinged skin makes it picture-perfect for preserving whole. Winter means country hams, cured and smoked the old-fashioned way over hickory or fruitwood, and a plate of sweet and milky Chesapeake Bay oysters eaten overlooking Baltimore harbor.

Today all of these vast resources are threatened from the great "protein factory" of the Chesapeake estuary to the fertile farms and rivers of the region. The Mid-Atlantic region is the second-most-threatened area of farmland in the United States, where—as a nation—we are losing 1.2 million acres of farmland per year. Instead of "eating our landscape," most of us now live in developments named for the farms destroyed to build our houses. Instead of relying on farmers and fishermen just down the road, we rely on farmers and fishermen 1,500 to 3,000 to 9,000 miles away to provide our food.

There is another way. We have options. As Wendell Berry said, "Eating is an agricultural act," and each time we eat, we can choose to vote with our food dollars for another way of life. We can shop at our farmers markets, join a Community Supported Agriculture arrangement with a local farm, purchase local produce offered by major regional grocery stores, or patronize restaurants serving local food. And when we shop or dine out and don't find these choices, we can ask for them. Remember: nothing is more persuasive than an informed and committed consumer.

As for a vision for the future, we have only to consult our past. When George Washington, our founding father and a farmer, looked around at the abundant natural resources of this region, he acknowledged "the great advantage which nature and circumstances have placed within our reach." Now it is time to honor our early and continuing debt to this beautiful land and to begin making choices that protect it. It's time for the delicious revolution. ▪

WINTER

EXPLORING THE CULINARY BENEFITS OF SMALL-SCALE, LOCAL AGRICULTURE & CELEBRATING THE FLAVORS OF WINTER IN THE MID-ATLANTIC

WINTER FARE

APPLE CIDER
APPLES
ARUGULA
ATLANTIC MACKEREL
BEEF
BEEF (FORAGE FED*)
BEETS
BISON
BLACK SEA BASS
BLUE CRAB
BOK CHOI
BRUSSELS SPROUTS
CABBAGE
CARROTS
CELERIAC
CLAMS
CLAMS (FARMED*)
CONCH
COUNTRY CURED HAM
CREECY GREENS
DAIKON RADISHES
EGGS (CHICKEN)
EGGS (FORAGE FED*)
FARMSTEAD CHEESES (AGED)
FLOUNDER
GARLIC
GREENS
HAYMAN POTATOES
HONEY
JERUSALEM ARTICHOKES
KALE
LEEKS

MONKFISH
MOZZARELLA (FRESH)
MUSHROOMS
ONIONS
OYSTER MUSHROOMS
OYSTERS
PARSNIPS
PEANUTS
PEARS
PERCH (WHITE & YELLOW)
PORK
PORK (FORAGE FED*)
POTATOES
PUMPKINS
RABBIT (FARM RAISED*)
RABBIT (FORAGE FED*)
RADISHES
RAINBOW TROUT (FARMED*)
RICOTTA (FRESH)
ROCKFISH (STRIPED BASS)
RUTABAGAS
SALSIFY
SCALLOPS
SCUP
SEA TROUT (GRAY)
SHAD & SHAD ROE
SHALLOTS
SHIITAKE MUSHROOMS
SPINACH
SQUID
TILAPIA (FARMED*)
TOMATOES (GREENHOUSE)
TURNIPS
VEAL
WINTER SQUASH

* SEE PAGE 233

CREECY GREENS

(for Aunt Sadie)

Christmas shopping in Roanoke I saw them:
sandy spiders for sale in the farmers market,
a treat few outside Appalachia would recognize.

From the barren flats above the cliffs,
those riverbank rocks time raised to mountainside,
you gathered creecy greens, age and autumn
stiffening your spinster stoop. Over the sink
you hunched them, rinsing off grit.
How long they simmered I do not know,
the shy child I was choosing the affections
of moss and oak, the elfin fancies of ferns.

Like the Mann farm, slopes too steep for surplus,
you were too stern for me, slapping my back
your only touch, made formal by poverty.
Perhaps you thought me weak, loving
books over gardens as I did. I preferred
the Ferrells, my father's other family branch,
all the abundance that permits warmth,
the closest to landed gentry West Virginia ever had,
huge bottomland farms portioned off
and lost long before the deed descended to me.

As you died long before my manhood,
long before I knew how few are arable bottomlands
or any abundance, how the sediments of solitude
may silt up a lifespan like yours or mine,
the way a small pond slowly fills with sedges
and cattails. It is your mountain blood that allows
this endurance, as I clean meticulous a batch
of creecy greens, snow blowing in again beyond
the steamed windowpanes. I am strong enough now,
boxing away a silver ring, raking leaves off graves
as frost seizes the limbs, as silver petals
in my weary beard. This skill you embodied:
how to live on weeds, how the wilderness feeds us
if we know which plants to pluck. How to season
spareness with fatback, how rich pot-liquor is:
with homebaked biscuits we sop up every drop.

—JEFF MANN

FARM LIFE IN WINTER

Cold, crisp, clear, quiet—the enormous stillness of winter on the farm. People who think life in the country is quiet have never lived on a farm. Gone in winter are the sounds of a tractor rumbling by, day after day pulling plows, tillers, mulch layers, and planters. Gone are the sounds of delivery trucks bringing various fuels, parts for machinery built long ago, seeds, seeds, seeds, and more seeds, soil mixes and flats for transplants, baskets, containers, and tools of the trade. Gone is the constant noise of trucks and tractors carrying the people who work on the farm. Missing are the voices as the produce is picked, pulled, cut, washed, and stored for market. Voices, honed by years on the farm, that carry their message without the use of radios or cell phones. Good strong lungs are our communication tools.

The quiet in the winter evening is the time for lists. There are never-ending lists of things to do, fix, and buy. We make lists of equipment, well used during the season, that needs repairs. We make lists of equipment that just gave up—that will not be coaxed for another year's service—and that needs to be replaced. There are lists of farm chores that never get done during the season and that might be done only in the quiet pace of winter. There are lists of household tasks that are tackled only in the slower days of winter. We make lists for nursery stock orders and seed orders. Hours are spent reading, studying, and dreaming over seed catalogs. Decisions made now as to when, where, and what to plant will affect all of next season. Choices made now determine how many employees will be needed next year, how much capital will be needed to start the season, and how much profit is possible for the farm operation. If too much is planted, you can lose most of your crops due to lack of management and insufficient labor. If too little is planted, there is inadequate cash flow to continue the farming operation. There is a very fine line between success and failure for vegetable farmers. Choices made concerning orchard operations—more trees, fewer trees—affect production in three to five years. And pruning and trimming decisions affect next year's crop.

Winter is a season of contemplation. It is a chance to revisit seasons past, a chance to enjoy the beauty that surrounds you. An afternoon walk takes you through crisp air. Leaves crunch as they fall. Staring at freshly plowed earth, you remember what has been there before and you imagine what will be there next. Winter is the time to reevaluate the life choices we make. Farming is a rewarding occupation on many levels, though very rarely economically rewarding. In order to maintain the farm and a rural lifestyle, most small family farmers live simply, without many of the modern capital goods. And the quiet beauty of winter reaffirms the farmer's decision to stay on the land.

Cold, crisp, clear, quiet—the first snow of the season blankets the earth. Clean and white, spreading across the landscape until the scene becomes surreal. Failures of the past year are forgotten. Even memories of successes are slowly fading away. Work stops. The land is still. Like a parent with a newborn, the farmer and the land sleep. ∎

Sunnyside Farm & Orchards is home to some of the region's freshest and best-tasting fruits and vegetables. The 245-acre farm—with its sloping land, greenhouse, and antebellum main house—has been tended by the Huyett family since the Civil War. Today Jim and Barbara Huyett spend the winter boning up on food trends in preparation for spring planting. In season, they can be found in the fields and orchards with their nectarines, plums, strawberries, bok choi, eggplants, and Asian melons or at the local farmers markets.

by Barbara B. Huyett
Sunnyside Farm & Orchards, Charles Town, West Virginia

THE CONNECTION BETWEEN GREAT FLAVOR & GREAT FARMING

by Chris
Fullerton
Tuscarora
Organic Growers
Cooperative

Many who are serious about eating well accept it as given that the most flavorful foods start with basic ingredients from small-scale local farms. The best chefs base their menus on the fruits and vegetables and the eggs and meats that are in season and from regional sources. And what backyard gardeners haven't sworn taste allegiance to their vine-ripened tomatoes above all others? Such biases for the flavors of the locally grown and for the family grown are opinions built on experience that is based on season after season of satisfying meals. But why should that be so? Why should these foods taste so good?

Before we can explore those questions, it is important to inquire about the nature of flavor itself. What we refer to as the taste of food is a combination of the chemical sensory stimuli detected by taste buds on the tongue and—to a greater degree of discrimination—the olfactory cells within the nose. Brillat-Savarin described it more poetically: "Smell and taste form a single sense, of which the mouth is the laboratory and the nose is the chimney." Our smell and taste receptors have evolved over eons to detect and distinguish between thousands of different chemical compounds at the molecular level. Although still poorly understood, it is believed that what we experience as flavor is the recognition by these receptors of the differing molecular shapes of various chemicals.[1]

The chemicals are primarily in the form of volatile gases. Food scientists interested in flavor use sophisticated equipment to detect the compounds at extremely low levels and can create a flavor map for any particular food. They have discovered two things: first, that chemicals can communicate flavors at extremely low concentrations, such as a few parts per trillion, and second, that some rich aromas are composed of volatile gases from nearly a thousand different chemicals. That basic scientific understanding of flavor, in conjunction with the emergence of large-scale food processing, has led to the creation of a flavor industry, which seeks to recreate the flavors that have been lost in the food manufacturing process.[2] Whether or not the scientists have succeeded is a matter of debate.

This focus on the flavor restoration of processed foods has largely shaped the agenda of agricultural researchers. Most serious study of flavor by the mainstream agricultural establishment involves attempting to correct off-odor or off-flavor in foods produced through new industrialized processes.[3] One of the first commercial products developed by means of genetic engineering was the inappropriately named Flavr Savr tomato. The real aim was not better flavor but longer shelf life (slowness to rot) and better shippability. Its lackluster taste was probably a good part of the reason for its failure.

I work with a farmer who grows about 25 acres of mixed organic vegetables, roughly 2 acres of which are devoted to tomatoes. For years he asked his local extension agent for help to grow a more flavorful tomato, and all he got was a brush-off. Flavor preferences are too variable, insisted the well-trained agricultural expert; it's no use trying to work on such an elusive, unquantifiable problem. The agent much preferred to work on increasing production or preventing diseases. But the farmer insisted in pursuing his own research into flavor; he had tasted better tomatoes—he loved to eat a great-tasting tomato, in fact—and he wanted to find out why his farm wasn't producing tomatoes that met his exacting flavor standards.

One of the reasons this grower is well versed in competing tomato flavors is that he's a member of the marketing cooperative I manage: Tuscarora Organic Growers. One of the things I've learned by working with our group of farmers over the years is that certain fruits and vegetables do much better on some farms than on others. And I'm not talking only about yields and resistance to diseases. One farm might have the most flavorful melons around but might turn out blackberries that are too sour to sell. Another might succeed at producing sweet berries but fail at sweet bell peppers. These are farms less than 50 miles from one another in the same river valley, growing during the same season, and sometimes growing identical varieties of melons or berries or tomatoes. Small differences in soil, elevation, and microclimate lead to drastically different flavors in the harvested crops.

The French have a name for the phenomenon: *terroir.* It's actually an abbreviation of *goût de terroir*, which translates literally as "flavor of the soil." The term is heard most often in discussion of wines, although it has also been applied to cheeses and other artisanal products produced in traditional ways in particular regions. Those who speak of *terroir* are referring to more than the minerals and other soil components that contribute to a distinctive flavor. The term has a broad connotation that embraces the entire physical environment of a place, the people who live there, and the traditions that have been passed down through generations. It's unfortunately not surprising that the French have a word for this idea—that flavor is inextricably tied to place—and Americans do not.

Soils are complex communities of both animate and inanimate components. Given that flavors themselves are complex mixtures and are detected at infinitesimal concentrations, it's no surprise that one farm's soil and climate will produce flavors different from another's. That view, which recognizes that food production occurs within diverse ecological communities, is most definitely not the view of the agricultural industrialists who control most of U.S. food production. The industrial model of food production strives to standardize as much as possible, the goal being efficiency and uniformity. Industrial farms are more likely to be owned by corporations, to operate monocultures on a huge scale, to use synthetic chemical fertilizers,

cooperative

Tuscarora Organic Growers Cooperative (TOG) connects organic family farms in the highlands of the Chesapeake Bay watershed with restaurants and retailers in and around Washington, D.C. The co-op was founded in 1988 by six growers, who that first season shipped about 1,500 cases of fresh, local produce. Fourteen seasons later, 16 farmer-owners and other growers produced more than 150 different crops— including fruits, vegetables, herbs, plants, decoratives, eggs, and cheese— and hope to ship 60,000 cases. The TOG warehouse is located on New Morning Farm near Three Springs, Pennsylvania. Chris Fullerton has managed the co-op since 1993.

and to ship their products long distances. Ecological farms are more likely to be owned and operated by families, growing a diversified selection of crops on a smaller scale, building soil health organically, and serving local or regional markets. And the latter farms will produce more flavorful food for four reasons.

1. **Fresher food is more flavorful.** Big industrial farms move their products from farm to consumer through clunky supply chains that can take weeks or months. Smaller farms, primarily through direct marketing, can cut the time down to days or even hours. The reason time makes a difference is the very nature of flavor: those flavor-producing chemicals are volatile, remember? That means they exist for only a brief time, and they then float away or break down. (That's why many recipes call for fresh herbs to be added at the very end, allowing just enough time to release their flavors but not so much time that the flavors fade). In order to help fresh produce survive long supply chains, modern farmers pick some crops underripe—especially fruits—before a full, complex flavor has had time to develop; they then use whatever technology is available to keep their crops from rotting in storage or on the shelves, thereby preserving the external appearance for a long time perhaps but not preventing the subtle internal changes that result in degraded flavor and texture.

   The word *fresh* in the past used to have a specific meaning: just made, or just picked. Now, in our preservative-happy world (with so many products stamped with a "fresh until" date), the definition seems to have become "not rotten." But those of us who've enjoyed truly fresh food know how quickly a ripe raspberry or ear of sweet corn can "get tired," long before it would be considered inedible. A farmer who cares about flavor respects these narrow flavor windows and acts accordingly.

2. **Food produced in healthier soil is more flavorful.** We know that soil and flavor are inextricably linked (remember *terroir?*). Many of the larger, industrial-model farms treat soil as little more than a sterile medium for delivering chemical fertilizers to plants—nitrogen, phosphorous, and potassium (N-P-K)—but in fact, soil is a complex ecological community. While the big three elements N-P-K are important, so too are other components: soil tilth (the amount of organic matter present), soil pH, the living community of microorganisms and invertebrates present in the soil, and the existence of trace elements and minerals. Farmers who don't appreciate that complexity are bound to lose it over time by practicing a kind of farming that mines the soil until it's depleted. Organic farmers, on the other hand, follow a long-term soil-building plan and have their fields tested frequently to monitor the

fields' progress. Rather than use simple chemical fertilizers, they add composted manure, plant cover crops that enhance the soil, and spread rock dusts to provide trace minerals, among countless other strategies.

It is a long-held maxim that healthy soils produce healthy plants that are more resistant to pests and diseases. But it also follows that healthy soils, because they're more complex, provide more of the building blocks that contribute to a plant's flavor. And animals fed on these healthier, more flavorful plants should in turn produce healthier, more flavorful eggs, milk, and meats.

3. **Independent farmers can choose practices that optimize flavor.** Much of U.S. food production occurs under contract to large corporations. Those corporations end up calling a lot of the shots: they provide—for a so-called fair cost—the feed, or seed, or fertilizer, or whatever, along with detailed production procedures that are not to be deviated from. Most of the farmers our co-op serves have been able to resist that neoserfdom. But the choice to farm independently is getting harder to make, as multinational, investor-owned corporations tighten their stranglehold on the U.S. agricultural markets. One of the problems with this corporate-controlled system is that it creates cookie-cutter farms, replicating one system across a diverse landscape. If farmers aren't allowed to make most of the decisions about the farming, that means they cannot choose a variety of plant or breed of livestock that may be better suited to their farm than the one stipulated by corporate fiat. And they're not allowed to decide to let concerns about flavor or quality direct their farming practices if the corporation has already set things up to maximize output, extend shelf life, and minimize variation. Farming is practiced in the complex, highly variable world, and farmers growing the best food can do so only by adapting to their local environments. One-size-fits-all corporate farming is not flexible enough to allow that variation, and flavor is often a casualty.

4. **Farmers operating on a smaller scale know their farms—and their farm products—intimately.** Someone once recommended that farmers shouldn't farm more land than they could walk over in a day. Even that seems like a lot for some of the more-intensive agricultural production like fruit and vegetable growing. The farmers I know think of and manage their farms as a series of patches or fields: This place here is the first to warm in the spring; that place there has always grown good eggplant; fields up top drain more quickly than those in the bottom, et cetera, et cetera. And because their farms are patchworks—not only over space but also over time—they notice things: things like, These Brussels sprouts taste more bitter than the ones grown over there, This

Mid-Atlantic Farm Facts

"Northern Maryland lies within the second-most-threatened U.S. agricultural area, and much of Maryland's Eastern Shore is within the ninth-most-threatened region."

—AMERICAN FARMLAND TRUST'S 1997 FARMING ON THE EDGE REPORT

cheese made in a wet year has texture and color that differ from the cheese made in a dry year, These turnip greens are sweeter after the frost. Such valuable observations can be made only if a farm has diversified into many different crops, if the crops get rotated over time from place to place, and if the farmer and the farmer's family are actually feeding themselves from the land. If those three conditions are met, farming becomes an ongoing experiment, with the kitchen and dinner table as laboratory.

Remember that tomato grower I mentioned who wanted to find out how to grow flavorful tomatoes? I've seen how he responds to a tomato at lunchtime. A bite into a particularly flavorful candidate immediately sets in motion a flood of interrogation, reminiscence, and speculation: What patch did this tomato come from? Which variety is it? How often was the patch irrigated? How was the land there prepared in the spring? What grew there the year before and the years before that? His mind turns over the myriad details, like a plow turning fresh earth, trying to tease out the complex, patterned story that culminated in the sweetly acid burst of "real tomato flavor." During more than 30 years of this kind of intensive lunching, he has seen his farm's tomato flavors improve, even though he hasn't got it all figured out yet. Would this kind of flavor evolution be possible on a farm that grew, say, 3,000 acres of spearmint every year?

There is a common thread throughout these four principles: flavorful food is a natural by-product of farming practices that recognize, honor, and adapt to a complex, ecologically rich world. Just as the industrial science of "flavor creation" cannot compete with the art of fine cooking, the implementation of industrial agricultural practices is not really comparable to the art of nurturing a soil and crops that yield exceptional flavors. In both practices (cooking, farming), the complexity of the real world acts as a kind of foil to reductionist thinking. Those who do not remain open to the incredible diversity of the natural world, who instead attempt to work against it (or in spite of it) will find as their reward an awful blandness. But choosing a world of rich flavors and smells and of variety and diversity and complexity is a challenge. Achieving great flavors—from fields as well as from kitchens—requires intuition, tradition, and artistry as well as a healthy respect for the limitations of scientific knowledge and a basic faith in one's own direct experiences. As long as we have our tongues and noses, some of us will continue to take this challenging, but ultimately delectable, path. ■

1 Harold McGee. *On Food and Cooking: The Science and Lore of the Kitchen* (Collier Books, 1984). Pp. 560-74.
2 Eric Schlosser. *Fast Food Nation: The Dark Side of the All-American Meal* (Houghton Mifflin, 2001). Pp. 120-28.
3 See studies reported by the Agricultural Research Service at www.ars.usda.gov.

Creecy Greens: The Flavor of Home

Creecy greens represent the flavor of home for many in the southeastern United States. *Creecy greens* is also one of the many common names for *Barbarea verna*—a naturalized European native that is both cultivated and gathered in the wild. The young leaves of this extremely hardy cold-weather green are harvested from midwinter until the plant begins to flower in the spring. Ardent fans of creecy greens claim that their sweetness is enhanced by the frost. Although also known as upland or dryland cress, creecy greens are unrelated to watercress or garden cress.

Occasionally used as a winter salad green, creecy greens are eaten most often as cooked greens—like spinach or kale. They're tart, delicious when warmed, and usually served with smoked ham or alone with corn bread and a couple of shakes of vinegar.

Cooking Mixed Greens

A recipe from George Swingler

Clean and wash greens (mustard, kale, and turnip).

Simmer country meat in water for ½ hour before adding greens.

Add greens and make sure there's enough water in the pot to cover them. Boil hard for 15 to 20 minutes.

Lower the heat, cover the pot, and cook for 2 to 2½ hours.

This recipe cooks all fresh greens, including creecy greens.

"Creecy greens are always found growing wild—
USUALLY IN RICH BOTTOMLAND. THEY'RE BEST IN SPRING, WHEN THERE MAY STILL BE A LITTLE ICE ON THE LAND. I RECALL GOING OUT TO PICK THEM THROUGH TIRED AND MELTING SNOW.

MY GRANDMOTHER OLLIE MAE NEELY LILLY WOULD GET SOME CREECY GREENS, RINSE THEM WELL, PUT THEM IN A POT WITH SOME BACON DRIPPINGS AND A BIT OF WATER, AND COOK THEM UNTIL TENDER. SHE MIGHT HAVE ADDED A TOUCH OF CIDER VINEGAR. THAT, WITH CORN BREAD, WAS HARD TO RESIST."

—BEN MAHMOUD, CHARLESTON, WEST VIRGINIA, NATIVE & DISTINGUISHED PROFESSOR EMERITUS, NORTHERN ILLINOIS UNIVERSITY, DEKALB, ILLINOIS

Local Foods Local Flavors

Common names for *Barbarea verna* and its close relatives include:

- American cress
- American yellowrocket
- Belle Isle cress
- Cassabully
- Creasy greens
- Creasy salad
- Creecy greens
- Dryland cress
- Early winter cress
- Early yellowrocket
- Garden yellowrocket
- Highland creasy
- Land cress
- Poor man's cabbage
- Southern winter cress
- Upland cress
- Winter rocket

FOOD, FLAVOR & A SENSE OF PLACE: MAKING THE CULINARY CONNECTION

There is, perhaps, no more powerful connection to our culture, our landscape, and our personal histories than food: The flavor of a perfectly ripened peach awakens long-dormant memories of childhood summers. The oven door opens—filling the kitchen with the smell of roasting lamb—and we are transported to Sunday dinners with relatives long gone. A taste of farmhouse cheese, and we are lost in the memory of last summer's trip to France. Food has the power to connect us to a specific place. Food has the power to bring us home.

Where traditional, regional foods once united and defined communities, consolidation in food processing and agriculture is now homogenizing the American diet. As a result, we are losing the opportunity to experience a place through food. The fast-food chains that now supply a significant portion of meals in the United States strive to be the same everywhere and are, therefore, disassociated from any place that is specific or unique. And global agribusiness has trained the market to value uniformity and cosmetic perfection over regional flavor and seasonal change. Thus, even in our own hometown, we find comfort and familiarity in foods that are unrelated to season or place—foods that are made or grown to taste the same no matter where they're harvested, processed, or served—while the regionally unique, the distinctive, the seasonal, the local are becoming unfamiliar and strange. But locally grown foods and their seasonal nature can tell you much about the place where you live. And for however long you opt to stay put, it is through local foods that you can deepen your connection to your local community.

Physical proximity used to be a defining characteristic of community, and the agriculture and natural features within that community determined the ingredients upon which the region's traditional cuisine was based. But in a new world, we have become unstuck. Community has become detached from place, and proximity has been replaced by shared interest—such as work, hobbies, or religious or political ideology—and the global sourcing of raw and processed foods. Gone are many of the reciprocal relationships upon which community once relied. Gone too is the recognition of culinary, economic, and social destinies that are intertwined.

Farm families that inhabit and work the land they own—as well as watermen who harvest a livelihood from a region's bays and rivers—are local industries that are firmly rooted in place. When they market their products directly to the public, such farmers and watermen stake their financial future on their ability to offer the community superior flavor and on being directly accountable to the people who buy their food. Buying, preparing, and sharing the foods they raise is a wonderful—and delicious—way to strengthen your own local roots and to build a face-to-face commu-

by Fran McManus
Eating Fresh Publications

nity that is dynamic, vibrant, and diverse. And sharing in both the bounty and the lives of regional food producers has the reciprocal benefits of keeping local farming viable while preserving the landscape that you love.

Exploring your region through local foods enables you to experience your community in a variety of ways: It can help you develop both familiarity with the physical attributes of the region and appreciation for what it takes to wrest a living from that land. It can strengthen your emotional connection to the place you live and deepen your relationships with the members of your community. It creates a new way to build a social network and a spiritual and cultural connection to the history of a place. And it can provide an opportunity for you—and your family and friends—to experience the natural world in your hometown. Local foods can give you all of that plus the delicious flavors that come only from food that is truly fresh and raised with a skilled and loving hand.

How to Make the Culinary Connection

- **Explore the Mid-Atlantic Region through Its Food**
  Understanding where, how, and by whom a food is produced enhances your personal sense of the value of that food. Begin by picking a regional food such as oysters. Through the works of such writers as Tom Horton and John Shields, learn about the regional history of oyster gathering, about the life cycles of the native and the introduced species, and about the culture of communities in which the watermen who harvest Chesapeake Bay oysters work and live. Familiarize yourself with the oyster's native habitat and the forces that threaten its long-term health. Visit the places where oysters are harvested, and meet the people who are doing that work. Buy some oysters, take them home, and cook them. Share your meal and your stories with friends. And invite those friends along on your next adventure into vintage apples, country hams, blue crabs, Hayman potatoes, or some other interesting regional food.

- **Eat with the Seasons**
  Farmers understand the effect that seasonal change and weather have on the taste of food. Eating more seasonally will help you develop an understanding of the impact of local weather that extends beyond its ability to determine the success or failure of an outdoor party. You'll taste the connection between rainfall and flavor and understand a farmer's pain when the region is hit by a late frost or a violent hailstorm. You'll tune in to which foods thrive on heat and which are sweetened by the arrival of frost. Eating with the seasons will also help you appreciate the exquisite pleasure of anticipation and be deliberate and totally present as you savor a flavorful food that is available only for a short time in a specific place.

"Food history is as important as a Baroque church. A cheese is as worthy of preserving as a 16th-century building."

—CARLO PETRINI, PRESIDENT AND FOUNDER OF SLOW FOOD

Slow Food

- **Take Weekend Outings That Center on Food**

  Through the work of local food harvesters and within the landscapes in which they work, we find certain visual, auditory, and olfactory signals that define a place as unique. So, the next time you plan a weekend road trip, make local foods a central theme. And while you're on the road, look for clues—like fishing boats, farmland, bays, rivers, and forests—that reveal the sources of local foods. Visit a farmers market, farm stand, or harvest fair. Grab a copy of Roger Yepsen's *Apples*, and seek out old apple varieties at roadside orchards. Spend the night at an on-farm bed and breakfast. When you stop for a meal, look for a restaurant that serves foods from local farms. Next time you visit a region's fine historic homes, pay attention to what's planted in the gardens. Visit the Museum of American Frontier Culture in Staunton, Virginia, to learn about the farmers who first settled the Shenandoah Valley. Make frequent trips to Monticello to examine the types of fruits, vegetables, and herbs that are growing in the gardens and orchards. By seeking out local food producers and tasting their products, you become an active participant in your landscape rather than just a casual observer.

- **Create a Cooking Club**

  Food is always more fun when it's prepared and eaten with friends. A cooking club is a great vehicle for exploring the sources and flavors of local foods. Together with a group of friends, you can forage for local foods and explore them by using new and historical recipes. Hold informal taste tests by buying and trying several varieties of a local food such as peaches, plums, apples, tomatoes, or farmhouse cheeses. Sample, compare, and search for ways to describe what you're tasting. Visit a community cannery and spend the morning working together to preserve some of the local harvest. Read Peter Hatch's *Fruits and Fruit Trees of Monticello*, and then take a field trip to the fall apple tasting at Monticello. Make the structure of the cooking club as formal or as loose as you like. The point is to have fun and to share your passion with other food fanatics.

- **Learn about Mid-Atlantic Regional Cuisine**

  Traditional regional foods reflect the combined culinary traditions of settlers and immigrants and the native and introduced food crops that thrive in that region's climate and soil. In this way, exploring the roots of regional cuisine connects us to local history: Delve into new and old cookbooks that explain the origins of traditional dishes. Host potluck dinners based on historical themes and recipes. And sample the menus of restaurants that build their image around authentic, regional cuisine. But beware: just because a place serves traditional dishes doesn't mean the ingredients were grown nearby. If the menu doesn't say, "We buy from local farmers," be sure to ask. ■

Hayman Potatoes

One of the joys of living along Virginia's Eastern Shore is a little-known but immensely popular gastronomic treasure called the Hayman potato. Described by various food writers as "lowly but noble" and "homely but sweet," these small, palm-size heirlooms are part of a special project of the Nature Conservancy to encourage sustainable agriculture and help preserve the unique environment of the Chesapeake Bay.

While the Hayman is an heirloom variety that has been grown for generations, growers generally grow them either for their own use or to sell locally. Haymans are grown almost exclusively on the Eastern Shore, where they thrive in the loamy soil and warm climate. You have to really love them to grow them, and because they're so delicate, they must be picked by hand and must not be refrigerated or the flesh will deteriorate.

"How dare Eastern Shore folk not share their Haymans! Such a scrumptious thing kept all to yourselves."

—C. L. ROBINSON, 1997

Once harvested, they're still not ready to eat; Haymans need to cure for two weeks to a month to develop their full flavor. Once they do, they're worth it. One columnist wrote that eating one is "as if nature already had blanketed it in a layer of marshmallows. And it's so juicy that when you bake it, you have to place it on metal foil, lest the syrup flood the oven." True Hayman devotees say the moist, smooth flesh doesn't even need butter or salt.

Treasured for their luscious, sweet flesh and smooth, creamy texture, Haymans were introduced in the early 19th century—local legend credits a ship's captain whose surname was Hayman—but production was so limited that nearly the entire crop was consumed by the 50 or so farmers and gardeners who raised them for the pleasure of their families.

Haymans are available from November to April. To get the full enjoyment from Haymans, peel and cut them into 2-inch cubes. Toss with olive oil, salt, pepper, and Herbes de Provence. Bake in the middle or upper third of a preheated 400°F oven for 25 to 30 minutes, turning occasionally or until soft and the exterior has browned.

Or scrub the Haymans and cut into ¼-inch slices. Preheat the oven to 400°F with a baking sheet inside. Spray the baking sheet with vegetable oil, place the Haymans on the sheet in a single layer, and spray the tops of the potatoes. Bake for 10 minutes, turn the slices with a spatula, and bake for an additional 8 to 10 minutes or until browned and crisp. Sprinkle with salt and serve immediately.*

Be warned: Because of their high sugar content, Haymans can turn your hands and utensils black. Peel Haymans quickly just before using them, and wash your hands and utensils immediately.

It's a small price to pay for such a deliciously sweet treat. ▨

Recipes courtesy of Eastern Shore Enterprises.

FINDING FOOD WITH FLAVOR IN THE MID-ATLANTIC

Once you've discovered the flavor of locally grown foods, you'll want to find the farmers.

Marketing is often a neglected part of the farm operation, especially among small farmers. When farmers spend so much time on production, it's difficult to find time to devote to marketing. So if you're looking for fresh, you may need to help yourself—and the farmer—by locating a farm or a farmers market nearby.

The Internet is a great place to start. In the Mid-Atlantic area, try www.farmerlink.com or your state's agriculture department Web site. Either one should land you in proximity to a farm or a farmers market. For example, in my home state, the Virginia Department of Agriculture's Web site is www.vdacs.state.va.us/vagrown. There one can quickly find pick-your-own farms, orchards, or nearby farmers markets. Farmerlink.com is easy to remember and covers the metropolitan Washington, D.C., area extensively. Produced by Therese Haar, the site has extensive farmers market listings. You might also try your county's Web page.

In Fauquier County, Virginia, the Agricultural Development Office is listed in the county government's directory, and the link you'll want is www.co.fauquier.va.us/services/Farm/index.html. On this site you can find an extensive listing of farm products offered directly by local Fauquier farmers: everything from beef, cheese, and chicken to hay, horses, llamas, and more. Your county may offer a similar service.

There's something special about going out and picking your own fruit. In Fauquier County, about 30 minutes (during nonrush hours) from the Washington beltway, two orchards—Heartland and Stribling Orchards—are close to each other and offer a variety of fruits and vegetables. They're located within a mile of I-66 in Markham, Virginia. You can locate both farms on the Virginia Department of Agriculture Web page. They make for a great outing to get fresh fruit, vegetables, and, naturally, fresh air. As a bonus, the bucolic views are some of the best in the world.

On a recent family journey, we visited Westmoreland Berry Farm, which, in our role as farmers, we sold next to at northern Virginia farmers markets years ago. Westmoreland Berry Farm is located near the birthplaces of George Washington and Robert E. Lee. It's a wonderful place that specializes in berries: strawberry, blueberry, and blackberry. But it grows many vegetables too. You haven't lived until you try Westmoreland's Red, White, and Blueberry Sundae. Oh, my! Westmoreland offers fresh-picked or pick-your-own produce, and if you can't make it out to the farm, Westmoreland sells at farmers markets in the D.C. area. Check it out on the Web at westmorelandberryfarm.com.

Last, a fantastic place to find fresh fruits and vegetables is a farmers market. Such markets are usually held one or two days a week in a parking lot, rain or shine. They offer a wide variety of fresh produce grown within

by Peter D. Mitchell
Fauquier County Agricultural Development Office

100 miles of the market, and some even offer meat products, eggs, breads, and jams. There's something wonderful about eating a locally grown tomato or ears of sweet corn fresh out of the field. Along those lines, if you want produce brought to you, many Community Supported Agriculture (CSA) groups have sprouted up. In a CSA, you pay the farmer in advance and receive a share of the bounty each week during the season. With CSAs you get a good variety of product in tune with the growing season.

You can't beat the taste of a homegrown tomato. Hope you can find one near you. ▪

Preserving
the Harvest

Dried Fruits & Vegetables

by Joy Lokey
L'Esprit de Campagne
(see page 109)

The Shenandoah Valley is one of the richest, most fertile valleys in the world. The farmers in this Virginia region are well-known for their delicious apples, peaches, cherries, and other fruits and vegetables. With its hot, sunny days, cool evenings, and languid breezes coming off the Blue Ridge Mountains, Virginia's temperate climate means flavor in farming.

Tomatoes were a viable crop here long before agribusiness was invented and commercial fruit and vegetable production moved to the west. There, chemicals are sprayed, the fruit is picked green by machines, and the tomatoes are gassed so they can be shipped thousands of miles away to the homemaker who demands a tomato for that midwinter dinner salad. Unfortunately, with long-distance production, flavor went out the door.

A new generation of farmers has come to the rescue by realizing there are other ways of farming and preserving their harvests. Just like in the good old days, when there was nothing like slicing a fresh-picked garden-grown tomato, people are again demanding quality in their fruits and vegetables. While there's nothing like a fresh garden tomato, a great alternative, especially during the winter months, is a beautiful, red, dried tomato. Dried tomatoes have a sweet, robust flavor and a soft, chewy texture that brings to mind summer's harvest.

Drying fruits and vegetables is one of the world's oldest preservation methods. In Italy, tomatoes and other fruits are dried right in the fields. In Virginia, apples are still sliced and laid out to dry on top of hot tin roofs in the summertime. Preserving your harvest by drying gives you a top-quality product while maintaining true flavor and nutritional qualities. The flavors are concentrated, so a little goes a long way.

Traditional recipes for, say, spaghetti sauce, pasta dishes, soups, and salads all are enhanced by using dried tomatoes. No need to rehydrate these dried ones, and you can cook them with no oil: moist-heat cooking plumps them up. The same goes for dried fruits. For instance, dried blueberries plump up beautifully in a muffin without the berries' running into your batter and turning it gray.

Dried tomatoes and fruits are fun and easy to use. Experiment with your favorite recipes. Your imagination is your only limitation. ▪

THE NATURAL SCIENCE OF CREATING FLAVOR ON THE FARM

by Joel Salatin
Polyface Farm

Virginia's Shenandoah Valley was the prairie of the Mid-Atlantic region before being settled by Europeans, who brought with them cultivation and cropping systems native to their German, Scotch-Irish, and English climates. At an elevation of nearly 2,000 feet and receiving a sporadic, 31-inch annual rainfall, this 2,000-square-mile valley figures prominently in any historical analysis of pre–Civil War America.

Known as the Breadbasket of the Confederacy, many of the Shenandoah Valley's highly eroded croplands returned to perennial pastures and forests after the opening of the western grain belt. Transferring an agriculture from Western Europe's temperate, misty rainfalls to this clay-soil, thunderstorm-prone, low-organic-matter area created deep gullies when millions of tons of topsoil washed into Chesapeake Bay.

Purchasing one of those worn-out, gullied farms in 1961, the Salatin family began planting trees, building ponds, composting, and healing the soil. Polyface, Inc., The Farm of Many Faces, is a tribute to land stewardship and livestock symbiosis. Entering its third generation, the farm is one of America's oldest nonchemical agricultural enterprises.

A visitor driving down the farm lane would see Feathernets, where a thousand nonhybrid laying hens enjoy a quarter acre of pasture in the safety of electrified portable netting that keeps predators out and the birds in. Shaded and sheltered under 20-foot-by-20-foot hoop structures on skids, the birds are moved every three days to a fresh "salad bar" of perennial prairie polyculture.

In the same field, the Lambrighini provides fresh pasture for forage-fattened lambs. The portable electric fence and shade-cloth shelter protect the lambs and promote succulent forage growth.

In another pasture, 50 portable 10-foot-by-12-foot-by-2-foot-high chicken shelters house 70 to 85 broilers apiece. Moved daily to a fresh spot, the shelters resemble a flock of migratory geese as they wend their way across the pasture. This gives the meat chickens a completely sanitary lounge area every day, protects the chicks from weather and predators, and ensures high forage ingestion due to its freshness.

Salad Bar Beef graces a pasture near the broilers, mowing the grass down to chicken length. Moved daily to a fresh paddock, the cattle mimic the mobbing and movement patterns of herbivores the world over. Never staying in the same spot, herbivores build soil and push plant succession forward by certain natural grazing principles that when duplicated domestically, create the same carbon-sequestering and soil-building grasslands found in rich prairies worldwide.

A portable electric fence offers livestock control to mimic those grazing principles, stimulating additional solar collection via photosynthesis in energy-equilibrium forage. The farm is actually a giant green solar collector, producing biomass to feed animals and producing the nutrient cycle that in turn maintains healthy biological activity in the soil. Forage-fattened beef contains high levels of conjugated linoleic acid.

Pigaerators enjoy the physiological distinctives of pigness in rotated pig pastures. Allowed to roam in quarter-acre pasture paddocks, the pigs receive a fresh paddock every 10 to 14 days. They cultivate with their nose plows, eat forages, wallow in self-made mud holes, and eat grain from a weatherproof feeder. This combination of exercise, salad greens, and carbohydrates produces pork that is rose-colored and dense. Coloring indicates high vitamin and mineral content.

Each plant and animal should be provided a habitat that most allows it to perfectly express and achieve physiological distinctiveness. The eating of food is fundamentally a biological function, not an industrial one. Any food system that views plants and animals as no different from copper fittings or extruded plastic dolls will inherently generate pharmaceutically dependent, immunodeficient, life-depraved people.

Just as birds in nature always follow herbivores, the Eggmobiles follow the cattle to sanitize the paddocks with free-ranging laying hens. The hens scratch through the dung pats, eating pathogens and parasite larvae and all the while incorporating the nutrients into the soil. In addition, the birds graze and eat crickets, grasshoppers, and other bugs.

Forage-based rabbits aid turkeys that are grazing, debugging, and fertilizing the vineyard and orchard. Vegetable gardens and currant tomatoes volunteering in the greenhouses where rabbits and laying hens spend the winter offer fresh-picked delicacies. Polyface is an attempt to balance the landscape with woodland, riparian zones, and grasslands supporting cattle (buffalo), sheep (elk and deer), and poultry (turkey, grouse, and pheasant). The natural flora and fauna, stewarded by the reverent farmer, yield far more nutritious, delicious, and ecologically enhanced food than does irradiated, chlorinated, genetically engineered, extruded, medicated, and adulterated factory fare.

In all livestock, the pasture-based, freedom-to-gambol lifestyle enhances texture and taste. Meat is firmer and more dense—not tough—and better colored. Pork especially carries a beautiful rose color, which is created by the carotenes in the forage and which indicates higher vitamin and mineral content. Egg yolks contain a natural deep-orange color, and the whites whip up significantly higher for meringues. Pastured eggs enhance moisture in pastries and often double shelf life. Yield in baked items actually increases up to 20 percent.

The majority of fresh produce consumed in the Washington, D.C., area is grown outside of the Mid-Atlantic region.

—FROM THE CAPITAL
AREA FOOD BANK'S
REPORT ENTITLED
FROM FARM
TO TABLE:
MAKING THE
CONNECTION IN
THE MID-ATLANTIC
FOOD SYSTEM

Lamb carries a naturally rich taste rather than the off taste—or gamy sense—associated with its grain-fed counterparts. Pastured turkeys probably carry more taste and texture positives over their factory-raised cousins than any other species. The meat has a naturally distinct flavor but carries a rich moistness all the way to the plate. Perhaps the most dramatic culinary response to pasture-based systems lies in the broths and stocks, from beef to poultry. Because the polyunsaturated fats are higher and the saturated fats are lower, broths yield remarkable clarity and softness, not to mention superior taste.

Polyface supplies roughly 400 families, 35 gourmet restaurants, several metropolitan buying clubs, and numerous farmers markets with superior food that celebrates the Shenandoah Valley's pre-European ecology. The proof is in the eating. ■

Regional Family Farms

Virginia Grown is the label to look for when you want to support Virginia growers and want to have access to a steady stream of the freshest food available anywhere. So, the next time you shop, look for the "Virginia Grown—Fresh from the Farm" slogan on posters, banners, and price cards. The promotion is the brainchild of the Virginia Department of Agriculture and Consumer Services, which offers a wealth of information on its Web site at www.vdacs.state.va.us/vagrown/. There you'll find a guide to pick-your-own and select-your-own Virginia farm products and farmers markets. The Special Comments section adds information about activities, festivals, tours, lectures, and other events and attractions planned for participating locations.

I spent the first 20 years of my life growing up in the city, blissfully unaware of how little I knew about where our food comes from and how much work is involved in producing it. For the past 30 years, I've been an organic farmer in rural Virginia, wondering how *everyone else* could be so ignorant of where food comes from and how good it could taste.

WHAT KIDS (& GROWN-UPS) ARE ASKING ABOUT FOOD

We raise organic beef and eggs and have had a pick-your-own strawberry business and market garden over the years. After a while, one forgets that not everyone knows about these things. About 10 years ago, we started offering farm tours and discovered that the things we took for granted were a great mystery to most others: things like how a chicken lays an egg without a rooster, or questions like, Aren't cows with horns bulls? and What do you have to spray to make your farm organic?

We find that most of the people who take our farm tours and classes are children. Fortunately, the children are comfortable asking the questions, thereby saving the adults—who also want to know—the embarrassment. No, chickens don't need a rooster to lay an egg, but without a rooster the egg won't hatch. Horns on a cow are indicative of the breed of cow, not the sex. For example, Jerseys grow horns—both cows and bulls—unless you cut them off when they're calves. Angus cows and bulls never grow horns, and *organic* basically means farming without toxic chemicals.

Other questions also come up from time to time, so we've compiled a list of explanations for the kids who will ask—and the adults who won't.

- **The older the chicken, the larger the egg.** Young hens—known as pullets—that are just starting to lay produce about 300 eggs per year per bird. It's about an egg a day, if you don't count the six-week vacation they take every year. Yes, it's a paid vacation. The color of the egg generally reflects the color of the bird and has nothing to do with the quality of the egg, which is determined by the quality of the feed, the fresh air, the exercise, and the green grazing that the hen has available.

- **There are basically two types of cattle: beef and dairy.** Beef cows produce bull (male) calves to be raised for steaks, roasts, and burgers, and they produce heifer (female) calves to be raised as replacement cows. Dairy cows produce milk for dairy products but only after they've had a calf. The only reason they produce milk is supposedly for the calf. The calf gets plenty of milk because the

by C. L. "Cory" Koral
Jordan River Farm

*Each year,
Delaware
harvests 4,000
to 5,000 acres of
potatoes, making
the vegetable the
state's number
one fresh-market
crop.*

—DELAWARE
DEPARTMENT
OF AGRICULTURE

dairy cow has been bred to produce about 10 times more milk than the calf needs. The richness of cow's milk varies during the year because of variation in the vegetation available to graze. Cows must be fed hay in winter; they have nothing else to eat. That's why during winter their milk is much less rich. You don't see the variation in richness with store-bought milk because it's adjusted at the creamery to be consistent year-round and because it's homogenized so that the cream never settles out.

- **Cheese can be made with any kind of milk from any kind of lactating animal.** The problem is, you have to have a lot of milk to make cheese. For instance, it takes approximately one gallon of cow's milk to make one pound of cheddar. There are many types of cheeses and many, many different methods for producing them. Basically, it requires coagulating the milk and then separating the coagulant, or curd, from the remaining liquid, or whey. Butter is made only from cream, and so it can't be made from homogenized milk.

- **What about flavor?** In the case of grass-fed cows, there are going to be variations in the flavor of the milk. Manufacturers of mass-produced milk adjust the fat content to create milk that is uniform and consistent throughout the year. On our farm, the cows are fed grass most of the year, although in winter they eat hay. That means the flavor of the milk is going to vary depending on the characteristics of the grass they're eating. In spring, when the cows are eating mostly onion grass, the milk will taste oniony. So we use that milk to make cheese. When the grass becomes more lush, the milk becomes more flavorful.

- **What about the flavor of beef?** In the beef industry, cows are fattened on corn in feedlots, which results in meat that is bland. Our cows are strictly grass fattened, which is hard to do in winter. Fattened on grass, cows get more variety in their diets, and the meat is more flavorful. ■

WINTER RECIPES

Baked Rutabagas

SERVES 2 TO 4

1 pound rutabagas, peeled and cut into ¹/₂-inch dice

1 to 2 tablespoons extra virgin olive oil

Sea salt

Freshly ground black pepper

¹/₂ teaspoon dried thyme

Preheat the oven to 400°F. Toss the rutabagas with some of the olive oil, salt, and pepper, and spread in a single layer on a sheet pan. Bake for 30 to 40 minutes until the rutabagas are golden brown and tender. Season with thyme, salt, and pepper and more of the olive oil.

COOKING FOR YOUR HEALTH AND WELL-BEING
Charlottesville, Virginia
Martha Hester Stafford
Chef/Owner

QUICK & BASIC RECIPES FOR WINTER PRODUCE

Braised Cabbage with Onions

SERVES 4 TO 6

2 cups vegetable stock

1 cup apricot juice

1 teaspoon lemon juice

1¹/₂ teaspoons sea salt

Freshly ground black pepper

1 to 2 tablespoons of sugar
(if the apricot juice is not very sweet)

1 tablespoon canola oil

2 medium onions, sliced

1 small head of white cabbage sliced thin

1 to 2 teaspoons caraway seeds

1 tablespoon unsalted butter — more if desired

1. Combine the vegetable stock, apricot juice, lemon juice, salt, and pepper. Bring the mixture to a boil, turn down the heat, and simmer for 5 minutes. Taste for seasoning. If it tastes sour, add a little sugar. The mixture should be very tasty.

2. Heat the oil in a heavy, medium saucepan with a lid. Add the onions and sauté until translucent but not brown.

3. Add the cabbage and caraway seeds, and pour in the seasoned stock. Bring to a boil, turn down the heat, and add the butter. Cover and simmer for about 15 minutes or until the cabbage is tender. Taste, and season with salt, pepper, and more butter if you wish.

Baked Winter Squash

Winter squash varieties develop a very thick skin. The thick skin allows them to be stored for up to 3 months in a cool, dry place, but it also makes them difficult to cut. I suggest preheating an oven to 300°F and placing the whole squash right on the oven rack. Bake it for 30 minutes. Warning: if you forget about it, it could explode! Remove the squash from the oven, and let it sit until cool enough to handle. Cut it in half and scoop out the seeds.

Turn the oven up to 350°F. Put the squash in a pan, cut sides down. Add a small amount of water. Place pan in the oven and continue baking until soft—30 minutes to 1 hour depending on the size and variety of squash.

Scoop out the soft flesh and use it for pies or soup, or mash it with butter or stock and serve with sea salt and pepper. Complementary spices are cinnamon, nutmeg, coriander, cumin, and curry.

Parsnips

Parsnips are delicious when steamed until tender. Their taste is sweet and comforting. While it is best to choose small or medium parsnips, even large ones can be steamed to tenderness if cut into small-enough pieces. Look for smooth, round, firm ones without blemishes. Peel the thin skin off, and if you notice a spongy appearance to the flesh, cut that portion off.

To enhance the natural richness of parsnips, add a little butter or extra virgin olive oil and a sprinkle of sea salt and freshly ground pepper. Herbs and spices that complement parsnips are oregano, thyme, tarragon, chives, cumin, cinnamon, and coriander.

Braised Parsnips

Fill a saucepan with the amount of water that you estimate will just barely cover the parsnips. It's all right if some of the pieces are above the water. Add a few sprinkles of sea salt, and bring the water to a boil. Add the parsnips and return the water to a boil. Turn down the heat, and simmer until tender, about 5 minutes. Serve plain or with any of the suggestions given above.

Braised Parsnips with Oregano

Parsnips

Vegetable stock or water

Fresh oregano

Butter

Sea salt and freshly ground pepper

1. Peel and slice the parsnips into $1/4$-inch coins. Then cut the larger coins into quarters so that all of the pieces are roughly the same size.

2. Create a braising liquid by estimating the amount of stock you'll need to almost cover the parsnips. You can adjust the amount after adding the parsnips. Sprinkle in some oregano—about $1/4$ teaspoon per cup of liquid is a good amount to start with—and a small piece of butter. Add a generous pinch of sea salt and a grind of pepper. Bring the stock to a boil, and taste it. It should be very tasty. If it tastes bland, add a little more salt, pepper, oregano, and butter until it tastes good.

3. Add the parsnips to the braising liquid. The braising liquid should cover about $1/2$ to $3/4$ of the parsnips. Cover the pot, bring the liquid to a boil, turn down the heat, and simmer for 5 to 8 minutes or until the parsnips are tender.

Steamed Parsnips

Peel the parsnip and slice it into coins about $1/4$-inch thick. Cut each coin into quarters or eighths depending on the size of the original coin. Try to keep the pieces a consistent size so that all of them cook in the same amount of time. Steam the pieces over boiling water in a steaming basket until tender, about 5 minutes. The time will vary according to the size of the parsnip pieces.

Serve plain or with any of the suggestions given earlier.

Quick
& Basic
Recipes
for
Winter
Produce
(continued)

Braised Collards with Smoked Turkey

SERVES 2 TO 4

2 bunches collard greens

2 tablespoons extra virgin olive oil

1 medium clove garlic, minced

Water

1 to 2 ounces smoked turkey—or ham
or smoked tofu—diced very small

Pinch of hot pepper flakes

Dash of vinegar

Sea salt

Freshly ground pepper

1. Wash the collards in a large bowl or a sink filled with water. Strip the leaves off the stems. Slice leaves into ½-inch strips. Heat the oil in a large sauté pan, add the collards, and sauté until they are wilted and dark green. Add the garlic and stir thoroughly to combine the flavors. Pour in enough water to cover the bottom of the pan by ¼ to ½ inch. Cover and simmer for 15 to 20 minutes or until the collards are tender. When they are tender, uncover the pan and cook away any remaining water.

2. Add the turkey and pepper flakes, and cook briefly just to heat the turkey. Season with a dash of vinegar, salt, and pepper.

Kale with Tamari & Mustard Seed

SERVES 2 TO 4

2 bunches kale

2 tablespoons extra virgin olive oil

Water

1 tablespoon yellow mustard seeds

1 to 2 tablespoons tamari

Dash of vinegar

Freshly ground pepper

1. Wash the kale in a large bowl or a sink filled with water. Strip the leaves off the stems, and tear or cut the leaves into bite-size pieces.

2. Heat the oil in a large sauté pan or large, heavy-bottomed pot over medium-high heat. Add the kale in batches, and, stirring often, sauté until it is wilted and dark green. As each batch cooks down, add another handful until all of the kale is wilted.

3. Add enough water to cover the bottom of the pan by ⅛ inch. Add the mustard seeds. Simmer, covered, until the kale begins to get tender, about 8 to 10 minutes. Uncover the pan and cook away any remaining water. When the kale is tender, season with the tamari, vinegar, and pepper.

**COOKING FOR
YOUR HEALTH
AND WELL-BEING**
Charlottesville, Virginia
Martha Hester Stafford
Chef/Owner

BLACK SEA BASS POACHED IN CALIFORNIA SPARKLING WINE

with Little Neck Clams & Arugula

SERVES 4

1 cup sparkling wine or champagne

1 cup fish stock

2 shallots, finely diced

3 button mushrooms, finely diced

4 seven-ounce black sea bass fillets (other winter fish that can be used with this dish include farmed striped bass or gray sea trout)

Salt and freshly ground pepper to taste

24 Little Neck clams

2/3 cup heavy cream

2 sprigs thyme, picked

3 tablespoons soft, unsalted butter

8 ounces arugula

1. Place champagne, fish stock, shallots, and mushrooms in a pan that is wide enough to hold all of the fish. Bring to a simmer. Season the fillets with salt and pepper and place in the liquid. Bring back to a very gentle simmer. Cover pan: first with parchment paper and then with a lid. Simmer until firm, approximately 7 to 8 minutes. Remove and discard parchment. Remove fillets and place directly on plates. Keep fish warm while cooking clams.

2. Turn heat up under pan. Add clams to poaching liquid, cover, and simmer until clams open. As clams open, place with fish on plates.

3. Once all of the clams have opened, add heavy cream and thyme to pan. Reduce to sauce consistency. Remove from heat and fold in butter. Spoon sauce over fish, reserving 1/4 cup in pan.

4. Wilt arugula in pan with sauce. Divide among 4 plates, season with additional freshly ground pepper to taste, and serve.

Chef's recommendation: Henriot Souverain NV champagne or another champagne with balance and style

MELROSE
Park Hyatt Washington
Washington
Brian McBride
Executive Chef

WINTER SQUASH SAVORY BREAD PUDDING

SERVES 6

For the squash:

2 acorn or other winter squash, about 1 pound each to yield 1$\frac{1}{2}$ to 2 cups cooked

4 tablespoons unsalted butter, softened

4 tablespoons maple syrup or 2 tablespoons dark-brown sugar

4 tablespoons fresh orange juice

Salt and freshly cracked black pepper to taste

For the onions:

4 tablespoons unsalted butter

2 large onions, julienned

$\frac{1}{2}$ cup dry sherry

Salt and freshly cracked black pepper to taste

For the glaze:

$\frac{1}{2}$ cup maple syrup

$\frac{1}{2}$ cup fresh orange juice

4 tablespoons unsalted butter

For the custard:

3 egg yolks

$\frac{1}{4}$ cup sugar

2 cups milk

Pinch of salt

4 tablespoons unsalted butter, melted

To assemble:

2 to 3 cups $\frac{1}{2}$-inch bread cubes, dried and lightly toasted; the more rustic and chewier the bread, the better

1. Preheat oven to 350°F.

2. To cook the squash, cut each squash in half and remove seeds. Rub inside and out with the butter and the maple syrup or brown sugar.

1789
Restaurant

1789
Washington
Ris Lacoste
Executive Chef

Place, cut side up, in a roasting pan, sprinkle with orange juice, and season with salt and pepper. Bake uncovered about 20 to 30 minutes until just done: fork-tender but firm. Set aside until cool enough to handle. The skin should peel right off and the flesh should be well caramelized, which adds great flavor. Cut into 1/2-inch cubes. Set aside until ready to use. The squash can be cooked a day ahead and kept covered in the refrigerator.

3. To cook the onions, melt the butter over medium-high heat and sauté the onions until soft, sweet, and golden, about 10 to 15 minutes. Deglaze with the sherry and cook until dry. Season with salt and pepper and set aside until ready to use.

4. To make the glaze, combine the maple syrup, orange juice, and butter in a saucepan. Bring to a boil, lower the heat, and, stirring often, simmer for 2 minutes.

5. To make the custard, whisk together the egg yolks and sugar. Meanwhile, heat the milk just to scald. Slowly add the milk to the egg yolk mixture, whisking continuously. When fully incorporated, add the salt and melted butter. Strain through a fine-mesh chinois or wire-mesh strainer.

To assemble:

6. With cooking spray, coat a 4x8-inch baking dish or six 8-ounce oven-proof ramekins. Layer with half of the bread cubes, onions, squash, and glaze. Press down to pack tightly. Repeat layers with the second half of bread cubes, onions, squash, and glaze. Press down again to pack tightly. Cover with warm custard. (Warm custard absorbs better. Cold is fine, but it takes longer.) Let sit for 30 minutes for the bread to absorb the custard.

7. Preheat oven to 325°F.

8. Refill the baking dish or ramekins to the top with the remaining custard, and cook in a water bath for about 75 minutes or until just firm to the touch. If cooking ahead, the pudding can be reheated, topped with a little glaze to remoisten before warming. To serve, cut the larger custard into 6 portions or unmold the individual ramekins.

Chef's recommendation: Alan Scott Dry Riesling or another aromatic white wine

BRAISED LAMB SHANK
with Winter Veggies & Lamb Jus

SERVES 6

$^1/_2$ cup grapeseed oil

1 cup flour

6 pounds lamb shanks

Salt and freshly ground pepper to taste

1 carrot, diced

1 onion, diced

2 celery ribs, diced

1 turnip, diced

4 cloves of garlic

1 cup white wine

1 cup tomato puree

2 quarts light veal stock or $1^1/_2$ quarts beef stock and $^1/_2$ quart water

1 herb bundle of rosemary, sage, and bay leaves tied up in cheesecloth

1. In a very large, ovenproof casserole, heat grapeseed oil to medium temperature. Flour lamb shanks, and season liberally with salt and pepper. Sauté shanks until golden brown on all sides. Remove shanks and set aside.

2. Heat oven to 300°F.

3. Add carrot, onion, celery, turnip, and garlic to casserole. Sauté mixture (*mirepoix*) for 5 minutes. Add wine, tomato puree, 1 quart of the veal stock, and the herb bundle. Return lamb to casserole, add stock to cover lamb, and bring to a simmer.

4. Place casserole in oven and simmer until shank meat pulls away from the bones—about $3^1/_2$ hours. (During cooking, add stock to keep meat submerged.) Remove shanks and keep warm. Remove herb bundle and discard.

5. Place cooled braising liquid and *mirepoix* in a blender and puree. Pour sauce through a fine-mesh strainer. Serve shanks with sauce ladled over the top. *Note:* Leftover sauce makes an excellent base for a bean and vegetable soup.

Chef's recommendation: Pinot Noir Talley or other smoky red wine that is rich in fruit

Equinox

EQUINOX
Washington
Todd Gray
Chef/Owner

TOASTED PECAN GRIDDLE CAKES
with Homemade Pumpkin Butter

MAKES 12 FIVE-INCH GRIDDLE CAKES

2 cups peeled, cubed pumpkin or butternut squash, divided use

1¼ cups all-purpose flour

1¾ cups whole wheat pastry flour

8 teaspoons sugar

2¼ teaspoons baking powder

¼ teaspoon salt

½ teaspoon ground cinnamon

½ teaspoon ground ginger

Dash of cloves

6 tablespoons coarsely chopped, toasted pecans

2 eggs

8 teaspoons melted butter

2¼ cups buttermilk (add a little more if batter seems too thick)

Pumpkin Butter (see sidebar)

Pure maple syrup

Yogurt

1. Steam cubed pumpkin until soft; set aside 1½ cups for pumpkin butter. Puree remaining pumpkin and set aside.

2. Preheat lightly greased griddle over medium heat.

3. Sift together flours, sugar, baking powder, salt, cinnamon, ginger, and clove. Add chopped nuts.

4. Combine eggs, butter, 2 tablespoons of the pureed pumpkin, and buttermilk; fold into flour mixture.

5. Cook about ⅓ cup of batter for each pancake on the prepared griddle. Serve with Pumpkin Butter and warm maple syrup. We like to add a dollop of plain yogurt.

Chef's recommendation: Jim's Organic Coffee and Fresh Orange Juice

Pumpkin Butter

1½ cups peeled, cubed, steamed pumpkin or butternut squash (from main recipe)

½ cup water

⅛ teaspoon ground cloves

1½ teaspoons ground cinnamon

2½ teaspoons ground allspice

½ teaspoon ground nutmeg

1 teaspoon ground ginger

Bring all of the ingredients to a boil; lower heat and simmer about 15 minutes until thick and shiny.

Don't expect a sweet pumpkin butter; ours is piquant and a perfect foil for these griddle cakes.

FOUR & TWENTY BLACKBIRDS
Flint Hill, Virginia
Heidi Morf
Chef/Owner

*Preheat oven to
350°F. Spread the
pepitas or
pumpkin seeds on
a baking sheet,
and roast in the
oven for 10
minutes or until
toasted. Remove
from the oven,
and set aside.*

PUMPKIN SOUP WITH PEPITAS

SERVES 4

1 small American pumpkin or large butternut squash, 2 to 2½ pounds

2 teaspoons canola oil

1 small onion, peeled and chopped

1 celery stalk, chopped

2 cups milk

2 cups water

2 tablespoons lemon juice

¼ teaspoon cumin

Pinch allspice

2 tablespoons dry sherry or Marsala

Salt and freshly ground black pepper to taste

2 tablespoons toasted pepitas or pumpkin seeds (see sidebar)

1. Preheat oven to 350°F.

2. Cut pumpkin in half, scrape out the seeds, and place cut-side down on a baking sheet or in a baking dish. Bake the pumpkin for about 40 minutes or until tender and easily pierced with a fork. Allow the pumpkin to cool for about 10 minutes before proceeding, because it will be easier to handle when it is not so hot.

3. While the pumpkin is baking, heat the oil in a small sauté pan, add the onion and celery, and sauté for about 3 minutes or until softened and clear. Set aside.

4. Scoop out the pumpkin pulp with a large spoon, place in a large bowl, and add the onion and celery mixture, milk, and water; stir to combine. Ladle some of this mixture into a blender and purée it in batches, being careful not to overfill the blender. Strain the soup through a colander to remove any remaining fiber and seeds. Add the lemon juice, cumin, allspice, sherry, salt, and pepper.

5. Transfer the soup to a small pot, and bring to a simmer. Divide the soup among 4 warmed bowls, and sprinkle each with the pepitas or pumpkin seed

Chef's recommendation: An Alsatian Riesling, such as Domaine Weinbach Cuvée Theo

Nora

RESTAURANT NORA
Washington
Nora Pouillon
Chef/Owner

HAYMAN SWEET POTATO SOUP
with Surry Ham

SERVES 6

4 large Hayman sweet potatoes, about 1³/₄ pounds

3 cups chicken stock

1½ cups Cream Base (see below)

Sea salt and freshly ground black pepper to taste

⅛ cup finely diced Surry ham or other dry-cured, hickory-smoked country
   ham for garnish

⅛ cup finely chopped chives for garnish

1. Peel and cube the sweet potatoes; cook in rapidly boiling salted water.
   When the potatoes are soft, place them in an ice water bath. Puree the
   chilled potato cubes in a food processor along with the chicken stock.

2. Push the puree through a fine-mesh strainer into a pan and add the
   cream base. Heat thoroughly and season with salt and pepper. Serve
   hot, in hot bowls, garnished with the diced ham and chives.

*Chef's recommendation: Gewürztraminer, Schlumberger, or another aromatic
Alsatian wine*

Cream Base

MAKES 2 CUPS

1 large onion, diced

4 shallots, sliced

2 tablespoons extra virgin olive oil

1 cup dry white wine

2 cups chicken stock

2 cups heavy cream

Cook the onion and shallots in the oil over medium heat until translucent.
Add the white wine, turn the heat to high, and reduce until almost dry.
Add the chicken stock and reduce until almost dry. Lower the heat and
add the cream. Reduce slowly for 10 minutes, stirring often. Strain.

*The onions from
the Cream Base
can be saved and
used as a filling
for omelettes or
an addition to
scrambled eggs.*

–CHEF JIMMY SNEED

SOUTHERN GRILLE
Richmond, Virginia
Jimmy Sneed
Former Chef/Owner

WINTER MUSHROOM SOUP
with Madeira Cream

SERVES 4

¼ cup unsalted butter

4 cloves garlic, minced

2 cups chopped mushrooms (portobellos, oysters, shiitakes)

3 leeks, cleaned and sliced, white parts only

2 stalks celery, chopped

2 carrots, peeled and chopped

2 tablespoons dried tarragon

Salt and freshly ground pepper to taste

2 to 2½ cups vegetable stock

5 tablespoons Madeira, divided use

¼ cup lightly whipped cream

1. To make the soup, melt butter over medium heat in a heavy-bottomed soup pot. Add garlic and sauté for 1 minute. Add mushrooms, leeks, celery, and carrots, and sauté until tender. Add tarragon, and season with salt and pepper. Add vegetable stock and 4 tablespoons of the Madeira.

2. Simmer, covered, until vegetables are soft, about 15 minutes. Allow soup to cool. Puree in a blender. Return soup to soup pot. Add more stock, if needed, to adjust thickness. Reheat over low heat, stirring gently. Adjust seasoning.

3. To make Madeira cream, combine the whipped cream and 1 tablespoon of the Madeira. Season with salt and pepper.

4. Divide soup among 4 bowls. Garnish each bowl with 1 tablespoon of Madeira cream.

Chef's recommendation: Rapidan River Semi-Dry Riesling or other aromatic white wine

C&O RESTAURANT
Charlottesville, Virginia
Thomas Bowles
Executive Chef

GOAT CHEESE SALAD ON FUJI APPLE CROUTON

SERVES 8

1 small spaghetti squash (3 to 3¹/₂ pounds)

Walnut Vinaigrette (see sidebar)

1 tablespoon finely chopped parsley

Salt and freshly ground pepper

2 Fuji apples

16 ounces goat cheese

¹/₂ cup pumpkin seeds, coarsely chopped, seasoned to taste with cayenne and salt, and toasted

8 cups mâche or arugula

24 red grape tomatoes

2 tablespoons pumpkin seeds, toasted and salted

1. Preheat oven to 350°F.

2. Bake the spaghetti squash either whole or split. If baking whole, pierce several times with a fork; if split, cut in half and remove and discard seeds. Place cut side up on a baking sheet, and bake until soft, about 90 minutes. Scoop flesh into a small bowl. Toss with enough Walnut Vinaigrette to coat—about 4 tablespoons. Add parsley, salt, and pepper, and toss. Chill.

3. Core apples and cut each crosswise into 4 slices.

4. Divide goat cheese into 8 pieces. Pat each piece into a flat disk the width of an apple slice. Pat and press the chopped pumpkin seeds into both sides of each disk.

5. Place one disk of goat cheese on top of each apple slice. Lightly heat goat cheese and apple croutons under broiler. Heating happens quickly; leaving the apple croutons too long in the broiler will burn the pumpkin seeds.

6. To assemble, toss mâche with vinaigrette to coat—about 4 tablespoons. Place 2 tablespoons of spaghetti squash in the center of each of 8 plates. Top with 1 goat cheese–apple crouton; surround with mâche. Garnish with grape tomatoes and toasted pumpkin seeds. Drizzle tomatoes with a little of the remaining vinaigrette, and grind black pepper around sides.

Chef's recommendation: Cape Mentelle Sémillon/sauvignon blanc or a weighty white wine from Graves-Bordeaux

Walnut Vinaigrette

¹/₄ cup white wine vinegar

2 shallots (2 ounces), coarsely chopped

2 heaping tablespoons Dijon mustard

6 tablespoons (3 ounces) walnut oil

6 tablespoons (3 ounces) salad oil

Salt and freshly ground white pepper

In blender, combine vinegar, shallots, and mustard; process until pureed. With the blender on, add walnut and salad oil mixture in a slow stream until thick. Taste, and season with salt and pepper.

BICYCLE
Baltimore
Barry Rumsey
Chef/Owner

BROILED OYSTERS
with Celery Cream & Virginia Ham

SERVES 6

36 Chincoteague oysters or any fresh medium-to-large variety (clean and save the top shells for serving)

1¼ cups heavy cream, divided use

½ teaspoon celery seed

2 bay leaves

1½ cups coarsely chopped flat-leaf parsley, leaves only

2 lemons, grated zest and juice

3 stalks celery, finely diced

2 to 3 ounces Virginia ham, finely diced

Sea salt and freshly cracked pepper

½ large celery root, peeled, coarsely diced, and reserved in acidulated water

2 tablespoons butter, unsalted

1. Shuck the oysters and drain, saving the oyster liquor for the sauce; set the shells aside.

2. In a noncorrosive saucepan, add the oyster liquor, 1 cup of the heavy cream, celery seed, bay leaves, parsley, and lemon zest and juice. Bring to a boil and let reduce slightly. Strain the mixture through a fine sieve; return to the saucepan. Add the celery and ham, and bring to a boil over medium-low heat. Check first for saltiness before adding salt, because the ham may add a great deal of salt to the mixture. If too salty (hams vary in saltiness), add a little more cream. Add the pepper. Keep warm.

3. Drain the celery root and put in another saucepan. Cover with fresh, salted water. Bring to a boil, lower heat, and simmer until tender. Drain.

4. In a food processor, add the celery root, butter, and remaining ¼ cup of cream, and puree.

5. Place ½ teaspoon of the celery root puree in each of the reserved oyster shells, top with one oyster, and spoon the celery-ham cream over the oysters. Place the filled oysters on a bed of sea salt on a sheet pan, and broil in the oven for about 5 minutes or until cream becomes brown and bubbly. Serve at once on heated dishes.

Chef's recommendation: Château Potelle sauvignon blanc or other dry white wine

KINKEAD'S
Washington
Bob Kinkead
Chef/Owner

SAUTÉED JERUSALEM ARTICHOKES & WALNUTS

SERVES 4 AS A SIDE DISH

1 pound Jerusalem artichokes

⅓ cup walnuts

2 large garlic cloves

1 tablespoon olive oil

Salt and freshly ground pepper to taste

1. Choose artichokes that are fresh and crisp. Scrape them with a paring knife to remove skin. If the skin is thick, you may need to peel it off entirely. Slice artichokes into thin cross sections, which will be irregularly shaped rounds. With a very sharp knife, slice the walnuts into thin cross sections. Finely mince the garlic.

2. To cook, heat the oil in a sauté pan over medium heat. Add the garlic, and as it starts to turn golden, add the sliced artichokes and walnuts. Toss to prevent the garlic from burning. Sauté until the artichokes are just tender and the walnuts lightly toasted. This takes only a matter of minutes, so it should be done minutes before you are ready to serve. Season with salt and pepper. This dish is excellent with roast pork.

Chef's recommendation: Le Cinciole Chianti Classico or a medium-bodied Dolcetto

**CASHION'S
EAT PLACE**
Washington
Ann Cashion
Chef/Owner

APPLE BLACK WALNUT PUDDING CAKE

SERVES 8 TO 10

1 pound golden raisins

1½ cups apple brandy

2 to 3 Granny Smith apples, peeled and cored (to yield 1 cup roasted apple puree)

1¼ cups sugar

1 tablespoon vegetable oil

1 teaspoon vanilla extract

1 cup all-purpose flour

1 teaspoon baking soda

½ teaspoon salt

½ teaspoon cloves

½ teaspoon cinnamon

½ teaspoon ground ginger

¾ cup coarsely chopped black walnuts

½ cup half-and-half

Mascarpone Cream (see sidebar on next page)

Two days before serving:

1. Combine raisins and apple brandy in a bowl. Cover and macerate at room temperature overnight.

The day before serving:

2. Preheat oven to 350°F.

3. Cut apples into eighths. Place in a single layer in a small baking dish. Cover loosely with foil and roast in oven until soft, about 30 minutes.

4. Puree roasted apples with fork or blender. Measure 1 cup of the puree and place in a large mixing bowl. Add sugar, vegetable oil, and vanilla. Mix manually until well incorporated.

TABARD INN
Washington
Huw Griffiths
Pastry Chef

5. Preheat oven to 325°F.

6. Sift together flour, baking soda, salt, cloves, cinnamon, and ginger. Stir into the apple mixture.

7. Stir together the walnuts, half-and-half, and raisin brandy mixture. Fold into the flour-apple mixture and pour into a well-greased 9- or 12-cup Bundt pan.

8. Bake cake until firm on top, about 40 to 50 minutes. (The cake will still be sticky in the center.) Cool and then chill overnight in the Bundt pan.

On the day of serving:

9. Carefully loosen sides of chilled cake with a knife. Place Bundt pan in several inches of hot water for 5 minutes. Unmold cake by flipping onto a flat serving plate. Serve topped with Mascarpone Cream.

Chef's recommendation: A dry rosé, such as Barboursville Rosato

Mascarpone Cream

1/2 pound mascarpone

1/2 cup light-brown sugar

1/4 cup brandy

1 cup heavy cream

Whisk together mascarpone, brown sugar, and brandy until smooth.

Add heavy cream and whisk until slightly thickened.

Serve a small amount with each slice of cake.

**Local Foods
Local Flavors**

***Everona Dairy Sheep's-Milk Cheese** is an artisanal product that retains the character and flavors of fresh milk and Virginia pasturage. Handmade from unpasteurized milk by using traditional methods, the cheese is made in small quantities, and only milk produced on the farm is used. Aged 2 to 9 months in a cool, moist environment, the cheese develops a natural rind and a firm texture. The cheeses are turned and washed two or more times a week with a salt brine that encourages the distinctive flavors to mature and intensify over time.*

SOUPE À L'OIGNON GRATINÉE
(Onion Soup)

SERVES 8

2 tablespoons unsalted butter

3 cups thinly sliced yellow onions

2 tablespoons flour

2 quarts beef stock

1 to 2 teaspoons salt

$^3/_4$ teaspoon freshly ground pepper

French bread, cut into 16 half-inch cubes for croutons

$^1/_4$ cup grated Gruyère

$^1/_4$ cup grated Parmesan

1. Melt the butter in a heavy saucepan or a Dutch oven. Add the onions, and stirring often, cook slowly over low heat—30 to 40 minutes—until golden brown.

2. When the onions are browned, stir in the flour; add the beef stock, vigorously blending it in with a whisk. Bring the soup to a full boil. Reduce heat, cover, and simmer for about 30 minutes. Taste for seasoning, and add salt and pepper as desired.

3. Preheat oven to 375°F.

4. Place the bread cubes on a baking sheet, and brown lightly in the oven for 5 to 8 minutes.

5. Pour the soup into 8 broiler- or ovenproof bowls, covering the surfaces with croutons. Combine the grated Gruyère and Parmesan. Top each soup with 1 heaping tablespoon of the cheeses. Place the filled bowls under the broiler or in a very hot oven to melt and brown the cheese. Serve immediately.

Chef's recommendation: Spielmann Pinot Blanc or other dry, crisp white wine

L'AUBERGE CHEZ FRANÇOIS
Great Falls, Virginia
Jacques Haeringer
Executive Chef

MUSHROOMS WITH MANCHEGO CHEESE

SERVES 2 AS A MAIN DISH, 4 AS A SIDE DISH

2 tablespoons olive oil

2 tablespoons chopped shallots

6 cups 1-inch pieces mixed mushrooms (oysters, cremini, shiitake, and, when making this dish in the fall, chanterelles)

1 tablespoon white wine

Kosher salt to taste

1/4 cup heavy cream

2 tablespoons finely minced parsley

4 ounces Manchego cheese or Everona Dairy Sheep's-Milk Cheese (see page 37), grated

1. Set sauté pan on high heat. When hot, add olive oil and shallots. Sauté until shallots brown slightly, add mushrooms, and sauté briefly until mushrooms soften.

2. Add wine and salt. Sauté another 30 seconds. Add cream, and cook, stirring, 30 seconds longer.

3. Add parsley and stir well. Place in a shallow bowl, sprinkle with cheese, and serve.

Chef's recommendation: Finca Valpiedra Reserva or another good, mature Rioja

JALEO
Washington
José Ramón Andrés
Executive Chef/Partner

SMOKED RICOTTA GNOCCHI

SERVES 4 TO 6

2 pounds boiling potatoes (select potatoes that are all the same size)

1 egg, beaten

$^1/_2$ cup Smoked Ricotta (see sidebar on next page)

$1^1/_2$ cups flour

1 tablespoon sea salt

1 teaspoon freshly ground white pepper

Several tablespoons unsalted butter

Light sauce or roasted vegetables (see next page), to finish

1. Preheat oven to 425°F.

2. Scrub the potatoes and boil in their skins in salted water until tender, about 15 minutes depending on size. Drain and peel while hot. Cut in quarters and spread on a baking pan. Dry potatoes in the hot oven for about 5 minutes.

3. In a large mixing bowl, rice or mash potatoes gently just until smooth with small lumps (do not overmash). Add egg and Smoked Ricotta; mix lightly. In a smaller bowl, combine flour, salt, and pepper. Add flour mixture to potatoes and combine with your hands to make a soft, dry dough. Do not overmix, because the dough will quickly become tough.

4. On a lightly floured surface, roll the dough, one handful at a time, into long sticks about $^1/_2$ inch in diameter. Cut into $1^1/_4$-inch lengths. Place a large handful in boiling, salted water. Cook until the gnocchi float, about 4 to 5 minutes. Lift them out of the water with a slotted spoon or mesh strainer and place immediately in an ice-water bath. Remove to a colander and drain. Repeat until all gnocchi are cooked. Separate drained gnocchi on baking sheets and set aside to rest until you are ready to serve.

NATIONAL PRESS CLUB
Washington
Jim Swenson
Executive Chef

5. When you are ready to serve, melt 1 tablespoon of the butter in a skillet over medium-high heat. When the butter begins to brown, add a single layer of gnocchi to fill the skillet. Sear the gnocchi in the light-brown butter to crust slightly on both sides. Repeat until all gnocchi are browned. Serve either in a light sauce or with some vegetables such as Oven-Roasted Butternut Squash (see below).

Chef's recommendation: A dry rosé, such as La Poussie Sancerre Rosé

Oven-Roasted Butternut Squash

3½ pounds butternut squash—or any other hard, orange squash—peeled and seeds removed

4 tablespoons olive oil

4 fresh sage leaves, finely chopped

Salt and freshly ground pepper to taste

1. Preheat oven to 375°F.

2. Cut squash into ½-inch cubes. Toss with olive oil. Spread on a baking sheet and sprinkle sage over all.

3. Roast, turning occasionally, until done, about 35 minutes. Season with salt and pepper.

**Local Foods
Local Flavors**

BLUE RIDGE DAIRY

Blue Ridge Dairy features handcrafted fresh mozzarella (fior di latte) cheeses and Italian-style ricotta made daily from the rich milk of registered Jersey cows. The mozzarella is crafted in the traditional Italian method, through lactic fermentation, which takes longer than commercial methods but which brings out distinctive and buttery flavor. All Blue Ridge Dairy fresh mozzarella is lactose free. The truly artisanal cheeses are made in small, 15-gallon batches. Three water buffalo are milked for production of mozzarella di bufala, and the resulting cheese is made by hand from 100 percent buffalo milk. Blue Ridge Dairy cheeses are available at farmers markets in and around Washington and Baltimore.

Smoked Ricotta

Hickory chips

1 pound fresh local ricotta

Ice cubes

Place a large handful of hickory chips in a bowl and cover with water. (To sweeten the smoke, add sour mash whiskey or scotch to the water.) Soak hickory chips for 30 minutes.

Light charcoal grill.

Place ricotta in a fine-mesh colander. Place colander in the center of a baking sheet with sides. Surround the colander with ice.

When coals are hot, place soaked chips over coals. Place pan of ricotta and ice on the grill, and close lid. Smoke for 5 minutes. Remove and stir to mix.

OYSTERS WITH CHAMPAGNE SAUCE

SERVES 4

20 oysters, shucked

Champagne Sauce (see below)

$1/4$ cup thinly sliced imported prosciutto, cut into $1/16$-inch julienne

$1/4$ cup coarsely chopped pistachio nuts

4 parsley sprigs, for garnish

1. Preheat oven to 450°F.

2. Place the oysters on a baking sheet and bake 3 to 4 minutes or until the edges of the oysters begin to curl.

3. Spoon Champagne Sauce over the oysters, and top with prosciutto and pistachios. Return the oysters to the oven for 45 seconds to warm the sauce. Garnish with a sprig of parsley.

Chef's recommendation: Veuve Clicquot Ponsardin or another full-bodied champagne

Champagne Sauce

1 tablespoon minced shallot

$1/2$ cup dry champagne

2 tablespoons champagne vinegar

$1/2$ cup heavy cream

4 tablespoons unsalted butter, cut into small pieces

Salt and freshly ground white pepper to taste

Place the shallot, champagne, and vinegar in a small saucepan (or the top of a double boiler) over medium heat. Bring to a boil and reduce mixture by one-third. Add the cream, return mixture to a boil, and reduce again by one-third. Remove the pan from the heat, but keep the burner on low. Whisk in the butter, one piece at a time. If the sauce cools too much to melt the butter, return the pot to the burner for a few seconds. Season the sauce with salt and pepper, adding a minimum of salt, because prosciutto is salty. Strain the sauce through a fine-mesh sieve, and keep warm over hot water that is in the bottom of the double boiler.

208 TALBOT
St. Michaels, Maryland
Paul Milne
Chef/Owner

ROCKFISH BRAISED IN APPLE JUICE
on Wilted Baby Spinach with Pine Nuts & Golden Raisins

SERVES 4

4 six-ounce rockfish fillets, skinned

Salt and freshly ground pepper to taste

1/2 cup all-purpose flour

6 tablespoons canola oil

3/4 cup apple juice

2 tablespoons unsalted butter

Wilted Baby Spinach (see sidebar)

1. Season rockfish fillets with salt and pepper. Dredge both sides in flour and shake off excess.

2. Heat a large sauté pan to medium hot and add oil. Sauté rockfish until golden brown. Turn fillets over and add apple juice to pan. Bring to a boil and add butter. Lower heat and simmer until fish is done—about 2 to 3 minutes depending on the thickness of the fish.

3. Remove fish to a warm platter. Continue simmering the liquid, stirring occasionally, and reduce until thick. Adjust seasoning with salt and pepper.

4. Divide spinach among 4 warm plates. Place a rockfish fillet on top of each serving of spinach, and drizzle the apple juice reduction over all.

Chef's recommendation: A dry white wine, such as White Hall Pinot Gris

Wilted Baby Spinach

4 teaspoons unsalted butter

3 tablespoons pine nuts

6 tablespoons golden raisins

9 ounces baby spinach, washed

Salt and pepper

Over medium-high heat, heat a very large sauté pan or a wide, heavy-bottomed pot large enough to hold all the spinach. Once the pan is hot, add butter, being careful not to let it burn. Add pine nuts and raisins, and sauté for about 1 minute. Add spinach. As spinach begins to wilt, season with salt and pepper. Cook the spinach just until soft—1 to 2 minutes only. Remove from heat and drain well.

ACACIA
Richmond, Virginia
Dale Reitzer
Executive Chef

FILETTO DI MANZO AL FORNA
con Prugne ed Albicocche
(ROASTED FILLET OF BEEF WITH PRUNE & APRICOT SAUCE)

SERVES 6

1 two-pound beef fillet

Salt and freshly ground pepper to taste

2 garlic cloves

1 stalk rosemary

4 fresh sage leaves

1 cup beef stock

2 tablespoons sugar

$\frac{1}{2}$ cup balsamic vinegar

4 ounces prunes (dried plums), julienned

4 ounces dried apricots, julienned

3 ounces pine nuts

2 cups reduced beef stock (4 cups stock reduced in half)

4 tablespoons olive oil

1. Preheat oven to 500°F.

2. Sprinkle the beef fillet with salt and pepper before cooking. Put fillet on a rack and place in a roasting pan with the garlic, rosemary, and sage. Place the pan in the oven, reduce the heat to 400°F, and roast until medium rare (140°F on an instant-read thermometer), about 40 minutes.

3. Remove roast and rack from pan. Add the beef stock and deglaze the pan. Strain the cooking liquid and reserve.

4. Place the sugar in a dry saucepan over medium heat. Keeping a very careful watch, let the sugar brown without stirring. Add the vinegar, turn up the heat, and reduce by half. Add the prunes, apricots, pine nuts, reduced beef stock, olive oil, and reserved cooking liquid. Simmer for 15 minutes.

5. To serve, thinly slice the beef, and spoon the sauce over top.

Chef's recommendation: A balanced Italian Chardonnay, such as Chardonnay Ceretto

GALILEO
Washington
Roberto Donna
Chef/Owner

BRAISED LAMB SHANKS
with Dried Cherries & Yukon Gold Mashed Potatoes

SERVES 4

3 tablespoons olive oil

2 white onions, cut in 1-inch dice

4 carrots, cut in 1-inch dice

4 parsnips, cut in 1-inch dice

2 celery stalks, cut in 1-inch dice

2 turnips, cut in 1-inch dice

12 garlic cloves, cut in 1-inch dice

2 bay leaves

2 tablespoons fresh thyme

2 tablespoons fresh rosemary

3 cups red wine

1 cup chopped tomato

4 cups chicken broth

4 one-pound lamb foreshanks, trimmed of fat and sinew

Salt and freshly ground pepper to taste

Yukon Gold Mashed Potatoes (see sidebar)

½ cup chopped parsley

1½ cups dried cherries

1. Preheat oven to 350°F.

2. In a large oven- and flameproof casserole, heat olive oil over medium-low heat. Add onions, carrots, parsnips, celery, turnips, garlic, bay leaves, thyme, and rosemary. Cover and sweat vegetables until soft, about 20 minutes.

3. Add red wine, tomato, and chicken broth. Stir well and add lamb shanks. Cover and bake for 3 hours or until shanks are tender.

4. Remove shanks from broth and set aside. Remove bay leaves and discard. Place casserole over high heat and reduce broth by half. Season with salt and pepper.

5. Place mashed potatoes in the center of each plate, and top with one shank. Finish the sauce with chopped parsley and dried cherries, and ladle over meat.

Chef's recommendation: A concentrated, full-bodied red wine such as Boscaini Amarone Marano

Yukon Gold Mashed Potatoes

8 Yukon Gold potatoes, peeled

Cut potatoes into 1-inch dice. Cover with water and simmer until soft. Drain well. Add milk, butter, and salt and pepper to taste. Mash to desired consistency, adding milk as necessary. Cover and keep warm.

**BISTRO
ST. MICHAELS**
St. Michaels, Maryland
David Stein
Chef/Owner

Our primary source for bison, Georgetown Farm, is in the mountains near Charlottesville, Virginia. Turnips and fingerling potatoes, grown by many of the small farmers from Manakin-Sabot to Nelson County, are frequently sold at farmers markets.

—CHEF ROBERT RAMSEY

FOX HEAD INN
Manakin-Sabot, Virginia
Robert Ramsey
Executive Chef

BRAISED BUFFALO HILL SHORT RIBS

SERVES 6 HUNGRY PEOPLE

5 pounds bison short ribs 2-inch cut, washed, trimmed of any excess fat, and tied in three-rib portions

Salt

8 ounces sliced smoked bacon, chopped into 1-inch bits

2 tablespoons cracked black peppercorns

1 cup dry red wine

2 quarts rich veal stock or Beef Consommé with Tomato Chips (see next page)

2 tablespoons tomato paste

2 tablespoons dried juniper berries

6 small (walnut- to golf-ball-size) turnips, scrubbed and trimmed

8 fingerling or small Yukon gold potatoes, washed thoroughly

1. Pat ribs dry with paper towels. Lightly salt meat on all sides.

2. Render bacon in a 10-inch iron skillet over medium heat until bacon is crisp. Remove bacon pieces and place in a stockpot. Raise heat under skillet and add peppercorns. Add bundled ribs—two bundles at a time—until all are seared. Do not crowd while searing. Place ribs in the stockpot after they brown. Remove peppercorns from skillet and add to stockpot.

3. Pour excess fat from skillet and deglaze with red wine.

4. Place ribs and deglazing liquid in stockpot, and cover with stock or consommé. Bring to a simmer over high heat for 5 minutes, skimming any fat that rises to the top. Reduce heat to slow simmer and add tomato paste and juniper berries. Cook for 90 minutes.

5. Add turnips and potatoes. Add enough stock to keep ribs and vegetables covered. After 2 hours, check ribs for doneness. They should be fork-tender.

6. Place ribs and vegetables in large, heated bowls, and ladle braising liquid over all.

Chef's recommendation: Jean Gagnerot Savigny-les-Beaune or a dry, medium-bodied red Burgundy

Beef Consommé with Tomato Chips

This makes a good substitute if you don't have veal stock handy. Tomato chips are easy to make, they keep forever in the freezer, and they add a boost of color, flavor, and body to soups, sauces, chilis, and stews or anytime you need a rich, roasted tomato flavor.

1 can tomato paste

2 quarts beef consommé

1. Preheat oven to 400°F.

2. Spoon 3 two-ounce dabs of tomato paste onto a well-greased, no-stick cookie sheet or frying pan.

3. Flatten each dab to approximately $1/4$-inch thick with the back of the spoon.

4. Bake for 30 minutes or until the edges are dark and crispy. Turn over with a spatula, and brown the other side until it is almost black. The chips will look like leather. Let cool.

5. Heat consommé to simmer. Add 1 two-ounce tomato chip and stir until it begins to color the consommé.

6. Store unused chips in a freezer bag.

**Local Foods
Local Flavors**

Georgetown Farm is located at the foot of the Blue Ridge Mountains in Free Union, Virginia. The farm produces 100 percent natural, antibiotic- and hormone-free meat products, including American Bison (buffalo) and Piedmontese Silver Beef. The lush green pastures and mild climate of central Virginia provide an ideal environment for producing exceptional meat products. Georgetown Farm's livestock is raised under strict guidelines and is processed in the family-owned abattoir.

Navy Beans

1 cup dry navy beans

Pick through beans to remove stones. Rinse beans and place in large saucepan with 3 cups of water. Bring to a boil, skim foam, and boil for 3 minutes. Set aside and let soak for 5 hours in cooking water. Drain. Wash saucepan, rinse beans with fresh water, and return to pan. Add 1 quart of water. Bring to a boil, reduce heat, and simmer until beans are well cooked, about 40 minutes.

LAMB STEW & NAVY BEANS
in Puff Pastry–Covered Crocks

SERVES 8

½ cup olive oil

2 pounds ¾-inch lamb cubes

1 small onion, diced into small cubes, or 1 pint pearl onions

2 carrots, sliced or coarsely diced

2 celery stalks, sliced or diced into large cubes

2 cups cooked Navy Beans (see sidebar)

3 tomatoes, diced into large cubes

2 sprigs thyme

2 sprigs rosemary

2 cloves garlic, coarsely chopped

2 cups red wine

5 cups lamb, veal, or beef stock

Salt and freshly ground pepper to taste

4 sheets puff pastry

1 egg, whipped

1. Place a saucepan on high heat, add olive oil, and heat until smoking. Add lamb and sauté until brown on all sides. Remove lamb from the pan and set aside. In the saucepan, add onion, carrots, and celery. Cook for 3 minutes or until soft. Add beans, tomatoes, thyme, rosemary, and garlic. Cook until they sweat, about 2 minutes.

2. Deglaze the pan by adding red wine and simmering until reduced by half. Add stock and lamb cubes. Season with salt and pepper. Remove saucepan from stove and let cool. Remove the thyme and rosemary sprigs.

3. Preheat oven to 375°F.

4. Use 8-ounce soufflé cups to finish cooking the stew. Cut puff pastry into 8 circles, 1 inch larger than the cups.

5. Divide stew evenly among the cups, filling each to within ½ inch of the top. Brush puff pastry on both sides with whipped egg; brush upper rim and outer ¼-inch edge of crocks with remaining egg. Cover cups with puff pastry. Be sure to seal well. Bake for approximately 15 to 20 minutes until pastry turns brown.

Chef's recommendation: Chalk Hill Winery Merlot (Sonoma) or a fruity, medium-bodied, slightly earthy red wine

BOAR'S HEAD Inn

BOAR'S HEAD INN
Charlottesville, Virginia
Alex Montiel
Executive Chef

SINGLE-FRIED OYSTERS
with Rémoulade Sauce

I own a restaurant and have access to just about anything I would like to eat. Every time I'm in my own establishment for dinner, I ponder the menu for quite a long time and then always order the single-fried oysters. I love them. The term single-fried *comes from towns in the lower Chesapeake Bay region. Another term —*fried oysters*— refers to an oyster fritter in which multiple oysters are contained in a large mass of batter that is lightly fried. The single-fried oysters, on the other hand, are, well, single fried.*

—CHEF JOHN SHIELDS

SERVES 4

1 pint (2 cups) shucked oysters

$^1/_2$ cup cracker meal crumbs (made from finely crushed saltine or oyster crackers)

$^1/_2$ cup all-purpose flour

$^1/_2$ teaspoon Old Bay seasoning

$^1/_4$ teaspoon salt

$^1/_4$ teaspoon freshly ground black pepper

Vegetable oil, for frying

Sauce Rémoulade, for dipping (see sidebar)

Lemon wedges

1. Drain the oysters, reserving the liquor, if desired. Combine the cracker crumbs, flour, Old Bay seasoning, salt, and pepper. Mix well. Dust the oysters with the crumb mixture, one at a time. Set aside on a rack for several minutes to dry.

2. Pour the oil into a frying pan to a depth of $^1/_2$ inch. Heat the oil and sauté the oysters until golden brown, about 3 to 5 minutes. Do not crowd the skillet, or the oysters will not get crisp. Add more oil as needed while you continue to cook additional batches. Remove oysters with a slotted utensil or tongs, and drain well.

3. Serve at once with Sauce Rémoulade and lemon wedges on the side.

Chef's recommendation: A dry, crisp white wine such as Sancerre Domaine de la Perrier

Sauce Rémoulade

$^1/_2$ cup mayonnaise

3 tablespoons finely minced celery

1 tablespoon finely minced green onion

$^1/_2$ tablespoon chopped parsley

$^1/_4$ teaspoon minced garlic

1 tablespoon coarse-grain mustard

$^1/_2$ tablespoon chopped capers

1 tablespoon ketchup

1 tablespoon Worcestershire sauce

$^1/_2$ teaspoon hot sauce such as Chile Man Louisiana Lightnin'

$^1/_2$ teaspoon paprika

$^1/_4$ teaspoon salt

Mix all of the ingredients together in a bowl. Cover and chill for several hours before serving.

GERTRUDE'S

GERTRUDE'S
Baltimore
John Shields
Chef/Owner

ROAST PORK LOIN
with Apple & Cranberry Coulis

SERVES 6

$1/4$ cup sugar

1 teaspoon ground ginger

$1/2$ teaspoon kosher salt

$1/2$ teaspoon freshly ground allspice

$1/8$ teaspoon ground cloves

1 two-pound boneless center cut pork loin, tied for roasting

Apple Coulis (see next page)

Cranberry Coulis (see next page)

Watercress for garnish

1. Preheat oven to 450°F.

2. In a bowl, combine sugar, ginger, salt, allspice, and cloves. Rub the pork loin with the sugar-spice mixture, coating it evenly.

3. Place the pork loin on a rack in a heavy roasting pan and cook at 450°F for 10 minutes. Reduce heat to 325°F and continue roasting until the internal temperature, measured by an instant-read thermometer, is 145°F, approximately 45 to 50 minutes. Remove from oven and let rest 10 minutes before slicing.

4. To serve, place a large spoonful of Apple Coulis in the center of a dinner plate. Using the back of the spoon, spread the coulis into a circle approximately 6 inches in diameter. Place a large spoonful of the cranberry coulis inside the circle of apple, and, using the spoon again, spread to the inside edge of the apple coulis. Slice the pork loin into pieces approximately $1/8$-inch thick, and place 3 or 4 of the pieces in the center of the concentric sauces. Garnish with sprigs of watercress.

Chef's recommendation: Château Montelena Chardonnay or another full-bodied, oaky Chardonnay

**RESTAURANT
COLUMBIA**
Easton, Maryland
Stephen Mangasarian
Chef/Owner

Apple Coulis

4 Granny Smith or other firm-fleshed apples, peeled, cored, and quartered

1 tablespoon unsalted butter

1/4 cup sugar

1/2 tablespoon freshly ground cinnamon

1 teaspoon fresh lemon juice

Zest of 1 small lemon

1 tablespoon brandy or cognac

1 tablespoon water

Place the apples in a heavy-bottomed saucepan. Add butter, sugar, cinnamon, lemon juice and zest, brandy, and water. Cover and cook over low heat, stirring occasionally, until a fork penetrates the apples easily. Cool slightly and process in a blender or processor until absolutely smooth and free of lumps.

Cranberry Coulis

1 cup fresh cranberries

3/4 cup sugar

1/4 cup fresh orange juice

1/4 teaspoon salt

1/4 teaspoon freshly ground nutmeg

1 cup water

In a heavy-bottomed saucepan, combine cranberries, sugar, orange juice, salt, nutmeg, and water. Bring just to a boil. Simmer, covered, 20 minutes or until cranberries split and become soft. Cool slightly and process in a blender or processor until smooth.

**Local Foods
Local Flavors**

Famous in San Francisco for its gourmet-quality beef, pork, and lamb, **Niman Ranch** *is now working with small-scale farmers in North Carolina to produce high-quality, humanely raised pork. Farmers who raise hogs for Niman develop flavor through good management, including choosing flavorful breeds, lowering stress on animals, and meeting husbandry standards established by the Animal Welfare Institute that require pigs to be on pasture or in bedded pens. All Niman meat is free of growth-promoting hormones and antibiotics.*

We have a
wonderful rabbit,
egg, and chicken
supplier in
Springfield
Farms in Sparks,
Maryland.

In spring, replace
the shiitakes with
a garnish of
sautéed morels.

—CHEF CINDY WOLF

BRAISED LOCAL RABBIT LOIN

with Sautéed Shiitakes

SERVES 2

8 slices applewood-smoked bacon, cut into small dice

1 onion, cut into small dice

1 carrot, cut into small dice

1 cup medium-diced portobello mushrooms

1 teaspoon fresh thyme, finely chopped

4 cups Rabbit Stock or reduced chicken stock (see sidebar on next page)

2 rabbit loins, bone in (see editor's note on next page)

2 tablespoons unsalted butter

2 cups shiitake mushrooms, sliced

Salt to taste

1. Over low heat, in a heavy, medium-size Dutch oven or ovenproof
   stockpot, slowly cook the diced bacon until the fat has melted and the
   bacon is browned but not crisp. Sauté the diced onion, carrot, and
   portobellos in the bacon fat for 5 minutes. Drain the bacon fat. (This
   will take several minutes. Push the vegetables to one side, tilt pot on a
   slight angle, and spoon the fat out as it drains.) Reserve the bacon fat
   for later use. Add the thyme and stock to the pot. Cover and simmer
   this broth 30 minutes.

2. Meanwhile, warm a medium-size sauté pan over medium-high heat, add
   the reserved bacon fat, and sear the rabbit loins until well browned on
   each side.

3. Add the seared loins to the broth, and braise until tender, about 1 hour.
   This can be done over low heat on top of the stove or, covered, in a
   325°F oven. It is important to be sure the pot is tightly covered so that
   the broth doesn't evaporate, scorching the meat. (If the broth does
   evaporate, add more stock.) When done, the meat should fall off the
   bone. Remove the rabbit from the broth, remove all remaining meat
   from the bone, and reserve.

CHEF CINDY WOLF
CHARLESTON

CHARLESTON
Baltimore
Cindy Wolf
Chef/Owner

4. Melt the butter over medium heat in a small sauté pan. Sauté the shiitakes until they just start to caramelize. Season with salt.

5. Over medium-high heat and stirring frequently, reduce the broth to sauce consistency, about 15 to 20 minutes. Add the rabbit meat and the sautéed shiitakes. Serve hot.

Chef's recommendation: A Côte de Nuits Pinot Noir, such as Morey St. Denis 1er Cru Clos des Sorbés Jacky Truchot

Local Foods Local Flavors

Springfield Farm *is located in northern Baltimore County in Maryland on land that has been owned by members of the same family since the 1700s. Twelve generations have lived on the farm, which is now owned and operated by David and Lilly Smith along with two of their daughters and their families. Springfield Farm raises chickens, turkeys, ducks, geese, guinea fowl, quail, rabbit, and veal to produce high-quality eggs and meat. Using only limited modern technology, Springfield Farm allows the animals to roam freely in lush green pastures so they can forage for that which nature intended. The animal feed is completely natural and consists of locally raised grains prepared specifically for Springfield Farm. No chemicals, hormones, or antibiotics are used in animal production, and processing is carefully accomplished by hand. Springfield Farm sells direct to restaurants and to individuals who come to the farm. Visitors are invited to come during daylight hours any day of the week and are welcome to help collect and clean eggs and feed the animals.*

Rabbit Stock

Remaining parts of 2 rabbits (about 5 pounds)

12 cups cold water

2 large carrots, chopped

2 small onions, coarsely chopped

2 large celery stalks with leaves

2 bay leaves

Place rabbit and water in a stockpot. Simmer, uncovered, for 30 minutes, skimming occasionally. Add remaining ingredients. Simmer, uncovered, for 2 1/2 hours, skimming. Strain, chill, and remove fat.

Editor's note: If your butcher offers only whole rabbits, have 2 three-pound rabbits cut into parts so that you have meat and bones available for the rabbit stock.

BOLOGNESE VENISON RAGU
with Butternut Squash Polenta Gnocchi

SERVES 4

2 ounces dried porcini mushrooms

¼ pound each onions, leeks, carrots, and celery

¼ pound (1 stick) unsalted butter

1 pound very lean ground venison (preferably trimmings from an aged saddle or loin) or lean ground sirloin

1¾ cups peeled, seeded, chopped tomatoes

2 cups good-quality dry, fruity red wine

1¼ pounds butternut squash

Olive oil

2 cups water

8 ounces instant polenta meal

1 tablespoon brown sugar, firmly packed

1 tablespoon finely chopped parsley

1 cup heavy cream

1 cup grated Parmigiano-Reggiano

Kosher salt and freshly ground white pepper to taste

For the ragu:

1. Reconstitute the mushrooms in 4 cups of warm water. Strain and finely chop (reserve the liquid for other uses). Set aside.

2. Grind the onions, leeks, carrots, and celery in a meat grinder, or shred in a food processor. Combine and set aside.

3. In a heavy stew pot, melt the butter over medium heat; add venison and stir gently to brown. Add the shredded onion, leek, carrot, and celery mixture. Reduce heat, stir thoroughly, and continue cooking slowly for approximately 30 minutes.

4. Add the mushrooms, tomatoes, and red wine. Lower the heat until the ragu comes to a bare simmer. Cook very slowly, stirring frequently, until the mixture becomes a dense, moist meat sauce, approximately 2 to 4 hours.

TABARD INN
Washington
David Craig
Former Executive Chef

For the gnocchi:

5. Preheat oven to 375°F.

6. Cut the butternut squash in half, remove seeds, and lightly brush the cut side with olive oil. Place, cut side down, on a cookie sheet, and bake until tender, about 30 minutes.

7. Remove from the oven and reduce heat to 350°F. When cool enough to handle, scoop flesh from the squash and puree in a food processor until smooth. Push puree through a fine sieve.

8. Spread puree in the bottom of a lightly oiled oven pan, and dry slowly in the oven to remove excess moisture, stirring frequently to prevent burning, about 25 minutes.

9. Pour water into a medium saucepan, add salt to taste, and bring to a boil. Slowly whisk in polenta meal in a continuous stream. Add sugar and stir well to combine.

10. Allow the polenta to thicken. With a spatula, fold in the squash pulp. Thoroughly mix the two.

11. Using olive oil, lightly oil a cookie sheet. Lay mixture out on a cookie sheet and spread evenly to a thickness of 1½ inches.

12. After the polenta cools, cut into small squares, triangles, and circles.

To serve:

13. Preheat oven to 450°F.

14. Spray a cookie sheet with vegetable oil, and evenly space the gnocchi on it. Bake in the oven until the outsides are slightly crisp, approximately 8 to 10 minutes, turning carefully halfway through the baking.

15. Reheat the meat sauce. Add the parsley, the heavy cream, and half of the cheese, and cook until thick. Adjust the seasoning with salt and pepper, if desired.

16. Spoon the sauce into the centers of 4 warmed dinner plates. Top with 3 or 4 gnocchi and sprinkle all with the remaining cheese.

DUCK CONFIT, GUMBO STYLE

SERVES 6 TO 8

4 tablespoons olive oil, divided use

$^1/_4$ cup chopped onion

$^1/_4$ cup chopped celery

3 garlic cloves, chopped

1 cup peeled and chopped tomato

$^1/_4$ cup red pepper, roasted, peeled, and chopped

1 cup chopped okra

6 ounces smoked country ham, diced

6 ounces smoked Surry sausage, cut into $^1/_4$-inch slices

1 fresh bay leaf

2 teaspoons Worcestershire sauce

1 pinch cayenne pepper

6 cups duck or chicken stock

2 cups Arborio rice

6 cups shredded Duck Confit (see next page)

2 teaspoons gumbo filé

8 teaspoons unsalted butter

2 tablespoons cilantro, chopped

1. In a medium-size saucepan, heat 2 tablespoons of the oil. Add the onion, celery, garlic, tomato, and red pepper. Cook for 3 to 5 minutes until transparent. Add the okra, ham, sausage, bay leaf, Worcestershire, cayenne, and stock. Simmer for 6 minutes. Keep simmering.

2. In a heavy-bottomed saucepan, heat the remaining 2 tablespoons of oil. Over medium heat, add the rice, stir and coat well. Add the boiling stock, a little at a time, and stir until incorporated. Continue to add stock and stir until all of the stock has been added, about 20 minutes. Add the duck confit and gumbo filé in the last few minutes. Rice should be creamy, with an al dente core. Fold in butter. Divide rice among 6 warmed bowls. Sprinkle with chopped cilantro.

Chef's recommendation: Edmunds St. John 1997 Durell Vineyard Syrah or other black-fruited red wine with hints of leather, bacon, and wood that are well integrated

VIDALIA
Washington
Peter Smith
Executive Chef

Duck Confit

recipe by George Cronk, adapted from *Cooking Fresh from the Bay Area*

YIELD: ABOUT 6 CUPS

8 duck legs

1 teaspoon cracked black pepper

2 teaspoons kosher salt

1/2 teaspoon fresh thyme

1 teaspoon chopped fresh bay leaf

6 tablespoons olive oil

6 cups Rendered Duck Fat (see sidebar)

1 carrot, chopped

2 celery stalks, chopped

1/2 onion, chopped

6 cloves garlic, chopped rough

Two days before cooking:

1. Clean duck legs of silver skin and excess fat. Sprinkle each duck leg, top and bottom, with pepper, salt, thyme, and bay leaf. Place legs on a wire rack, fat side down. Put the rack on a baking sheet and cover loosely with a dry dishcloth. Do not use plastic wrap. Refrigerate for 2 days.

The day of the meal:

2. Preheat oven to 250°F.

3. Wipe the herbs off the duck legs. Heat the olive oil in a medium-size skillet or sauté pan. The oil should be very hot. Sear the duck legs on both sides and remove from the heat.

4. Heat the duck fat in a pan large enough to hold the duck legs and the vegetables. Bring the duck fat to a simmer and place the duck legs, carrot, celery, onion, and garlic in the fat. The legs and chopped vegetables should be completely covered in duck fat. Cover and put in the oven for approximately 2 1/2 hours or until the legs are tender. Remove the pan from the oven. Carefully remove the legs from the fat, and let stand. When cool enough to handle, pull the meat from the legs.

Rendered Duck Fat*

yield: about 6 cups

6 pounds duck skin and fat

6 cups water

Dice the skin and the fat, and combine them with the water in a small saucepan. Bring the liquid to a slow simmer. Skim any impurities that may rise to the surface. Simmer the fat slowly for 1½ to 2 hours or until all of the water has evaporated and the fat has clarified. You will be able to tell when the fat is rendered by the way it looks: it will be very clear, and the simmering bubbles will be much smaller. Strain the fat through a fine-mesh colander or cheesecloth, and discard the skin. Rendered fat can be refrigerated for 2 months or frozen for up to 1 year.

* Recipe by Joseph George, adapted from *Cooking Fresh from the Bay Area*

SPRING

EXPLORING THE SOCIAL
BENEFITS OF SMALL-SCALE,
LOCAL AGRICULTURE &
CELEBRATING THE FLAVORS
OF SPRING IN THE
MID-ATLANTIC

SPRING FARE

AMERICAN EEL
APPLES
ARUGULA
ASPARAGUS
ATLANTIC MACKEREL
BEEF
BEEF (FORAGE FED*)
BEETS
BISON
BLACK SEA BASS
BLUEBERRIES
BLUE CRAB
BLUEFISH
BOK CHOY
BROCCOLI
BROCCOLI RAAB
CABBAGE
CATFISH
CATFISH (FARMED*)
CHICKEN
CHICKEN (FORAGE FED*)
CLAMS
CLAMS (FARMED*)
CONCH
CROAKER
DAIRY (PASTURED*)
DOGFISH
EDIBLE FLOWERS
EGGS (CHICKEN)
EGGS (DUCK, GOOSE, QUAIL,
    & GUINEA)
EGGS (FORAGE FED*)
FARMSTEAD CHEESES (AGED)
FENNEL
FLOUNDER
GOAT CHEESE (FRESH)
GREEN GARLIC

GREENS
GUINEA FOWL
HERBS
HERRING ROE
HONEY
KALE
LAMB'S QUARTERS
LEEKS
LETTUCES & SALAD GREENS
MONKFISH
MORELS
MOZZARELLA (FRESH)
MUSHROOMS
OYSTER MUSHROOMS
OYSTERS
PEANUTS
PEAS
PERCH (WHITE & YELLOW)
PORK
PORK (FORAGE FED*)
POTATOES
QUAIL (FARM RAISED*)
RABBIT (FARM RAISED*)
RABBIT (FORAGE FED*)
RADISHES
RAINBOW TROUT (FARMED*)
RAMPS
RHUBARB
RICOTTA (FRESH)
ROCKFISH (STRIPED BASS)
SCALLOPS
SCUP
SEA TROUT (GRAY)
SHAD & SHAD ROE
SHIITAKE MUSHROOMS
SHRIMP
SOFT-SHELL CRAB
SORREL
SPANISH MACKEREL

SPINACH
SPOT
SPRING ONIONS
SQUID
STRAWBERRIES
SWISS CHARD
TILAPIA (FARMED*)
TOMATOES (GREENHOUSE)
TURNIPS
VEAL

* SEE PAGE 233

SPRING PLANTING ON THE FARM

Spring is about hope. Planting seeds is about hope. It is a time of optimism. In the mind's eye, we can see and taste the perfect tomato, the most delicious melon. Spring is also marked by questions lurking in the back of the mind. By now, the planning for the year has been completed, and it is time to start the work of getting the plants and seeds in the ground. There is a growing sense of concern about just when the weather will break and the soil will be ready to work and be prepared for planting. Nice days are treasures, and a 2-inch rainfall is a certain delay. Seedlings are ready to transplant. Is it spring?

Other questions are in the mind. Each year's plans for the coming year are based on an accumulation of past years' lessons learned. Planning is difficult. The summer of 1999 was one of the hottest, driest summers on record. The summer of 2000 was one of the coolest, wettest on record followed by almost no rain in September and October. So, the Sunleaper tomatoes that we planted in 2000—because they like the heat and will set tomatoes when the temperature is above 90 degrees—did not do as well as they would during an average year. That's what most planning is about: the average. Questions are in mind about how well the new Lannen transplanter will handle lettuce transplants. Lettuce is our main crop and is difficult to transplant because depth is important and because unlike tomatoes, lettuce has no stem. There are lots of questions, the answers will unfold, and next year we will use the lessons learned.

We are market gardeners. Since we began selling in 1997, we have established rewarding relationships with three terrific restaurants, and we sell to two small markets and at the FreshFarm Farmers Market in St. Michaels, Maryland. This is a producers-only market, which means that we may sell only produce we ourselves have grown. Producers-only markets ensure the highest-quality produce from growers who take pride in what they grow. We are Maryland Department of Agriculture Certified Organic and intend to remain organic under the new U.S. Department of Agriculture regulations effective October 2002.

We made that choice because we eat what we grow and we want what we grow and sell to be as healthy as possible. We grow on approximately 3 to 4 acres, on raised beds with drip irrigation. Each year, we expand, but the *we* is only my husband, Mark, and myself, and along about August it can seem like a hundred acres.

Today we planted our first planting of lettuce in the field, and yes, with a little more tinkering, we feel the new planter was a wise investment. Each week, we plan to put out 432 lettuce plants. We had hoped to start the first week in March, but weather did not permit. As soon as the bed is planted, it is covered with row cover. Covering a 120-foot-by-6-foot bed

Butter Pot Farm

Surrounded by water, Butter Pot Farm in Cambridge, Maryland, is situated alongside the Little Choptank River, a tributary of Chesapeake Bay. Growers Mark and Linda Wilson have 80 acres, 24 of which are open field and 3 of which are organic farmland. The Wilsons grow organic vegetables for market—mainly lettuce and tomatoes but also beans, asparagus, beets, onions, broccoli, cabbage, and kale as well as melons. Their products are sold at two local farmers markets and two retail markets as well as to three area restaurants.

by Linda Wilson
Butter Pot Farm
Cambridge,
Maryland

with a cover that is almost like gossamer is always a challenge. If it has been calm for a week—which it never is in spring—the wind is sure to blow as soon as we start to roll out the cover. But the cover goes on and the plants are protected.

We started planting trays the end of January and have planted 99 trays with 72 cells for a total of 7,182 plants. Each tray is numbered and dated with entries in the planting book as to variety, germination, date of transplant, and date of sale. We'll plant about 30 varieties of lettuce and salad greens and about a dozen varieties of tomatoes. Once the harvest is finished, the bed will be tilled and planted in summer cover to enrich the soil. By September all beds will be tilled—except for fall crops—and winter cover planted. Growing organically, the aim is to enrich the soil by introducing green manures that add nutrients, attract beneficial insects, and prevent soil erosion. Each week from now until November, new trays of seeds will be planted and a new bed of lettuce will go out into the field. Lettuce seeds germinate in 3 to 7 days, spending 4 weeks afterward in the seedling tray and then 4 weeks in the field to harvest. In addition to our planting of lettuce, some Walla Walla onions and spinach also went out today. Seedlings for the first tomato and beet plantings are looking good. We also grow peppers, eggplant, melons, pole and asparagus beans, fall crops, and a smattering of other vegetables.

Much of the joy of market gardening is about being outdoors and being able to observe the evolution of the season: the return of the purple martins, the first flowers, the budding of the trees, the first strawberry blossoms. Some days—the really long ones when we're especially tired at the end of the day—market gardening is just work. Asparagus harvest begins the first week in April. It is the beginning of the marathon—plant, tend, harvest, and sell—and the hope for a good season. ■

CREATING A FOOD SYSTEM THAT WORKS

Where your food comes from really does matter.

The survival of small family farming is in the interest of all of us. It serves the common good. And contrary to the conventional wisdom, the demise of small farming is not inevitable. It is not the result of inexorable laws of economics or irresistible forces of nature. Rather, it is a result of decisions made by people—policy choices and buying choices— that can be reversed by people.

Each of us has a little power—and together we have a lot of power— to create a food system that serves the common good. We exercise that power by making thoughtful decisions about what food to purchase and by our participation in the democratic process.

We can have an environmentally sound, productive, healthy, and efficient agriculture based on small farms. They are, in fact, essential to a socially sound agriculture that supports healthy and just communities. The benefits of small family farming are many.

Societies and communities in which income, wealth, and power are more equitably distributed are generally healthier than those in which they are highly concentrated. A research report by University of California anthropologist Dean MacCannell says it well:

> Everyone who's done careful research on farm size, residency of agricultural landowners and social conditions in the rural community finds the same relationship: As farm size and absentee ownership increase, social conditions in the local community deteriorate. We have found depressed median family incomes, high levels of poverty, low education levels, social and economic inequality between ethnic groups, etc., associated with land and capital concentration in agriculture. . . . Communities surrounded by farms that are larger than can be operated by a family unit have a bimodal income distribution, with a few wealthy elites, a majority of poor laborers and virtually no middle class.

Community matters. The bonds and mutual obligations people form with others over time are a form of social capital.

Without community, people are more likely to follow their own interests and less likely to act in pursuit of the common good. Only within community are there constraints against negative behavior and reinforcement for positive behavior as well as a reasonable expectation that unselfish behavior will be reciprocated. But when small farms are destroyed, communities die with them.

by Chuck Hassebrook
Center for Rural Affairs

HEALTHY FOOD, HEALTHY FARMS, CLOSE TO HOME

Appalachian Harvest is a network of certified-organic family farmers in southwestern Virginia and northeastern Tennessee who are working with nature to nurture rich, living soils as the building blocks for healthy farms and healthy crops. Many of Appalachian Harvest's farmers are making the transition from tobacco farming and are working together to bring the highest-quality, best-tasting organic foods to local tables at affordable prices.

Maintaining the diversity of farm sizes by preventing total domination by large corporate farms enhances the resilience of American agriculture to resource shocks and other unforeseen problems.

Diversity enhances resilience. If one approach is rendered ineffective due to unanticipated events—such as climate change or energy crisis—society needs optional systems to fill the void.

Corporate agriculture is all about uniformity. The classic example is integrated hog and poultry production, wherein genetically uniform animals are fed uniform feed, in uniform buildings, following uniform management practices enforced by company field hands. This highly vulnerable system places our food supply in jeopardy.

Smaller is more sustainable. Megascale agriculture by its very nature involves more-difficult environmental compromises. For example, giant livestock operations concentrate more animals and more manure in a smaller area than the land, air, plants, and water can absorb. That turns manure into a pollutant. But on well-managed smaller operations, manure applied to fields at lower rates is an environmentally beneficial resource. It replaces chemical fertilizer and enhances soil quality, thereby increasing the infiltration of rain into the soil and reducing polluted runoff.

Not all small farms are good environmental stewards, and not all big farms are bad for the environment. However, modest-scale farming inherently allows for more environmentally friendly approaches.

In spite of the public interest in small farming, U.S. policy is biased toward bigness. We must demand that our senators and other government representatives establish farm policies that support the common good by strengthening small farms, rewarding environmental stewardship, and building new marketing channels that connect environmentally responsible family farmers and ranchers with consumers.

No less important are the buying decisions each of us makes. Increasing numbers of Americans are voting—via their purchases—for environmental responsibility. We must also vote with our dollars for socially responsible agriculture. We can ask stores to stock products grown on small family farms and seek them out. And we can seek food from farms that treat their farmworkers justly.

We all gain when we work together to ensure that our food system supports environmental stewardship, genuine opportunity, and community. ■

FAST FOOD & FAMILY LIFE

Fast food is doing to family life what expressways once did to city neighborhoods: cutting a swath of speed and anonymity through a place where people once walked, talked, and hung out together. When fast food invaded the family, it brought not just food products but also a new set of cultural practices. In the fast-food culture, you don't prepare and serve your food; you receive it from a stranger in handheld units served in paper and you consume it with a beverage hidden in an opaque paper cup. You are expected to scarf your food instead of savoring it (what's to savor?). The bright lights and colors of the restaurant implore you to not linger over conversation. You eat while doing something else or while on your way to somewhere else. If you bring fast food home, you consume it as quickly as it was prepared, probably in front of the television.

The fast-food culture robs family life of its core ritual practice: a daily meal, prepared and served in the home, where all family members come together to reconnect and feed their bodies and spirits. These meals include nearly all of the ingredients of healthy family living: work, conversation, pleasure, tradition, and ironing out differences. Through foods and recipes that we bring from our own childhoods and cultures, family meals are where the past meets the present, where stories are shared, where we figure out how to share conversational "air time," and where we learn to manage the tensions that sometimes mar family gatherings.

None of this happens without taking time, and time is the antithesis of fast food and its culture. Roasting, baking, simmering, and stewing all take time. Meal planning and shopping take time. Buying special foods takes extra shopping time, as does growing one's own food. Cooking with pots and pans and using real dishes instead of paper wrappers—all of it adds to the time required for a family meal. If time is money, family meals can never compete with fast food.

It's not that we are blind to the value of family meals. Surveys consistently show that most Americans say home-cooked family dinners are important and that they regret their decline, but we will not reclaim our family meals from the fast-food culture until we deal with the way our schedules create a chronic sense of time urgency. We fall prey to fast food and its culture because we're too busy to devote ourselves to family dinners, Sunday brunches, and other meals that take time and preparation and that call for being together in the same place at the same time.

Some of this overscheduling is economically driven and hard to change in a society in which two incomes are often necessary to maintain a middle-class lifestyle. When Mom is not home in the afternoon to start preparing dinner, it's easy to go out for burgers or to bring home tacos. That's when advance planning, getting everyone involved in cooking and

by William Doherty, Leslie Bautista, Barbara Carlson, Jane Guffy, Sue Kakuk & Bugs Peterschmidt
Putting Family First

cleanup, and preparing some foods ahead of time can make a difference. Many families with working parents manage to resist the fast-food culture and enjoy rich dinner traditions. But it takes conscious effort.

The other way we lose time for family meals is by overscheduling our children in extracurricular activities, many of which, from sports to music, to academic enrichment activities are held during the dinner hour. If you have more than one child in more than one activity, there's a good chance your opportunities for family dinners are drastically curtailed. And once you've lost your dinner rituals, it's hard to get them back. Kids and adults alike can get used to "special ordering" their food from the freezer or the macaroni-and-cheese box, and microwave ovens are convenient for allowing all to consume the frozen or reheated food of their choice.

We can fight this fast-food culture. The first beachhead lies in our individual homes, in which we can make family meals a higher priority than outside activities. We can say no to any activity that robs us of regular dinners. We can involve everyone in the family in conducting meal rituals, and we can make mealtime a time of conversation and connection. It's time to take back our kids, our families, and our meals from the expressway of the fast-food culture. ■

Resources for Living Local

From the Ground Up—A joint effort of the Chesapeake Bay Foundation (CBF) and the Capital Area Food bank, From the Ground Up brings fresh produce to the Washington area and educates the public about the relationship between agriculture, the environment, the food supply, and hunger. Produce is grown in an environmentally sensitive manner on CBF's Clagett Farm in Upper Marlboro, Maryland. At least half of the produce is distributed to low-income neighborhoods every week for 6 months. The other half is distributed to the organization's 125-member Community Supported Agriculture program.

VISION FOR A SUSTAINABLE FOOD SYSTEM

We "need to become independent of the world market economy because the world market economy is ultimately controlled by interests which seek power or profit and which do not respond to the need of the world's peoples" (*Basic Call to Consciousness*, Akwasasne Notes, p. 117).

The Haudenosaunee tell it like it is. If we want a food system that will serve our needs and the needs of our friends and neighbors regardless of creed, color, sex, or income, we must unlink from the present so-called global economy and create a new one. We can defend the new food system on the bases of economics, self-interest, and food security. We can also defend it on the basis of priceless values: an intimate relation with our food and the land on which it is grown; a sense of reverence for life; cooperation; justice; appreciation for the beauty of the cultivated landscape; and a fitting humility about the place of human beings in the scheme of nature.

Whatever words we find to justify it, we need a food system that begins with stewardship of the land; that produces food with respect for the ecology of the field, the farm, the watershed, the region, and the earth; that uses appropriate, nonviolent technology; and that distributes its benefits fairly. How do we get from where we are to where we long to be? Many of us across the United States are already working on this future food system. We have the ideas, the energy, the commitment—even when we lack many of the resources. To keep up our morale and give us clear direction, it would also help to share a vision of where we want to go. I offer these thoughts as a first sketch. It is what I daydream about during long hours weeding or sorting carrots.

Under a sustainable food system, every child will have the opportunity to share in a garden and learn how to raise and preserve food. Both urban and rural schools will offer programs in Future Farmers of America and 4-H clubs. All adults, including the unemployed and the homeless, will have the choice of participating in growing food on the scale they prefer: in an urban garden, by a few hours a season on a community farm, or by receiving training as a professional farmer and getting the financing to establish a full- or part-time farm enterprise. Training will include an understanding of ecology; acquiring the hands-on practical skills needed for growing, marketing, and working with other people; and holistic planning and management of resources. The land-grant schools will be accountable to the farmers and other citizens they were created to serve. Consumers, farmers, and academics will cooperate in establishing the agricultural research agenda.

Through a process of democratic and holistic planning, we will establish coherent regions and reasonable limits to farm acreage per family

by Elizabeth Henderson
Peacework Organic Farm

as the basis for the production and distribution of food staples. Instead of the average bite's traveling 1,200 miles, a much lower mileage will be the goal. The other determining parameter will be the use of energy: from expending 10 calories to produce 1 calorie of food, by David Pimentel's calculation, we will set our goal closer to the primitive achievement of 0.8:1. That need not exclude the possibility of exotic treats, but the basic foods we need for sustenance—grains, beans, potatoes, vegetables—will come from within our local region. Environmentally benign fuels from renewable sources will replace the polluting petrochemicals that fuel current farm equipment and the current transportation system.

A dense network of minifarms will surround each populated area and supply fresh vegetables from gardens and greenhouses all year round. Federal, state, and local policy will enable farmers to diversify their crops, use rotations, and institute other conservation practices. Soil erosion will be eliminated. Farm-raised animals will lead lives free from undue stress, pain, or suffering, and we will provide for their sustenance in a way that is respectful of the carrying capacity of the land. An enormous blossoming of biological controls and of the understanding of soil/plant interactions will narrow the gap in the use of toxic materials between organic and conventional farmers.

The development of regional infrastructures for marketing and distribution will reduce farmers' dependence on export sales. Farmers and consumers will have a variety of marketing choices: marketing cooperatives, food cooperatives, buying clubs, and Community Supported Agriculture projects. A food-banking system will store supplies for local emergencies or for shipping to other regions— either within the U.S. or abroad— where shortages occur.

The children of farm families will want to stay on the farm. Vital rural communities will become distinctive cultural centers. The rural economy will thrive, with many interesting job opportunities for local inhabitants both young and old, able-bodied and handicapped. Rural economic development will be guided by a policy of import substitution: instead of importing yellow peppers from, say, Holland, a local greenhouse will grow them. There will be an array of delicious local cheeses, breads, fruit drinks, wines, beers, and other specialty items to replace those imported from abroad. Processing plants and community kitchen and storage facilities will make it possible to preserve local food for year-round use. Food packaging will be designed so it can be recycled, reused, or eaten. All heavy metals and other pollutants will be carefully separated from organic wastes so those wastes can be efficiently composted and returned to the soil. Proposals for new processed foods will be judged for their contribution to nutritional needs and local self-sufficiency. Stores, schools, and other institutions will have the policy of purchasing locally produced food first.

No one will suffer from malnutrition. Access to a healthy supply of food will be considered a right. Instead of billions of dollars spent to subsidize megafarms, government subsidies will go to low-income consumers. Food stamps, farmers market coupons, and other support devices will place higher-priced foods within the reach of every consumer. Farmers will get off the dole. Farm gate prices will be based on a system of parity; that is, the prices farmers receive will be high enough to cover the costs of production and offer a decent wage to farmers and farmworkers and a reasonable return on investment. So-called externalities—such as soil erosion, water pollution, and the depletion of nonrenewable resources—will be factored into the price of food. Working people throughout the food system will enjoy safe working conditions and decent pay.

I am sure there are many things I may have forgotten—issues that are debatable and changes to be made. I offer this vision as a point of departure. Let's improve it together as we work together to transform the unjust, irrational, and wasteful food system we are saddled with today. If we farmers, gardeners, and citizens who care about soil, water, and food quality join with environmentalists, scientists, trade unionists, food justice activists, the civil rights movement, green entrepreneurs, members of religious groups of every faith, and universal health insurance advocates, we can create together a just and peaceful world in which all living creatures will coexist. We can create a global cooperative whereby human beings from diverse ethnic groups exchange seeds and recipes instead of bullets and missiles. ▪

Regional Family Farms

Maryland Certified Organic Growers Cooperative, Inc. (MCOGC), unites Maryland certified-organic farms committed to bringing the highest-quality organically grown fruits, grains, herbs, flowers, and vegetables to market. MCOGC's fourfold mission aims to (1) preserve Maryland farmland through economically viable organic farms; (2) offer an extensive variety of produce, fruit, and grains grown by family farmers in Maryland; (3) create an identification with the food supply by encouraging consumers to know who produces the food they eat and how it is grown; and (4) provide opportunities for area residents to participate in an innovative subscription program—known as Community Supported Agriculture—to ensure access to the best locally grown organic food available.

Ramps & Other Wild Mountain Greens

by George Ellison
adapted from materials in the writer's Back Then column dated March 28, 2001, in the Smoky Mountain News *(Waynesville, North Carolina) and his Nature Journal column in the* Asheville *(North Carolina)* Citizen-Times *dated August 3, 2001*

There was a time not so very long ago when just about everyone made it through the winter on cured meats, stored roots, and canned or dried vegetables. The first wild greens that appeared each spring were avidly sought after and prepared, using time-honored procedures. Even in this age of supermarkets and year-round produce, many of us still look forward to locating, harvesting, preparing, and chowing down on the real thing.

"Before there were many cars, the old folks used to walk all over the mountains gathering greens," Cherokee Lucinda Reed told me before her death several years ago. "You can eat off the land all year round if you want to."

Members of the remnant Eastern Band of Cherokees here in the Great Smokies region of western North Carolina are avid collectors of wild greens and other plants. Three of their favorite spring greens are well-known and widely collected: poke sallet (*Phytolacca americana*), ramps (see below), and branch lettuce (*Saxifrage micranthidifolia*). But if you attend a community club potluck in the spring on reservation lands, there's every chance you'll also have an opportunity to try less familiar potherbs as well. Bean salad (rosy twisted stalk, *Streptopus roseus*), stacey salad (small-flowered phacelia, *Phacelia dubia*), sweet salad (Solomon's seal, *Polygonatum biflorum*), bear grass spiderwort (*Tradescantia virginiana*), and sochan (green-headed coneflower, *Rudbeckia laciniata*) are collected as young plants, cleaned, and then parboiled or fried or both.

The early European settlers brought with them—often unknowingly—additional plants like watercress (*Nasturtium officinale*), dock (*Rumex ssp.*), dandelion (*Taraxacum ssp.*), and creasy sallet (*Barbarea verna*) that have also become spring staples in this region.

By my reckoning, raw or cooked wild greens are to be eaten with vinegar or lemon juice and a helping of buttered corn bread. If you so desire, by all means dish out the steaming greens right on top of the corn bread, then butter and pepper it liberally, and go to eating.

Ramps, also known as wild leeks, are no doubt the most famous plants here in the southern mountains. Ramp festivals abound every spring. According to one source, the word *ramps* comes from Europe, where it refers to the North American ramps' English cousin, the ramson (*A. ursinum*), also known as the bear leek or wood garlic. They are a member of the lily family and are, of course, placed in the same genus (*Allium*) as wild onions (*A. cernuum*) and wild garlic (*A. canadense*).

Many ramp fanciers aren't aware that our native ramp has two taxonomically recognized forms. Some botanical authorities consider these to be no more than varieties of the same species, while others, like this writer, assign each of them distinct-species status.

Wide-leaf ramps (*A. tricoccum*) have red-tinged leaves more than 2 inches wide and stalked leaf bases that are pinkish in color. Narrow-leaf ramps (*A. burdickii*) have untinged leaves that are less than 2 inches wide with unstalked leaf bases that are whitish in color. Wide-leaf ramps are by far the more common. They taste about the same, but in my opinion the narrow-leaf species has a more delicate flavor.

Ramps are sometimes available at roadside stands, but the Cherokees and white residents mostly gather them in early spring on the rich mountainsides either on their own lands or—with a permit—on U.S. Forest Service lands. Ramps have gained a wide reputation for having a powerful taste and a lingering, odoriferous smell. This has, unfortunately, discouraged the fainthearted from enjoying a succulent treat. What's all the fuss about? They're just onions. I find them to be delectable and pleasingly aromatic. Eat the bulbs raw, and see what I mean. Or cook and mix them with other greens or scrambled eggs. ■

FOOD & COMMUNITY

For three years now, the weather has made our work growing food much more difficult than it might have been. My partners and I grow organic vegetables on 18 acres for a Community Supported Agriculture project that has 270 member households. First, we had a drought; then a cold, wet year; and then an even more severe drought. When you spend hours and hours in a field moving a heavy hose from plant to plant to give each one just enough water to keep it from dying, it's hard not to question why you even bother. There is so much food in the markets. The United States is rich enough to import vegetables from anywhere in the world. Why should we struggle so hard to keep a small farm going?

While we represent a tiny part of the world food market, small farms that sell directly to the public provide a significant portion of the fresh in-season vegetables and fruits in our local regions. We can supply local consumers with food that is fresher and thus more nutritious than food shipped hundreds of miles. Those of us who are determined to continue farming know that we cannot compete with the big boys on price. The top 100 growers farm from 2,000 to 65,000 acres by using big, expensive, specialized machines and poorly paid farmworkers. We work with our hands and with machines we can adapt to many purposes. Since storage and shelf life are not issues, we choose varieties that taste best and have the highest nutritional value. In a very real sense, the food we produce is handcrafted: we invest more care per acre and per plant than do industrialized farms. As ancient wisdom teaches, "The best fertilizer is the footstep of the farmer." Our livelihood depends on our integrity and the quality of our food. We would not want to sell anything but the safest, finest food to the friends and neighbors who support our farms.

Our little farms also make big contributions to the local economy. Unlike the biggest growers, who ship supplies by the truckload straight from the manufacturer, we shop at local stores. We hire people from the community to supplement the work done mainly by members of our families. By selling close to our farms—at farmers markets, farm stands, or Community Supported Agriculture projects—we reduce the food-miles traveled by so much of what is sold in the supermarkets.

Running a farm is a dream for many people. On a small farm, you express your deepest values through your work. Often, people who go on farm tours are struck by how different each farm is from every other. A farm is a unique creation and its own particular blend of soil quality; climate; farmer's personality and abilities; physical, mental, and spiritual resources; and available markets.

So while you perform the everyday task of buying your food, you can simultaneously do something of great significance: you can vote with your

by Elizabeth
Henderson
Peacework
Organic Farm

food dollars for the kind of farms you would like to exist. By taking a little extra care to seek out local farm products, you are saying no to industrialized megafarms with their intense use of chemicals and their dependence on underpaid farmworkers. You are also much more likely to take home food that is fresh, nutritious, and full of flavor. And you are making it possible for people like me to partake in the ancient miracle of begetting food from the land, practicing the craft of farming, raising our families close to nature, and surviving in the global supermarket. ▪

Resources for Living Local

The **Virginia's Finest** trademark program was introduced in 1989 to identify, differentiate, and promote top-quality, Virginia-produced and -processed agricultural products. Since it began, the program has grown to include more than 500 participating agricultural, food, and beverage companies. The label covers fresh produce, specialty foods, hams, peanuts, wines, potted plants, Christmas trees, and many other products. Virginia's Finest products are easily identified by a red and blue check mark and can be found in most gift, gourmet, and specialty shops; grocery stores; nurseries; greenhouses; orchards; and farms. Quality standards used in the program are established by industries, agricultural groups, and similar representatives and are approved by the Virginia Department of Agriculture and Consumer Services. A two-step procedure for participation involves the development of industry standards and certification. Processed foods are approved by a special committee.

KNOW YOUR FARMERS

Who grows our food? That's a question too few Americans ever ask. In fact, we may have a whole generation of young-sters who not only don't know but who also have lost the knack of enjoying and cooking fresh food, believing that everything they eat comes from neatly wrapped packages; forget the farmer.

As a member and coleader of Slow Food USA and as a strong sup-porter of American Farmland Trust (AFT) with its national headquarters in Washington, D.C., I urge people to visit their weekly community farmers markets in Virginia and Maryland as well as in Washington, where the big blockbuster—the FRESHFARM Market at Dupont Circle—takes place every Sunday morning. The market has built a community neighbor-hood within the heart of the nation's capital. As Ann Yonkers, the farm market's manager, says, this market is building a connection for shoppers, because they actually face and talk to the people who raise their food.

Meeting farmers face-to-face is the best way to understand what it takes to put food on your table. Take the case of James Huyett, a lifelong farmer from West Virginia who's spent long hours of planning and toil on acreage that has been in his family since Civil War days. Tanned, bearded, and dressed in work clothes, Huyett greets customers at his farm stand at the Dupont Circle market—that is, when he's not busily sorting out his produce and arranging it along his display tables. From him you'll learn cooking tips, what's in season now, and what will be available next week. Huyett even hands out printed recipes showcasing what's freshest at the market.

But what really makes him tick is his passion for the land and his love of farming. His typical day during the growing season starts well before 5 a.m., by which time he's checked his equipment and talked to his fore-man about the day's work. Then he, his wife, and the farm helpers set about the day's tasks, whether the tasks be weeding, picking, planting, plowing, fighting off pests, or readying produce for market. In winter Huyett's schedule slackens slightly, but he is already making detailed plans for the crops he plans to plant the next growing season.

Huyett is only one example among many. Once you've made the rounds of the area's farmers markets, you may get to know something about the farmer who sells fresh eggs and honey or about the couple that oversees the stand selling delicious baked goods at Maryland's Takoma Park market. Maybe you'll strike up a conversation with the herb seller wearing the funny hat or with the young pair that sells peaches and toma-toes at Virginia's Reston market or with the one who bakes wonderful cheese breads at the Falls Church market or with the elderly plant seller at the Arlington County market. Each person surely has a story to tell, and you may want to hear them all.

by Alexandra Greeley
Vegetarian Times *magazine*

Most important, getting to know the farmers is the best way to support the work they do for all of us. It is, after all, the AFT's motto—"No Farms, No Food"—that should make us stop and ask the question, Who grows our food? Without farmers, we wouldn't eat. ■

Preserving Strawberries in Virginia

by Susan Tedder
Gentleman's
Ridge Farm
(see page 91)

Preserving fruit has been an essential part of family life since the invention of the mason jar in the 1850s. In leaner times, families relied on canned fruits and vegetables for food during the winter months. Today most families can and preserve because they enjoy carrying on the tradition taught to them by their mothers and grandmothers. As a jam maker, I love the satisfaction of seeing jars of fresh preserves lined up on the table as they cool. And, of course, it's hard to top the taste of home-cooked jams and jellies.

Strawberries are loved by almost everyone. While we grow a large variety of fruits and vegetables on our farm commercially, it is the month of May—strawberry time—that finds us swamped with customers. The sandy, loamy soil of Southside Virginia is favorable for the sweetness of the fruit and produces healthy plants with bold green leaves. Many home gardeners enjoy planting and caring for strawberries. Commercially, however, it is a time-consuming crop that is subject to damage from spring frosts and freezes.

Making strawberry preserves is a simple process. Prepare the fruit by washing, capping, and either quartering or crushing the berries. Add sugar and pectin, and cook to desired thickness (refer to canning recipes for the number of minutes). Strawberry preserves are my favorite. I loved strawberry preserves as a child and enjoyed helping my mother pick the fruit and make preserves. In fact, strawberry preserves were the inspiration for our jam and jelly business. Although we now prepare more than 20 different varieties, we add strawberries to many of them, often using this fruit as our symbol. ■

WHY FARM COMMUNITIES THRIVE

One of the more disheartening indictments of American social priorities at the dawn of the 21st century is that in the past few years, the number of Americans sitting in prison has surpassed the number of Americans who farm.

Farmers still produce the most important ingredient in the food chain, but they've become the most marginalized link in that chain. A hundred years ago, the farmer retained the majority of every dollar an American spent on food. Today the farmer gets a fraction—roughly 7 cents out of every dollar, or about as much as is spent on packaging. Agribusinesses—from seed and agrochemical companies to food processors and supermarkets—now capture the lion's share of the food dollar. There's plenty of money in the food system, but only a trivial share gets to the farmer.

It's no surprise then that most farm-raised children aren't interested in farming; farming has become the equivalent of economic suicide. As the average age of someone living in farm country increases—the number of American farmers older than 65 years is three times the number of those younger than 35 years—most farm communities are teetering on the brink of extinction. Although it might not be immediately apparent, that's the sort of trend that should concern anyone who eats.

Luckily, the story of American agriculture isn't all dismal. In fact, people who are fed up with the way most food is grown are hatching something exciting, beautiful, and quite hopeful for farm communities: Ordinary people are taking a fierce interest in any and all of the details of the food they purchase. As a country, we're beginning to ask whether our food was doused with pesticides. What crops were in the rotation? Does the livestock have access to the outdoors? How did the farming affect the watershed? Were farmworkers treated fairly? And we're seeking out farmers to get the answers.

Seeking out farmers may seem difficult to those who live in cities thousands of miles away from where food is grown and raised. But farmers markets, Community Supported Agriculture, and restaurants that feature local food all offer ways to shorten the distance between food consumers and food producers. Most of us would be surprised at how many ways there are to support local farmers in our area and therefore benefit from the freshest, most delicious food possible.

The advantages are clear for the consumer: Control over the quality of one's food grows with increasing proximity to the farmer raising that food. Buying direct from farmers means greater freshness, increased variety, and fewer preservatives needed to ship and store food. Everyone benefits from less food packaging, less transportation, and less energy use, in addition to less pollution. And a landscape defined by many small and

by Brian Halweil
Worldwatch
Institute

diverse farms dotting the countryside offers a variety of community and conservation benefits that are not readily provided by a small number of corporate megafarms.

Face-to-face interaction with the person who produced your food offers a reconnection with the land and living things that can bring great joy and satisfaction—a kind of culinary solidarity. Compare the social interactions at an open-air farmers market with the doldrums of a sterile supermarket.

For the farmer, selling local means fewer middlemen and a greater share of the food dollar. Money spent at farmers markets goes straight into farmers' pockets. That money flows through farm communities to support businesses, schools, hospitals, newspapers, and other entities that make communities tick.

And that is, ultimately, how farm communities will flourish in the U.S. once again: because people need them, care about them, and actively support them. ▪

Resources for Living Local

American Farmland Trust

The **American Farmland Trust** (AFT) is a private, nonprofit organization founded in 1980 to protect farmland in the United States. The AFT works to stop the loss of productive farmland and to promote farming practices that lead to a healthy environment. Its action-oriented programs include public education, technical assistance in policy development, and direct farmland protection projects. To find out more about the specific steps your community can take to create a farm plan, contact the American Farmland Trust.

SPRING RECIPES

Spring Salad

SERVES 4

Wash 8 to 9 ounces of lettuce in a large bowl or sink full of water. Agitate the leaves and allow the dirt to fall to the bottom of the sink/bowl. Lift the leaves off the top. Repeat until there is no grit at the bottom of the bowl. Spin dry.

Dress with:

1 tablespoon low-sodium soy sauce

1 tablespoon brown rice vinegar

3 tablespoons extra virgin olive oil

Whisk together and add to the salad as much as needed. Finish with a little fresh ground pepper.

COOKING FOR YOUR HEALTH AND WELL-BEING
Charlottesville, Virginia
Martha Hester Stafford
Chef/Owner

QUICK & BASIC RECIPES FOR SPRING PRODUCE

Roasted Asparagus

SERVES 4 TO 6

2 pounds fresh asparagus, trimmed

2 tablespoons extra virgin olive oil

Sea salt

Lemon wedges

1. Preheat oven to 475°F.

2. Rinse the asparagus stalks and drain on paper towels. Spread the stalks out on a cookie sheet. Brush the asparagus with oil, and then sprinkle with salt.

3. Roast the asparagus 10 to 12 minutes or until tender.

4. Serve with lemon.

Philip's New Potatoes

SERVES 4 TO 6

1½ pounds small red new potatoes cut in halves or quarters

1 tablespoon dried thyme or 2 tablespoons fresh thyme, minced

1 to 2 tablespoons brown rice vinegar or Japanese rice wine vinegar

¼ cup extra virgin olive oil

1 teaspoon sea salt

Freshly ground black pepper

1. Place the potatoes in a heavy, medium-size saucepan. Fill the pot with cold water to cover the potatoes by 1 inch. Bring the water to a boil, turn down the heat, and simmer for 5 to 10 minutes. Test to see if they are done by inserting a sharp knife into a piece of potato. If it slides in easily, they're done.

2. Drain the potatoes and put them back in the pan. Sprinkle with thyme. Add vinegar, olive oil, salt, and pepper. Toss gently until liquid is absorbed.

Strawberries in Virginia Wine

SERVES 4

1 cup young, fruity Virginia red wine (Horton Vineyards Route 33 is a good choice)

$^1/_2$ cup sugar

2 to 3 cups sliced strawberries

1. Stir together the wine and the sugar, and allow the mixture to sit until the sugar dissolves. To speed up the process and eliminate the alcohol in the wine, put the wine and sugar in a small saucepan and bring to a simmer over low heat. Simmer for a few minutes to boil away the alcohol.

2. Toss the wine and sugar with the strawberries, and let them sit for at least an hour. Serve alone or over vanilla ice cream.

Spinach with Spring Onions, Butter & Dill

SERVES 4 TO 6

2 bunches young spinach

2 tablespoons fresh, unsalted butter

1 bunch scallions or 4 Egyptian onions, green and white parts sliced into thin rounds

2 tablespoons minced fresh dill or 1 tablespoon dried dill

Sea salt and freshly ground pepper

More butter, if desired

1. Wash the spinach in a large bowl or sink full of water. Lift the leaves off the top, and repeat until there is no grit at the bottom of the bowl (usually 3 times is best). Break off and discard the tough stems. Place the clean and trimmed spinach in a colander, but do not dry it. The spinach will cook in the water that is clinging to the leaves.

2. Melt the butter in a medium-to-large sauté pan. Add the scallions and sauté until wilted and tender. Put the spinach in by handfuls, adding more as it cooks down. If you are using dried dill, add it now to give it a chance to rehydrate. The spinach needs to cook for only 2 to 3 minutes. Once it's tender, add the fresh dill if you are using it, and season with salt, pepper, and more butter.

Sugar Snap Peas with Tarragon

Wash the snap peas, trim the stems, and pull off the tough string that runs down one side of the bean. Blanch the peas briefly — no more than a minute — in a large pot of boiling salted water. To serve, toss with chopped fresh tarragon, extra virgin olive oil or butter, sea salt, and freshly ground pepper.

CHESAPEAKE BAY CRABMEAT & PEANUT TEMPURA FRITTERS
with Mango Salsa

SERVES 6

Mango Salsa (see sidebar)

For the fritters:

¹/₂ pound crabmeat

1 teaspoon finely chopped thyme

2 teaspoons finely chopped tarragon

2 tablespoons finely chopped basil

1 teaspoon finely chopped chives

¹/₂ teaspoon finely chopped shallots

1 cup fine white bread crumbs (from loaf of fresh bread)

¹/₄ cup heavy cream

1¹/₂ cups flour, divided use

¹/₂ cup olive oil

For the tempura batter:

1 egg

³/₄ cup milk

³/₄ cup finely crushed peanuts

Salt and black pepper to taste

1. Make the Mango Salsa (see sidebar) and set aside.

2. In a mixing bowl, combine the crabmeat, thyme, tarragon, basil, chives, and shallots. Add breadcrumbs and heavy cream. Mix well, add salt and pepper to taste, and mix again. Form into 1- to 2-ounce cakes. Use ¹/₂ cup of the flour to dust both sides of the patties. Set aside on a rack.

3. Put olive oil in a medium-size sauté pan over medium heat.

4. Make tempura batter immediately before using. For the tempura batter, whisk together the egg and milk. Add the remaining 1 cup of flour, and whisk until well blended. Add the peanuts and salt and pepper to taste.

5. When the oil is hot, carefully coat the crabmeat patties with the tempura mix and—without crowding them—panfry until crisp on both sides. (As it sits, the tempura batter will thicken and may need to be thinned with milk as you go along.)

6. Place even portions of the salsa in the centers of 6 dinner plates. Top each with a crab fritter.

Chef's recommendation: Matanzas Creek sauvignon blanc (Sonoma) or a dry crisp white wine with full acidity

BOAR'S HEAD INN
Charlottesville, Virginia
Alex Montiel
Executive Chef

SHRIMP WITH GARLIC & OLIVE OIL

SERVES 2

6 tablespoons extra virgin olive oil

8 small garlic cloves, thinly sliced

20 large shrimp, peeled and deveined

1 small dried spicy chili pepper, crushed

1 bay leaf (fresh or dried)

1 large, firm, ripe tomato, either cut in half and grated or blanched, peeled, and finely chopped

1 tablespoon sherry

Kosher salt to taste

1 tablespoon finely chopped parsley for garnish

1. Set sauté pan on high heat. Add olive oil and garlic. Sauté until garlic begins to brown.

2. Add shrimp, chili pepper, bay leaf, and tomato. Sauté just until shrimp turns pink.

3. Add sherry and salt. Sauté briefly to meld flavors. Sprinkle with parsley and serve.

Chef's recommendation: An aromatic, racy white wine like Fillaboa Albariño — Rias Baixas

JALEO
Washington
José Ramón Andrés
Executive Chef/Partner

A plum thicket
grows nearby,
and in spring—
when the plums
are too ripe for
tarts—we make
this simple palate
cleanser. We also
love using local
raspberries at
their peak, but
you can substi-
tute any ripe fruit
for the plums.

—CHEF ROBERT
RAMSEY

GOLDEN PLUM SORBET

MAKES 5 CUPS

3 cups water

12 to 14 tablespoons granulated sugar

1 cup pureed, ripe plums or fruit of your choice

Zest and juice of half lemon

Additional lemon zest for garnish

The day before serving:

1. Bring water to a boil and add sugar. (If the puree is very sweet, add 12 tablespoons sugar. If the purée tastes like just-ripe fruit, add 14 table-spoons.) Stir and simmer for 5 minutes or until sugar is completely dissolved and syrup is clear.

2. Remove from heat, and chill in refrigerator to room temperature.

3. Add fruit puree, zest, and lemon juice. Place in freezer and leave overnight.

On the day of serving:

4. Remove from freezer and let temper for 10 minutes.

5. When soft enough to mix, pulse in food processor, gradually adding small chunks and pulsing only until smooth. Store in the freezer in an airtight container. Remove from freezer 15 minutes before serving. Garnish servings with additional lemon zest.

Chef's recommendation: Horton Vineyards Viognier or a shot of Absolut Mandarin

FOX HEAD INN
Manakin-Sabot,
Virginia
Robert Ramsey
Executive Chef

FRESH BERRY CLAFOUTIS

SERVES 6

This is a great way to use overripe berries.

—CHEF CINDY WOLF

¹/₂ cup sugar, plus extra for dusting of ramekins

3 tablespoons flour

¹/₂ teaspoon baking powder

¹/₄ teaspoon baking soda

Pinch salt

3 whole eggs

6 tablespoons milk

¹/₂ cup melted unsalted butter

2 cups fresh berries (Blackberries, raspberries, and blueberries are especially good. If using strawberries, cut the larger ones in half.)

1. Butter 6 four-inch ramekins or small quiche pans. Lightly dust each with sugar.

2. Preheat the oven to 400°F.

3. Sift together the sugar, flour, baking powder, baking soda, and salt.

4. Beat eggs. Make a well in the center of the dry ingredients; pour eggs into the well. Add milk and melted butter. Slowly stir the dry ingredients into the center until all ingredients are mixed.

5. Divide fruit among the ramekins or pans. Pour batter on top.

6. Bake 25 to 30 minutes until set.

Chef's recommendation: A medium-sweet white, such as Muscat des Rivesaltes, Domaine Piquemal

CHEF CINDY WOLF
CHARLESTON

CHARLESTON
Baltimore
Cindy Wolf
Chef/Owner

FRESH ENGLISH PEA
& FAVA BEAN SOUP

SERVES 4

1½ pounds fava beans, in pods

1½ pounds English (garden) peas, in pods

1 medium leek (white part only) or ½ small onion, coarsely chopped

1 stalk celery, coarsely chopped

1 medium carrot, coarsely chopped

1 small clove garlic

8 peppercorns

3 branches fresh thyme

6 cups cold water

6 tablespoons butter

6 shallots, finely chopped

Salt and freshly ground pepper to taste

3 small, fresh spearmint leaves

Chives, for garnish

1. Shell the favas, discarding pods; shell the peas, reserving pods. Set aside a small handful each of the shelled peas and favas for garnish.

2. Prepare a simple vegetable stock using the pods from the English peas, leek or onion, celery, carrot, garlic, peppercorns, and thyme. Don't bother sautéing the vegetables first; just cover them with the cold water and let the flavors infuse as you bring the stock to a boil. Half an hour of simmering should be sufficient. The resulting stock should have a pronounced, fresh pea flavor. Strain stock and allow to chill in the refrigerator or freezer.

3. In a large pot, bring plenty of water to a boil, and blanch the fava beans for 1 minute. Drain and plunge the beans into ice water to stop their cooking. Remove and discard the outer skin from each bean.

4. Blanch the reserved peas and favas for 1 minute or until just tender. Drain and plunge into ice water to stop their cooking. Set aside to use as garnish.

**CASHION'S
EAT PLACE**
Washington
Ann Cashion
Chef/Owner

5. Heat the butter in a soup pot. Sauté the shallots for 3 or 4 minutes until soft. Add peas and favas and just enough vegetable stock to cover. Season with salt and pepper to taste. Allow stock to come to a simmer. Cook the peas and favas until they are tender but still bright green, about 5 minutes. Remove from heat.

6. Puree cooked peas in a blender or food processor, using as much chilled vegetable stock as required to achieve a smooth, light consistency. The chilled stock stops the cooking process and helps the soup maintain its bright color and fresh flavor. Add the spearmint leaves to one of the batches as you puree.

7. Pass the soup through a medium sieve to remove skins. Do not use a fine-mesh sieve, or you will lose too much of the creamy solids that give this soup its consistency. Adjust seasoning. Reheat soup just before serving. Garnish with finely minced chives and the reserved blanched peas and favas. You may also serve this soup cold, although I prefer it heated.

Chef's recommendation: Domaine Weinbach Pinot Blanc or a dry Alsatian Riesling

**Local Foods
Local Flavors**

Bergey's Dairy Farm *is a family-held cooperative located near Chesapeake, Virginia, that produces premium milk in glass bottles, homemade ice cream, and other dairy products. The cows are never given bovine growth hormones or steroids, and the Bergeys grow most of the feed for their cows on their family farm. The dairy operation has a small, farm-owned retail store on site and makes door-to-door deliveries of milk products.*

Vinaigrette

3 tablespoons balsamic vinegar

Salt and freshly ground pepper to taste

1/2 cup extra virgin olive oil

In a small bowl, combine vinegar, salt, and pepper. Whisk in the olive oil.

SNEAD'S FARM ASPARAGUS, VIDALIA ONION & NEW POTATO SALAD

SERVES 8

2 pounds new potatoes, quartered

2 pounds fresh asparagus (preferably grown by Emmett Snead*)

1/2 pound mesclun

Vinaigrette (see sidebar)

1/4 cup thinly sliced Vidalia onion or other sweet onion (see note on page 89)

Sea salt and freshly ground pepper to taste

4 hard-boiled eggs, coarsely chopped, for garnish

1. Bring a pot of salted water to a rapid boil. Blanch the potatoes until just cooked. Remove to an ice water bath to cool.

2. Snap off and discard the woody ends of the asparagus spears, and blanch spears in another pot of rapidly boiling salted water. Depending on the thickness of the stalks, they will take 2 to 5 minutes to cook. Once they are tender but still bright green, plunge them into an ice water bath.

3. In a medium bowl, dress the mesclun with some of the vinaigrette, and divide evenly among 8 chilled plates.

4. Cut the asparagus into 2-inch pieces. Put the asparagus, onion, and potatoes in the bowl, and toss with the rest of the vinaigrette. Adjust seasoning with salt and pepper.

5. Mound some of the asparagus mixture on top of each mesclun pile, and garnish with chopped egg.

Chef's recommendation: Tokay Pinot Gris Vieilles Vignes, Siegler, or another full-bodied, dry Alsatian wine

* *Editor's note:* When asked why his asparagus is so delicious, Emmett Snead says that freshness and proper harvesting make all the difference. Snead cuts his asparagus plants by hand, gets it quickly out of the sun, and keeps it well hydrated before and during the short trip to local customers. The result is asparagus with superior texture and flavor.

SOUTHERN GRILLE
Richmond, Virginia
Jimmy Sneed
Former Chef/Owner

LEMON GOAT CHEESE TART
with Sliced Fresh Strawberries

SERVES 8

1 cup unsalted butter

2/3 cup sugar

1/4 teaspoon salt

2 small egg yolks

1 teaspoon vanilla

2 1/3 cups flour

Goat Cheese Filling (see sidebar)

2 pints strawberries

Sugar to taste

1. Preheat oven to 375°F.

2. Blend butter, sugar, and salt. Mix in egg yolks, one at a time, and add vanilla. Mix well, and then add flour. Roll out to a thin (1/8-inch) crust. Place in a 10-inch tart or springform pan with a removable bottom. Chill crust in refrigerator 30 minutes or longer.

3. Remove crust from refrigerator, line with foil, and fill with dry beans or pie weights. Bake for 15 minutes. Remove weights and foil and bake about 10 more minutes until golden.

4. Pour Goat Cheese Filling into prepared pie crust and bake until set, about 25 to 30 minutes.

5. Slice strawberries and toss with a small amount of sugar. Cut tart into 8 slices and spoon strawberries onto each slice before serving.

Chef's recommendation: Linden Riesling Vidal or some other off-dry white wine

Goat Cheese Filling

1 pound fresh goat cheese

1/2 pound cream cheese

1/4 cup mascarpone

4 tablespoons soft, unsalted butter

3/4 cup sugar

1/3 cup whipping cream

4 eggs

Zest of 1 lemon

1 teaspoon vanilla

Blend goat cheese, cream cheese, mascarpone, and butter until smooth. Beat in sugar. Add cream, eggs, lemon zest, and vanilla. Stir until combined.

FOUR & TWENTY BLACKBIRDS
Flint Hill, Virginia
Heidi Morf
Chef/Owner

Orange Hollandaise

In a 1-quart metal bowl, combine:

2 egg yolks

1½ teaspoons fresh orange juice

1 teaspoon water

Pinch of salt and white pepper

Cook egg mixture over boiling water, whisking constantly until slightly thickened. Remove from heat and add a drop or two of cold water to stop the cooking process. In a slow, steady stream, add:

4 tablespoons clarified butter

Whisk constantly while a slightly thick emulsion forms—about 2 to 3 minutes. If the sauce breaks (separates), whisk in a small amount of ice water.

RESTAURANT COLUMBIA
Easton, Maryland
Stephen Mangasarian
Chef/Owner

ASPARAGUS CUSTARD
with Orange Hollandaise

SERVES 4 AS AN APPETIZER

1 pound fresh asparagus, 2 inches of the stem end discarded, remaining coarsely chopped (reserve 4 of the best-looking tips for the garnish)

1 tablespoon unsalted butter

1 small shallot, coarsely diced

½ teaspoon kosher salt

⅛ teaspoon freshly ground white pepper

Scant ⅛ teaspoon freshly ground nutmeg

½ cup chicken stock

½ cup heavy cream

2 egg yolks

1 egg

Orange zest for garnish

Orange Hollandaise (see sidebar)

1. Preheat oven to 325°F.

2. Place the asparagus, butter, shallot, salt, pepper, and nutmeg in a heavy-bottomed saucepan. Cover and cook over low heat, stirring occasionally, until the asparagus turns bright green and the shallot turns translucent, approximately 10 minutes. Add chicken stock, bring to a boil, lower heat, and simmer uncovered for 10 minutes. Slowly add the cream and bring back to a simmer. Cool slightly, place in small batches in blender, and run on high until smooth. Then force through a fine sieve.

3. In a medium-size bowl, beat the egg yolks and whole egg thoroughly. Add the asparagus mixture, stirring all the while.

4. Butter 4 six-ounce ramekins, and ladle the custard into the ramekins. Place the ramekins in a pan with hot water to one-third the height of the ramekins. Bake for 45 minutes or until a knife inserted into the custard comes out clean.

5. To serve, run a thin-bladed knife around the edge of the custard. Invert onto a plate garnished with orange zest and the reserved asparagus tips cut in half. Serve with Orange Hollandaise.

Chef's recommendation: Chalone Pinot Blanc or a quality Chenin Blanc

VIDALIA'S BAKED ONION

SERVES 4

6 tablespoons unsalted butter, divided use

4 jumbo Vidalia onions, whole

3 tablespoons dark-brown sugar

4 teaspoons finely chopped fresh thyme

4 teaspoons finely chopped fresh rosemary

2 tablespoons finely chopped garlic

4 tablespoons beef broth

8 tablespoons sherry vinegar

8 shiitake mushrooms, roughly chopped

4 ounces country ham, cut into thin strips

4 tablespoons tomato (blanched, peeled, seeded, and chopped fine)

2 tablespoons capers

4 teaspoons chives, finely minced

1. Preheat the oven to 375°F.

2. Set out 4 tablespoons of the butter to soften at room temperature. Peel onion skin in ¼-inch strips, from the flower end back to the root end of the onion, leaving intact at the root. Cut four 12-inch-by-12-inch squares of aluminum foil. Place 1 tablespoon of the softened butter in the center of each square of foil. Mix together the brown sugar, thyme, rosemary, and garlic; divide into 4 portions, and top each of the butter centers with the mixture. Place the onions on top in the centers of the foil squares with root ends facing up. Gently pull up the strips of skin, and draw the foil up from the four corners to the center, forming a pyramid. Lightly crimp the foil around the neck of the onion with the skins pulled straight up. Pour 1 tablespoon of the broth and 2 tablespoons of the vinegar into the top opening of each foil packet.

3. Bake for about 1 hour and 10 minutes or until soft. Remove onions from foil and place on serving plates. Reserve the juices.

4. Heat a medium-size sauté pan. Add the remaining 2 tablespoons of butter, shiitake mushrooms, and country ham. Sauté until mushrooms soften. Add the reserved juice from the baked onions and then the tomato, capers, and chives. Cook for several minutes to reduce liquid so that it coats the back of a spoon. Season to taste. Spoon sauce into the centers of 4 plates. Top with an onion and drizzle more sauce over all.

Chef's recommendation: Horton Viognier 1999, Miner Viognier 1999, or other white wine with good acidity and hints of apricot and white peach

Editor's note: *Vidalia onions are grown in Georgia. Farmers near the town of Courtland, Virginia, are growing an onion that has the sweetness of a Vidalia, but because of the cooler spring weather, it is not the Vidalia's equal in size. To prepare this recipe using a local onion, substitute large, sweet yellow onions.*

VIDALIA
Washington
Peter Smith
Executive Chef

SOUFFLÉ GLACÉ AUX FRAISES

(FROZEN STRAWBERRY SOUFFLÉ)

SERVES 8

$2\frac{1}{2}$ pounds whole strawberries (to yield $3\frac{3}{4}$ cups puree)

$\frac{1}{2}$ cup water

1 cup sugar

6 egg whites

Pinch of salt

$1\frac{1}{2}$ cups heavy whipping cream

4 tablespoons strawberry brandy or kirsch

Unsalted butter to grease soufflé collar

8 whole strawberries for garnish

Coulis de Fraises (Strawberry Sauce) (see next page)

1. Wash the strawberries in a bowl of cold water. Be sure to lift the berries out of the water so as to leave all grit behind. Hull the berries, and puree in a food processor. Set aside.

2. Prepare an Italian meringue by combining the water and sugar in a heavy saucepan, and, stirring often, heat until the mixture reaches 280°F, or the soft-crack stage on a candy thermometer. When the thermometer reaches 250°F, begin whipping the egg whites and salt in an electric mixer; whip until soft peaks form. When the sugar syrup reaches 280°F, remove the pan from the heat. With the electric mixer on low, slowly pour the hot syrup into the beaten whites; continue whipping 4 to 5 minutes until meringue cools.

3. Whip the heavy cream in a chilled bowl.

4. Stir the strawberry brandy into $1\frac{3}{4}$ cups of the strawberry puree; set the balance aside (the remaining puree will be used in Coulis de Fraises). Fold the puree into the cooled meringue. Then gently fold the whipped cream into the strawberry-meringue mixture. Chill in the refrigerator while preparing the soufflé molds.

To assemble the soufflés:

5. Butter eight 5-ounce ramekins. To make the collars, cut eight 12-inch-by-6-inch strips of parchment paper or aluminum foil, fold in half lengthwise, and butter one side. Wrap a strip of foil, buttered side facing in, around the outside of each mold. Secure the ends with several pieces of masking tape. The foil must stand 1 inch above the rim of the molds.

6. Divide the meringue mixture evenly among the 8 ramekins, filling each to the top of the collar. Freeze several hours. Before serving, remove the collar and top each soufflé with one of the whole strawberries. Serve with the sauce on the side.

Chef's recommendation: A dry, Pinot Noir–driven champagne such as Trouillars Brut Rosé

Coulis de Fraises (Strawberry Sauce)

³/₄ cup sugar

2 tablespoons kirsch

2 cups strawberry puree (from step 1 of main recipe)

Mix sugar and kirsch with the remaining 2 cups of puree. Refrigerate until time to serve.

Gentleman's Ridge Farm *is a pick-your-own fruit and vegetable operation serving customers throughout southeastern Virginia. Located in Blair, Virginia, Gentleman's Ridge also creates an assortment of delicious jams, jellies, and preserves in a variety of flavors made with farm-fresh ingredients. Gentleman's Ridge features its own line of gift and specialty baskets as well as its recently introduced pasta sauce.*

ROMAINE HEARTS & SHAVED PECORINO SALAD
with a Creamy Black Pepper Dressing

SERVES 6

For the dressing:

2 egg yolks (see Food Safety note on page 233)

8 teaspoons red wine vinegar

1 tablespoon Dijon mustard

Pinch of salt

$^1/_2$ teaspoon Worcestershire sauce

$1^1/_2$ teaspoons cracked black peppercorns

$^1/_4$ cup sour cream

$^3/_8$ cup olive oil

$^1/_4$ cup salad oil

For the salad:

6 hearts of romaine, root end trimmed

2 cups shaved Pecorino Romano (shave with a carrot peeler)

$^1/_4$ cup pine nuts, lightly toasted

3 eggs, hard cooked and coarsely chopped

$^1/_2$ pint cherry tomatoes, sliced in half

1. In a mixer or blender, combine egg yolks, vinegar, mustard, salt, Worcestershire sauce, and peppercorns. Mix for 3 minutes. Slowly add the sour cream, olive oil, and salad oil; blend for 5 minutes.

2. Divide romaine among 6 chilled plates. Drizzle dressing on and between the leaves; top with Pecorino, pine nuts, chopped egg, and cherry tomatoes.

Chef's recommendation: Vincent Delaporte Sancerre or another Loire sauvignon blanc

**BISTRO ST.
MICHAELS**
St. Michaels, Maryland
David Stein
Chef/Owner

EGG LINGUINE WITH GARLIC & HERB SHELLFISH SAUCE
& Fried Calamari

SERVES 4 AS AN APPETIZER

12 ounces egg linguine, cooked and drained

Shellfish Sauce (see below)

Garlic Butter (see sidebar)

Canola oil for frying

Flour

12 calamari (squid) tentacles

4 teaspoons chopped parsley

4 teaspoons chopped tarragon

4 teaspoons chopped chives

1. Toss linguine in 12 ounces of the Shellfish Sauce. Add 4 tablespoons Garlic Butter.

2. While heating the oil to 350°F, coat the calamari with flour. Fry coated calamari in the hot oil.

3. Mound pasta and sauce in a warmed bowl. Place calamari in a ring around the pasta; sprinkle all with chopped parsley, tarragon, and chives.

Chef's recommendation: Sancerre Domaine de la Perrier or another medium-bodied Sauvignon Blanc

Shellfish Sauce

1 cup Chardonnay

2 cups clam or shellfish stock

2 cups heavy cream

Combine the Chardonnay and stock in a saucepan. Bring to a boil and reduce by half. Add cream and reduce until thickened stock coats the spoon.

Garlic Butter

¼ pound unsalted butter, softened

1½ teaspoons finely minced garlic

1½ teaspoons finely minced shallots

½ teaspoon salt

⅛ teaspoon freshly ground black pepper

1½ teaspoons finely chopped parsley

Combine all either in a blender or by hand.

(Freeze leftover butter for later use.)

208 TALBOT
St. Michaels, Maryland
Paul Milne
Chef/Owner

CORNMEAL-CRUSTED CROAKER

on Grilled Green Asparagus
with Yellow Tomato Sauce

SERVES 4

1 gallon water

1 cup kosher salt

2 pounds large, green asparagus spears

2 tablespoons olive oil

Salt and freshly ground pepper to taste

Canola oil

8 croaker fillets, checked thoroughly for small bones

1 cup flour

3 eggs

2 cups cornmeal

Yellow Tomato Sauce (see next page)

Chopped parsley for garnish, optional

1. Bring water and salt to a boil in a large pot.

2. Remove and discard woody bottoms from asparagus. Cook asparagus in the boiling water for 4 minutes. Immediately shock in an ice bath— which sweetens the asparagus—and drain well. (This can be done ahead of time.)

3. Prepare and light the grill. Toss asparagus with olive oil and a pinch of the salt and pepper. Grill until hot with nice grill marks—about 2 to 4 minutes. Do not burn.

4. Heat a cast-iron pan on medium-high heat. Fill with ¼ inch of canola oil. Dust the croaker fillets in flour and shake off the excess.

5. In a wide bowl, whisk eggs until well mixed. Lay each fish fillet in egg wash, and then coat in cornmeal so it is evenly breaded. Repeat until all fillets are breaded.

ACACIA
Richmond, Virginia
Dale Reitzer
Executive Chef

. Fry fillets for 1 to 2 minutes or until they are a rich golden brown on each side. If you don't have a pan large enough, fry in batches. Place cooked fillets on a plate with paper towels, and keep warm in the oven until served.

. Divide the grilled asparagus among 4 hot plates; place flat in the center of each plate. Lay 2 croaker fillets on top of the asparagus, and spoon Yellow Tomato Sauce around the asparagus. Garnish with chopped parsley. (A note from the chef: Garlic mashed potatoes are great with this dish.)

Chef's recommendation: A medium-bodied Chardonnay, such as Naked Mountain

Yellow Tomato Sauce

shallot, finely diced

teaspoon unsalted butter

/2 cup white wine

yellow tomato, stemmed and chopped

/4 to 1 cup vegetable stock

basil leaves

Salt and freshly ground pepper

tablespoons olive oil

In a saucepan over low heat, sweat shallots in butter until soft. Add white wine, turn up the heat, and boil until reduced to 2 tablespoons. Add the chopped tomato and enough vegetable stock to just cover. Bring to a boil. Reduce to a simmer and cook until thickened—about 10 minutes depending on juiciness of tomato and on personal preference.

Remove from heat and allow to cool completely. In a blender, puree with the basil and strain. Season with salt and pepper to taste. Finish by whisking in the olive oil.

ROCKFISH WITH TOMATOES, CAPERS, LEMON, ARTICHOKES & FENNEL

SERVES 6

3 large globe artichokes

2 lemons, zest and juice

6 cloves garlic, peeled

1 cup extra virgin olive oil, divided use

2 bulbs fennel, finely sliced lengthwise

Salt and freshly ground pepper

2 tablespoons peanut oil, for sautéing

6 six-ounce rockfish fillets

4 Roma tomatoes, peeled, seeded, and cut in large dice

1 cup dry white wine

1 cup fish or chicken stock (optional)

2 tablespoons capers

1 tablespoon basil leaves, cut into thin ribbons (chiffonade)

1. Trim the artichoke stems to 1 inch. Remove the tough outer leaves, and trim the sharp tips of the leaves with scissors. Slice off the top third of each artichoke. Using only enough water to cover, blanch the artichokes in salted, boiling water with a little of the lemon juice. When tender — after about 20 minutes — remove from the water and let cool. Save the leaves for another use and discard the hairy choke. Slice the hearts and stems into $\frac{1}{8}$-inch slices.

2. Place the garlic cloves in cold water in a small saucepan. Bring to a boil, boil for 1 minute, then strain. Repeat 3 times total. Slice the garlic and set aside.

3. In a sauté pan over high heat, add 1 tablespoon of the olive oil. Add fennel, and sauté until tender. Add salt and pepper to taste. Spoon into a bowl and keep warm.

KINKEAD'S
Washington
Bob Kinkead
Chef/Owner

4. Wipe out the sauté pan, add the peanut oil, and bring to medium-high heat. Salt and pepper the rockfish fillets. Sauté 2 or 3 fillets at a time, browning on one side about 4 to 5 minutes, turning and sautéing 2 more minutes, and removing from the pan. Keep warm and repeat with remaining fish.

5. Add the sliced garlic to the pan along with 8 tablespoons of the remaining olive oil. Cook 2 minutes. Add the sliced artichokes and sauté until starting to brown. Add the tomatoes, white wine, stock, lemon zest and juice, and the remaining 7 tablespoons of extra virgin olive oil. Turn up the heat and reduce the liquid by ¼.

6. Reduce heat and return the rockfish to the mixture. Add the capers and the basil, and adjust salt and pepper. Cook 2 more minutes until fish is just flaky, and again adjust salt and pepper.

7. Divide the fennel among 6 warm dinner plates, and top with the rockfish fillets. Sauce with the vegetable mixture and serve.

Chef's recommendation: Coulée de Serrant or another Loire dry white wine

**Local Foods
Local Flavors**

VIRGINIA SEAFOOD

*The **Virginia Seafood** logo identifies seafood that has been harvested or processed in the state. Virginia's quality control and regulatory standards for water quality and seafood-processing facilities are recognized as among the most stringent in the nation. The state's water and the products it yields are reviewed and regulated by many state and federal agencies. Virginia's watermen and processors continually inspect the seafood they catch and sell, and every processor is required to have a knowledgeable food safety person in each plant.*

Fontina Sauce

¹/₂ pound Fontina cheese

2 tablespoons flour

1 cup milk

¹/₂ cup heavy cream

2 egg yolks

Dice the cheese into small cubes and toss with the flour until well covered. Cover the cheese with the milk and allow to sit in a warm place for 2 hours to let the cheese soften. Heat the cream slowly in a double boiler; add the cheese-and-milk mixture. Cook slowly until the cheese completely dissolves. Remove from the heat. Very slowly stir in the egg yolks, one at a time, fully incorporating into the cheese mixture after each addition. Do not reheat after adding egg yolks.

GALILEO
Washington
Roberto Donna
Chef/Owner

GNOCCHI ALLA FONTINA

SERVES 4

1¹/₂ pounds Yukon Gold potatoes

2 extra-large egg yolks

²/₃ cup durum flour (semolina)

Salt and freshly ground white pepper to taste

Fontina Sauce (see sidebar)

1. Preheat oven to 425°F.

2. Place the potatoes, with the skins on, on a baking sheet. Bake, uncovered, for 50 minutes or until completely cooked. Remove potatoes from the oven; immediately peel and rice them through a food mill.

3. Once the riced potatoes are cool enough to handle, add the egg yolks and most of the flour. Season with salt and white pepper, and fold all together by hand until incorporated. Test the consistency of the gnocchi dough by cooking a small piece in a little boiling water. If the dough is too wet, add a bit more flour. If too dry, add a small amount of water. Allow the gnocchi dough to relax for 10 minutes before rolling.

4. Roll a small piece of dough between your palms into a tube the diameter of your index finger. Drop on a lightly floured board and cut into ¹/₂-inch sections. Roll each section across the tines of a fork or a gnocchi board.

5. Cook the gnocchi in small batches in rapidly boiling salted water. When they float on the surface, skim them off with a strainer.

6. Toss the cooked gnocchi in Fontina Sauce. Serve at once.

Chef's recommendation: Barbaresco, Ceretto, or a Barolo

MORELS SAUTÉED IN WHITE WINE
with Asparagus Vinaigrette & Shaved Parmesan

SERVES 4 TO 6

1 bunch asparagus, ends trimmed

1 shallot, coarsely chopped

¼ cup champagne vinegar

1 teaspoon fresh lemon juice

1 to 1½ cups extra virgin olive oil

Salt and freshly ground pepper to taste

4 tablespoons unsalted butter

1 pound fresh morels

½ cup good dry white wine

Parmesan cheese, for garnish

1. Blanch asparagus for 1 minute in plenty of boiling salted water. Drain
   and plunge into ice water. Chop asparagus coarsely and put in blender
   with the shallot, champagne vinegar, and lemon juice. Purée on high
   speed, drizzling in the olive oil until creamy and of pourable consistency.
   Season with salt and pepper.

2. Melt butter in a sauté pan; add morels and sauté for 1 minute. Stir in the
   white wine and continue cooking until morels are just soft. Season with
   salt and pepper.

3. To serve, put a few tablespoons of asparagus vinaigrette in a circle on
   each plate, place sautéed morels over the circle, and shave a few curls
   of fresh Parmesan over all.

*Chef's recommendation: A complex, full-bodied South African sauvignon blanc,
such as Thelema*

C&O RESTAURANT
Charlottesville, Virginia
Thomas Bowles
Executive Chef

DANDELION SOUP

SERVES 4

1½ pounds tender dandelion greens

4 tablespoons unsalted butter

1 small onion, finely diced

3 cups chicken or vegetable stock

2 egg yolks

1 teaspoon Dijon mustard

1 cup heavy cream

Salt and freshly ground black pepper to taste

Dash pepper sauce such as Chile Man Louisiana Lightnin' (optional)

1. Remove and discard the bottom few inches of the dandelion stems, and if the stems are large, strip greens from stems. This should yield about 12 to 16 ounces of edible greens. Wash the greens several times; discard the water. Soak the greens for 10 minutes in cold water to cover. Then drain. Chop greens finely.

2. In a soup pot, melt the butter and cook the onion for several minutes until soft. Add the greens and continue cooking until they are wilted. Add the stock and bring to a boil. Lower the heat, cover, and simmer for 30 minutes. Cool slightly and puree ⅔ of the soup in a blender. Return to the soup pot, but remove from the heat.

3. In a small bowl, beat together the egg yolks, mustard, and cream. Slowly add to the soup, stirring rapidly with a wire whisk. If needed, thin the soup with additional stock.

4. Reheat the soup, but do not bring to a boil. Season to taste. Serve hot or very cold.

Chef's recommendation: A full-bodied Chardonnay, such as Sonoma Cutrer Russian River

My "other" mother, Mealy Sartori, would get so excited every spring, when the dandelions were just poking their heads out of the damp soil. She always reminded us, "Use only the young, tender ones, or they'll be too bitter!" And she was right. Around the Chesapeake, dandelion greens have always been regarded as a spring tonic: they clean out your blood after a long, cold winter.

—CHEF JOHN SHIELDS

GERTRUDE'S

GERTRUDE'S
Baltimore
John Shields
Chef/Owner

CRAB NAPOLEON

SERVES 4

For the pastry:

2 sheets phyllo dough

1 egg, slightly beaten

1/4 cup melted unsalted butter

Kosher salt and freshly ground black pepper

For the filling:

1 avocado

1 heaping tablespoon sour cream

1 scant tablespoon grainy Dijon mustard

1 teaspoon fresh lime juice

Salt and freshly ground pepper

8 to 10 ounces jumbo crabmeat, picked

For the garnish:

2 large handfuls grape tomatoes, cut in half

4 small handfuls micro or baby greens

1/2 red bell pepper, finely diced

Extra virgin olive oil

Aged balsamic vinegar

1. Set rack in lower half of oven and preheat oven to 350°F.

2. Lay 1 sheet of phyllo on a buttered baking sheet. Brush with egg wash, and cover with other sheet. Brush with melted butter. Cut into twelve 4-inch-by-4-inch squares. Sprinkle with salt and pepper. Bake for 12 minutes.

3. Mash avocado, keep somewhat chunky. Mix lightly with sour cream, mustard, lime juice, salt, and pepper.

4. To assemble, place a phyllo square on each plate. Top with 1 tablespoon avocado mix, then crabmeat. Repeat for 3 layers, ending with a layer of avocado and crab.

5. Garnish each plate with tomato halves, micro greens, and red pepper. Drizzle with olive oil and balsamic vinegar.

Chef's recommendation: La Crema Chardonnay or another creamy, oak-barrel-fermented, Sonoma Chardonnay

BICYCLE
Baltimore
Barry Rumsey
Chef/Owner

STEAMED BLACK BASS
with Spring Vegetables & Carrot Broth

SERVES 4

1 tablespoon butter

10 to 12 fresh cilantro stems

1 stalk fresh lemongrass, sliced

4 five-ounce black bass fillets (check for and remove small bones)

Salt and freshly ground pepper to taste

1 cup dry white wine

2 tablespoons olive oil

1 carrot, julienned

10 snow peas, picked and julienned

1 red pepper, julienned

1 yellow pepper, julienned

4 green onions, trimmed and split in quarters

1 daikon radish, peeled and julienned

1/2 teaspoon black sesame seeds

4 cups Carrot Sauce (see next page)

1 tablespoon fresh cilantro leaves, washed

1. Preheat oven to 450°F.

2. Cut four 18-inch-by-18-inch squares of parchment paper. Fold each sheet of paper in half, and cut into a half-heart shape. When open, the paper will be in a heart shape. Open the heart-shaped parchment on a work table and divide the butter among all four, greasing the middle of each evenly. Distribute the cilantro stems and lemongrass over the butter. Place the fillets, skin side up, on one side of the heart and sprinkle with salt and pepper. Fold parchment paper over bass. Beginning at the top of the heart, turn edges under in small, overlapping folds to seal, leaving a 1-inch opening at the end. Pour 2 ounces of wine through the opening in each papillote, and twist each end to seal. Put the paper packages on a baking pan, and place in oven for 7 minutes.

Melrose

MELROSE
Park Hyatt Washington
Washington
Brian McBride
Executive Chef

3. Heat olive oil in a sauté pan. Quickly sauté the carrot, snow peas, peppers, onions, and radish. Season with salt, pepper, and sesame seeds. When just tender—about 5 minutes—remove from heat. Divide vegetables among 4 bowls.

4. Remove bass from the oven. Open parchment paper, and remove and discard lemongrass and cilantro stems. Place 1 fillet in each bowl on top of the vegetables.

5. Pour the wine from the parchment paper into the pan used for sautéing the vegetables. Add Carrot Sauce and cilantro leaves. Bring to a boil and adjust seasoning. Ladle over fish and serve.

Chef's recommendation: Martin Schaetzel Cuvée Reserve Pinot Blanc or a crisp Alsatian Pinto Gris

Carrot Sauce

4 cups strained carrot juice

1 ounce fresh lemongrass, chopped

1 ounce Thai ginger (galangal root), thinly sliced

2 tablespoons unsweetened coconut milk

½ jalapeño pepper, seeded and chopped

2 large cloves garlic, split in half

1 dash cinnamon

5 sprigs basil

5 sprigs cilantro

4 cups fish stock

Combine carrot juice, lemongrass, ginger, coconut milk, jalapeño, garlic, and cinnamon in a nonreactive pot. Over medium-high heat, reduce by half, about 25 minutes. Remove from heat, add basil and cilantro, and let steep for 20 minutes. Strain carrot mixture into fish stock. Place back on stove and reduce to yield 4 cups. Adjust seasonings. Will keep for 7 days in refrigerator.

TARRAGON & GARLIC ROASTED SPRING CHICKEN

SERVES 4

1 four-and-one-half-pound
  free-range chicken

$^{1}/_{2}$ ounce fresh tarragon, divided use

20 cloves garlic, peeled

$^{1}/_{4}$ pound unsalted butter

Salt and freshly ground pepper
  to taste

$^{3}/_{4}$ pound medium-size asparagus

8 ramps (wild leeks)

1 pound English peas, in shells

$1^{1}/_{2}$ pounds fingerling potatoes

1 cup dry white wine

1. Preheat oven to 350°F.

2. Prepare chicken by filling the inside with $^{3}/_{4}$ of the tarragon and all of the garlic. Rub chicken heavily with butter on all sides, and season with salt and pepper. Place on a rack in a roasting pan and roast upside down, which allows the leg juices to permeate the breast meat. Roast until thoroughly cooked, about 75 minutes.

3. To prepare the veggies, snap the woody ends off the asparagus stems. Lightly peel the asparagus and ramps. Shell the peas and set aside in a cool place. Blanch the asparagus and ramps separately in plenty of boiling salted water until just tender, and plunge into ice water to halt the cooking. With half of the reserved tarragon, boil the potatoes until easily pierced with a fork but not mushy.

For the tarragon sauce:

4. Remove the chicken from the pan. Drain the fat.

5. Add the wine to the pan, stir with a wooden spoon to release the browned bits, and incorporate the roasting juices. Stir in the remainder of the chopped tarragon.

6. Reheat the asparagus and ramps in boiling salted water. Remove and drain. Quickly blanch the peas in boiling water. Remove and drain. Combine the asparagus, ramps, and peas in a serving bowl, and season to taste with salt and pepper. Serve the sliced chicken on warmed dinner plates with the veggies and potatoes. Season all to taste with salt and pepper. Serve the tarragon sauce separately.

Chef's recommendation: Dry, medium-bodied white wine such as Barboursville Pinot Grigio

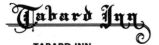

TABARD INN
Washington
Andrew Saba
Executive Chef

WARM GOAT CHEESE & BEET SALAD

with Walnuts & Sherry Vinaigrette

SERVES 4

8 baby red, gold, and white beets

3 tablespoons walnut oil

1/4 cup sherry vinegar

Salt and freshly ground pepper to taste

8 ounces mixed salad greens

Maple Sherry Vinaigrette (see sidebar)

1/2 cup finely chopped scallions

1/3 cup walnut halves

1/2 cup finely chopped red onion

6 ounces fresh goat cheese

1. Preheat oven to 400°F.

2. Wash and trim beets. Wrap in foil with a small splash of water. Roast until tender, about 35 to 40 minutes. Cool, peel, and dice beets. Toss beets with walnut oil and vinegar. Season to taste with salt and pepper.

3. Toss mixed greens with 6 tablespoons of the Maple Sherry Vinaigrette.

4. Combine scallions, walnuts, and red onion. Toss with 4 tablespoons of the Maple Sherry Vinaigrette.

5. Divide goat cheese into 4 slices. Place on a baking sheet and warm in oven at 400°F for 2 minutes.

6. To serve, divide greens among 4 plates. Top with sherried beets, the scallion-walnut-onion mixture, and a slice of warmed goat cheese.

Chef's recommendation: La Famiglia di Robert Mondavi Barbera or another fruit-driven red wine

Maple Sherry Vinaigrette

1 tablespoon finely diced shallots

1/2 teaspoon Dijon mustard

2 tablespoons sherry vinegar

2 1/2 teaspoons maple syrup

2 tablespoons walnut oil

1/2 cup peanut oil to taste

Salt and freshly ground white pepper to taste

Combine the shallots, mustard, sherry vinegar, and half of the maple syrup. Slowly whisk in the walnut and peanut oils. Adjust seasoning with salt and pepper. Add remaining maple syrup, as necessary, to taste.

1789 Restaurant

1789
Washington
Ris Lacoste
Executive Chef

BEET-CURED MAHI MAHI

SERVES 4

3 medium-size beets

6 to 8 teaspoons coarse sea salt

1¼ cups cold water

4 six-ounce mahi mahi fillets

Olive oil

Potato Salad (see below)

1. In a food processor, blend beets and sea salt until beets are shredded. Add cold water and process until smooth.

2. Place mahi mahi fillets in a stainless steel or glass bowl. Pour beet mixture over fillets. Add more water if needed to cover fish completely. Cover bowl and marinate overnight in refrigerator.

3. When ready to serve, rinse mahi mahi well to remove excess salt. Dry with a paper towel and sear in a hot frying pan with a small amount of olive oil until golden. Turn and cook for 3 to 5 minutes.

4. Serve over Potato Salad or Harvard beets.

Chef's recommendation: Aragones, Joao Portugal Ramos, or another dry, earthy red wine

Potato Salad

¼ cup mayonnaise

¼ cup sour cream or yogurt

2 tablespoons sliced scallions

1 tablespoon chopped dill

¼ onion, finely minced

Salt and pepper to taste

2 pounds red bliss or Yukon Gold potatoes, unpeeled

1 hard-boiled egg, finely chopped (optional)

1. Blend mayonnaise, sour cream, scallions, dill, and onion. Season to taste with salt and pepper. Chill for 1 to 2 hours.

2. Scrub potatoes, place in a saucepan, and cover with cold water. Bring to a boil, cover, and simmer until potatoes are tender. Drain and cut into chunks. While still warm, mix well with sauce. Add egg, if desired.

NATIONAL PRESS CLUB
Washington
Jim Swenson
Executive Chef

GOAT CHEESE FRITTER
with Asparagus & Truffle Vinaigrette

SERVES 6

Truffle Vinaigrette (see sidebar)

3 ounces fresh goat cheese

1/2 cup all-purpose flour

1 egg, whipped

1 1/2 cups brioche bread crumbs, toasted

2 bunches asparagus, blanched and cut on the bias into 1-inch pieces

1/2 cup shallots, sliced and sautéed

1/2 cup tomatoes, peeled, seeded, and diced

Baby greens for garnish

The day before serving:

1. Prepare Truffle Vinaigrette (see sidebar). Cover and refrigerate overnight.

On the day of serving:

2. Form goat cheese into 6 small rounds for fritters. Dredge each fritter first in flour, then in egg, then in bread crumbs, then again in egg, and again in bread crumbs. Cover and refrigerate.

3. Without cooking further, combine and warm the prepared asparagus, shallots, and tomatoes. Season with salt and pepper. Keep warm.

4. Sauté goat cheese fritters in a lightly oiled, nonstick sauté pan until golden brown on both sides and warmed through.

5. Heat 6 medium-size plates. Place a fritter in the center of each plate. Arrange asparagus around fritter and drizzle plate with truffle vinaigrette. Garnish with baby greens such as tatsoi or mâche. Serve immediately.

Chef's recommendation: Araujo sauvignon blanc or another crisp, clean white wine

Truffle Vinaigrette

2 tablespoons sherry vinegar

2 tablespoons balsamic vinegar

3/4 cup extra virgin olive oil

1 small black truffle, minced

1/4 teaspoon dry mustard powder

Salt and freshly ground pepper to taste

Combine vinegars, olive oil, truffle, mustard powder, and salt and pepper.

Whisk vigorously to prepare vinaigrette. Adjust seasonings.

EQUINOX
Washington
Todd Gray
Chef/Owner

ASPARAGUS *&* VIRGINIA MOREL MUSHROOM SALAD

with Roasted Garlic *&* Lemon Dressing

SERVES 4

For the roasted garlic and lemon dressing:

1 head garlic, unpeeled

Zest of 1 lemon for garnish

Juice from 1 lemon

1 teaspoon Dijon mustard

1 green onion, trimmed and coarsely chopped

Sea salt and freshly ground pepper to taste

$1/2$ cup olive oil

1. Preheat the oven to 400°F.

2. Cut off the top third of the garlic head to expose the insides of the cloves. Wrap the garlic in aluminum foil, and bake 30 to 40 minutes until very soft.

3. Squeeze the garlic pulp into a blender. Zest the lemon and set aside. Squeeze the juice of the zested lemon into a measuring cup, add enough water to make $1/2$ cup liquid, and pour into the blender with the mustard, green onion, salt, and pepper. Puree until smooth. With the machine running, add the olive oil in a thin stream, blending until the vinaigrette emulsifies.

For the asparagus:

$3/4$ pound asparagus, trimmed and peeled, if large

4. Steam or boil the asparagus for about 4 minutes or until tender. Drain in a colander and rinse with cold water to stop the cooking. Drain on a kitchen towel. Cut the bottom third of the asparagus stalks into $1/2$-inch diagonal slices, and set aside; reserve the upper $2/3$.

Nora

RESTAURANT NORA
Washington
Nora Pouillon
Chef/Owner

For the salad:

1 tablespoon olive oil

10 ounces morels, rinsed, drained, and trimmed

8 green onions, trimmed and sliced into ¼-inch rounds

2 teaspoons balsamic vinegar

1½ teaspoons tamari

⅓ cup chopped flat-leaf parsley for garnish

5. Heat the olive oil in a sauté pan, add the morels, and sauté for about 2 to 3 minutes. Add the green onions, balsamic vinegar, and tamari. Continue to sauté for about 2 more minutes, stirring from time to time or until soft and blended. Remove from the heat, add the sliced and cooked asparagus stems, and stir to combine. Season to taste with salt and pepper.

6. To serve, pour the garlic-lemon dressing into a pool covering half of each of 4 salad plates. Fan the asparagus spears over the dressing. Place a large spoonful of the morel and asparagus mixture at the base of each asparagus fan, dividing the portions evenly among the 4 plates. Sprinkle with parsley and lemon zest.

Chef's recommendation: A quality Chablis such as Verget 1er Cru Vaillons

L'Esprit de Campagne is located in the Shenandoah—one of the world's richest, most fertile valleys. In 1984, from their farm kitchen within this mountain-girded valley near Winchester, Virginia, Joy and Carey Lokey began L'Esprit de Campagne, now the largest farm-based manufacturer of sun-ripened dried tomatoes and dried fruits on the East Coast. Roma tomatoes and regional fruits are grown on small farms like the Lokeys'. Handpicked at their sun-ripened peak, they are carefully washed and individually prepared for drying in L'Esprit's custom-designed, low-heat wind tunnel dehydrators. Drying time is carefully monitored to retain their rich natural colors and high nutritional value.

PROSCIUTTO-WRAPPED SHAD ROE
with Asparagus, Ramps, Shallots
& Sweet Peas with a Sweet Pea Coulis

SERVES 4

8 ramps (wild leeks), same size and diameter as the asparagus

8 perfect spears of medium-size asparagus

2 cups shelled sweet peas, divided use

Kosher salt and freshly ground white pepper to taste

Sugar

1/4 pound (1 stick) unsalted butter, divided use

1 cup thinly sliced shallots

2 sets jumbo shad roe, split

4 large, paper-thin slices of prosciutto

Canola oil to sauté

1. Preheat oven to 375°F.

2. Rinse ramps well, trim off root ends, and remove outer layers from the bulbs. Blanch asparagus spears, peas, and ramps separately in plenty of boiling salted water. Shock each in ice water. Drain and reserve separately.

3. Bias cut the asparagus into 1-inch lengths, discarding any tough or wooded stems.

4. Puree half of the sweet peas in a blender, scraping down and adding a little water if necessary to achieve a very smooth puree. Pass through a fine sieve, and season with salt and a little sugar to taste.

5. Melt 6 tablespoons of the butter in a sauté pan. Sauté the shallots over low heat until translucent and tender. Toss the ramps, asparagus, and the remainder of the peas with the shallots and keep warm. Season to your liking.

6. Warm the pea puree very gently, and swirl in the remaining 2 tablespoons butter to melt and enrich the sauce.

TABARD INN
Washington
David Craig
Former Executive Chef

7. Carefully rinse the shad roe sacs and pat dry. Lay out each slice of prosciutto and place a roe sac at one end. Prick the shad roe several times with a skewer, and season with pepper to taste. Wrap the roe in the prosciutto, keeping the bundles tight and as uniform as possible.

8. Heat enough canola oil in a sauté pan to come halfway up the roe bundles. Sauté to a nice golden brown on each side. (The cooking shad roe will pop and shoot off hot oil, so stand well back or place a splatter guard screen over the pan.) Remove roe to a baking pan, and place in the oven for 3 to 4 minutes—for medium rare (pink in center)—or longer if you prefer. Remove and allow to rest.

9. Spoon the pea coulis into the centers of 4 warmed plates. Place the vegetable ragout in the centers of the coulis. Slice the roe on the bias, and shingle around the vegetables.

Local Foods
Local Flavors

SHAWNEE SPRINGS

Shawnee Springs is one of the few remaining canneries that grow and can their own peaches. The peach varieties used for canning—Red Haven, Glow Haven, Loring, and Jim Wilson—are chosen for their superior flavor and texture. The peaches are grown and canned on site and are peeled by hand with steam instead of a lye solution, thereby ensuring both the highest quality and unsurpassed flavor. The short time and distance between growing and canning also contribute to the flavor. Owned and operated by the Whitacre family, the business began in the early 1900s as an apple orchard, which grew into a successful apple- and peach-growing business. The Shawnee Springs cannery was purchased from neighbors, and the business continues today as both an orchard and a canning operation.

SUMMER FARE

AMERICAN EEL
APPLES
APRICOTS
ARTICHOKES
ARUGULA
ASIAN PEARS
BASIL
BEEF
BEEF (FORAGE FED*)
BEETS
BISON
BLACKBERRIES
BLACK-EYED PEAS
BLACK SEA BASS
BLUEBERRIES
BLUE CRAB
BLUEFISH
BROCCOLI
BRUSSELS SPROUTS
CABBAGE
CANTALOUPE
CARROTS
CATFISH
CATFISH (FARMED*)
CAULIFLOWER
CELERIAC
CELERY
CHANTERELLES
CHERRIES (SWEET & SOUR)
CHICKEN
CHICKEN (FORAGE FED*)
CLAMS
CLAMS (FARMED*)
COLLARDS
CONCH
COUNTRY CURED HAM
   (HANG TO EAT IN WINTER)
CROAKER
CUCUMBERS
CURRANTS
DAIRY (PASTURED*)
DOGFISH
DUCK (FARM RAISED*)
EDIBLE FLOWERS
EGGPLANT
EGGS (CHICKEN)

EGGS (DUCK, GOOSE, QUAIL,
   & GUINEA)
EGGS (FORAGE FED*)
FARMSTEAD CHEESES (AGED)
FAVA BEANS
FENNEL
FIGS
FLOUNDER
GARLIC
GOAT CHEESE (FRESH)
GOAT MEAT
GOOSE (FARM RAISED*)
GOOSEBERRIES
GRAPES
GREEN & YELLOW BEANS
GREENS
GUINEA FOWL
HERBS
HONEY
HORSERADISH
KALE
KOHLRABI
LETTUCES & SALAD GREENS
LIMA BEANS
MELONS
MONKFISH
MOZZARELLA (FRESH)
MUSCADINE GRAPES
MUSHROOMS
NECTARINES
OKRA
ONIONS
OYSTERS
PAWPAWS
PEACHES
PEANUTS
PEARS
PEAS
PEPPERS
PERCH (WHITE & YELLOW)
PLUMS
PORK
PORK (FORAGE FED*)
POTATOES
QUAIL (FARM RAISED*)
RABBIT (FARM RAISED*)
RABBIT (FORAGE FED*)
RADISHES
RAINBOW TROUT (FARMED*)
RASPBERRIES

RICOTTA (FRESH)
ROCKFISH (STRIPED BASS)
RUTABAGA
SCALLOPS
SEA TROUT (GRAY)
SHALLOTS
SHIITAKE MUSHROOMS
SHRIMP
SOFT-SHELL CRAB
SORREL
SPANISH MACKEREL
SPINACH
SPOT
SQUASH BLOSSOMS
SQUID
SUMMER SQUASH
SWEET CORN
SWISS CHARD
TILAPIA (FARMED*)
TOMATOES
TURKEY (FORAGE FED*)
TURNIPS
VEAL
WATERMELON

* SEE PAGE 233

SUMMER

EXPLORING THE ECONOMIC
BENEFITS OF SMALL-SCALE,
LOCAL AGRICULTURE &
CELEBRATING THE FLAVORS
OF SUMMER IN THE
MID-ATLANTIC

CRAB FARMING IN SUMMER

Life as a Chesapeake Bay waterman is a unique and life-fulfilling experience. As soft crab producers, our summer day starts at 3:30 a.m., when we check the crab floats for soft crabs. We grab a bagged breakfast and head to the local gas station for a cup of java and to talk with fellow crabbers about yesterday's catch. Then it's to the boat.

While we head out to the creek, the cull boy sets up baskets to sort the catch. Just as we round the bend, we can see the first line of peeler pots dead ahead. The cull boy reaches for the buoy hook and snatches the first cork out of the water. With a smooth rhythm, he places the line in the pot puller, and we hear it sing as the pot comes to the surface. He unlatches the trap door and empties the catch onto the culling board, returning to the water any undersized crabs, fish, and other juvenile species. By the time we reach the next pot, everything's been sorted and he's reaching for the next buoy. The process goes on until about 11 a.m., when we head back to the truck and go home.

The day has just begun. The cull boy places his peelers in the floats and takes the rest of his catch to the seafood market. It's now 3 p.m. We continue checking the crab floats every 4 hours for soft crabs. Yes, even all through the night, they must be removed from the water or they will return to being hard crabs.

The fisherman's reward is having put in a hard day's work and in producing a premier, high-quality product that is in high demand. You see, there are a variety of fish but only one Chesapeake Bay Soft Crab. Even though we're governed by unpredictability—crab supply, weather, competition, and government regulations both domestic and overseas—the worst day soft crabbin' is more fun than a lot of things I could be doing to make a living. The freedom to soft crab gives me only one boss, and that's the mailbox. ■

Buster's Seafood & Crab Farm

Launched in 1991, Buster's Seafood & Crab Farm uses the recirculating aquaculture system developed by the Virginia Institute of Marine Science. For more than 10 years, Buster's Seafood & Crab Farm has been successfully shedding soft crabs. Says crab farmer Paige Hogge, "The hours are lousy—24 hours a day for 5 months—and there's always work to do, but the reward is finding that soft crab swimming in the float: it's our crop."

by Paige Hogge
Buster's Seafood
& Crab Farm
Urbanna, Virginia

BUYING LOCAL MEANS HEALTHIER LOCAL ECONOMIES

Wal-Mart Stores' TV advertisements feature a sunny-yellow ball with a smiley face, dressed in Zorro regalia, slashing price after price as it bounces down the aisles. Were the United States to have better truth-in-advertising laws, those commercials would also show the cartoon swordsman smashing storefront windows on Main Street and placing "Closed" signs on thousands of family-owned businesses that once constituted the heart of America.

Many certainly celebrate the emerging world of Wal-Mart America, in which a small number of chain stores sell for bargain prices and under one roof every product consumers need. Economy and convenience have become our new mantras. But the chain store world is hardly Nirvana.

The first problem is that a community that depends on chain stores becomes vulnerable to some nasty surprises. If you and your neighbors buy groceries only from Wal-Mart, then other locally owned food stores will gradually go out of business and your grocery choices will become only as broad as the imagination of a low-level ordering clerk in Bentonville, Arkansas. If Wal-Mart headquarters then decides to shut down your store and build a larger one 75 miles away, you've suddenly lost your food supply altogether. In fact, as you become a link in the global food chain, any crisis anywhere in the world—say, an oil embargo that raises fuel prices, an outbreak of mad cow disease that cuts off supplies of beef, or sudden bankruptcy like the kind Enron experienced—can reverberate in your weekly grocery shopping.

A second problem is that a community in which everyone is a consumer of someone else's products—and no one is a producer—is an economic disaster zone. In a typical Wal-Mart, as noted in the recent documentary *Store Wars*, only a small fraction of every food dollar goes to paying the part-time, minimum-wage employees operating the store. Most of the money is sucked out of the community and into the pockets of the Waltons in Arkansas—one of the richest families in the world. At a locally owned grocery store, in contrast, a much higher percentage of each dollar spent winds up being respent, by employees and owners alike, in the local economy. Every time a dollar is spent in a community—on local suppliers, local hardware dealers, local farmers—its impact multiplies. With a much higher multiplier, a locally owned economy enjoys more income, more wealth, and more jobs.

by Michael Shuman
Community Ventures

To get a sense of how much money it was losing from the local economy, the state of Vermont, with funding from the U.S. Department of Agriculture, recently undertook a study called the Leaky Bucket. The study found that on an annual basis, Vermonters purchased nearly

$2 billion of nonlocal food, spent $1 billion in energy, and paid $240 million in interest alone on out-of-state credit cards. If Vermont made a concerted effort to become self-reliant in those three areas, it would have more than $3 billion of additional multiplier available for its economy.

The third problem afflicting Wal-Mart America is that a community without a strong economic base also crumbles in a hundred other ways. Most taxation on income, property, sales, and employment occurs at a distant corporate headquarters where imported goods are produced. Once drained of public dollars, a community with only chain stores finds it has to cut police and fire services, scale back schools, postpone road upgrades, and cancel environmental protection projects. Sure, the chain stores pay some local taxes; they're just a lot less than what equivalent local businesses pay. A study of a proposed Wal-Mart in Saint Albans, Vermont, estimated that three-quarters of all of the store's sales would be drawn from existing businesses, thereby reducing total employment and tax revenues within the community.

Fortunately, Wal-Mart economies are not inevitabilities; they are choices. And every time you choose to buy local, you bring your economy back under control, boost the multiplier, and strengthen the public sector. And there's no better place to begin to go local than with your food purchases. Despite the spread of supermarkets and other chain stores, most communities still have some locally owned food markets. If yours doesn't, then search for a nearby farmers market or just a farmer. Plus, there are a growing number of Community Supported Agriculture arrangements that link farmers directly with consumers through annual subscriptions.

Those involved in the direct purchase of fresh food from local farmers soon discover something remarkable. All of those bargains advertised by Wal-Mart turn out not to be such bargains after all. One of the dirty secrets of the globalized food system is that its distribution costs are huge—and rising. For every dollar you spend at a supermarket, about 67 cents goes to retail markup, transportation, packaging, refrigeration, and advertising. This means that family farms can produce cheaper food than supermarkets can—even if their per-unit production costs are higher—by dealing directly with consumers and cutting most of those wasted 67 cents.

To be sure, compared with the highly sophisticated global food business, local food systems are in kindergarten. The linkages among small-scale farmers, food processors, markets, consumers, and Internet companies—eviscerated by more than a generation of mergers, buyouts, and consolidations in the food industry—are only now being repaired and revitalized. But history is on their side.

Many trends suggest that the competitiveness of locally grown food is steadily improving. As the price of oil increases—which over the next decade or so seems almost inevitable—food transported over long distances will become relatively more expensive. That price rise will be nudged along by environmental measures to slow global warming that place green taxes on fossil fuels and by the increased vulnerability of long supply lines to terrorism. The proliferation of niche markets—such as antibiotic-free chickens, organic peas, heirloom vegetables, and micro-brewed beers—also favors local producers.

If the market is increasingly favoring local food systems, then why worry? If local farmers, linked with local stores, can provide cheaper food, won't the Wal-Marts just go out of business? Maybe. Unfortunately, as annual reports by the Green Scissors Coalition show, the conventional food business is propped up by tens of billions of dollars of federal subsidies each year. The subsidies go to big agribusiness, big cattle, big chicken, big water, and big fertilizer. If consumers don't vote with their wallets to counteract such market distortions, we will lose generations of family farmers and small businesses before they ever have the opportunity to compete on a level playing field.

A tremendous choice lies ahead of us. We can continue to get snookered by the Wal-Marts of America and exchange our community welfare for a few bargains here and there—most of which turn out to be illusory. Or we can increasingly buy food from local farmers, local food processors, and local retailers and thus enjoy the independence and prosperity that come with strong, self-reliant economies. As Benjamin Franklin once wrote, "Anyone who is willing to trade independence for security deserves to wind up with neither." ■

Resources for Living Local

The **Virginia Independent Consumers and Farmers Association** (VICFA) is made up of small-scale farmers and citizens who seek to preserve the quality, diversity, wholesomeness, and availability of locally grown and home-produced food products. With its motto of "From Home and Farm Direct to You," the organization works to promote and preserve unrestricted, unregulated trade between farmers and their customers. VICFA holds that barriers to access include growing regulation of small-scale farmers and the rise of industrial technologies such as genetic engineering and irradiation.

THE SOUL OF COMMUNITY IN ACTION

Urban and rural communities need each other to survive and to thrive. Folks in the city rely on farmers—now less than 1 percent of the U.S. population—to feed them, while folks in the country rely on people in town to buy their products so they can stay on the farm. As sprawl, global economics, and other matters divert people, money, and businesses away from urban neighborhoods and rural areas, there has never been a greater need for mutual support among those two groups.

The growing popularity of farmers markets is one indication that rural feeders and urban eaters are acting on this healthy codependency. Farmers markets have been growing by leaps and bounds throughout the United States, and very much so in the Washington, D.C., region. And for good reason: vegetables and fruit taste better and are better for you when they are eaten soon after harvesting. It takes just one visit to a farmers market to discover that tomatoes aren't supposed to bounce and apples don't have to come with that sparkling floor-polish sheen.

For farmers, direct marketing of produce—through either farmers markets, Community Supported Agriculture programs or food-buying clubs—carries significant economic advantage over selling to wholesale buyers. According to a study conducted by organizers of the Rally for Rural America—held in Washington in March 2000—farmers receive 9 cents on the wholesale market for lettuce that sells for $1.29 on local supermarket shelves. And with prices hovering near historical lows, growers of traditional commodity crops such as corn and soybeans make even less.

When farmers sell directly to the consumer, they get the whole dollar, which makes it possible for them to keep planting melons instead of selling the land for malls. The good news for farmers in the Washington area is that demand for healthy, affordable, locally grown food exceeds the supply. The level of public awareness of the health, economic, and social benefits of buying directly from local farmers has been rising faster than the rate of new farmers growing for the new markets, and of experienced farmers ready or willing to make the transition to selling their produce directly to the public.

Despite the clear economic advantages of doing so, some family farmers simply don't have the time, the staff, or the desire to drive two hours to the city to sell their produce. For those farmers, marketing cooperatives offer an attractive alternative. The Tuscarora Organic Growers Marketing Cooperative (TOG) assembles and delivers a wide variety of produce on behalf of 17 small family farmers in south-central Pennsylvania to restaurants, health food stores, and farmers markets in Washing-

by John Friedrich
Community Harvest

ton. By working together with their neighbors and hiring a small team of sales and distribution staff, farmers participating in TOG are able to focus on what they do best: growing quality vegetables, fruit, flowers, herbs, and other products.

Cooperative marketing efforts benefit farmers by providing a means to get their produce directly to full-price-paying consumers and a means to benefit communities by increasing the supply of locally grown food. This is especially important to low-income communities, which have a difficult time recruiting farmers to participate in their markets because of competition from markets in wealthier communities, in which customers turn out in greater numbers and are able to pay higher prices.

Farmers are discovering that cooperation pays, and so are residents of urban neighborhoods. When urban communities organize markets to buy directly from farmers, they develop a more reliable connection with the growers of their food—a connection less dependent on the vagaries of the food industry. Establishing a greater degree of security over the food supply is particularly important for residents of low-income neighborhoods, who have watched a steady stream of grocery stores become boarded up during the past 30 years.

Beyond the economic and health benefits of farmers markets, marketing cooperatives play an important role in strengthening the communities that run them. The new Columbia Heights Community Marketplace in Washington grew out of a series of meetings that had been called in response to a heated dialogue about race and gentrification in that very diverse community. The idea of the marketplace emerged as a way of bringing the community together on a regular basis for dialogue and unity while supporting local farmers, vendors, and performers. Organized as a cooperative effort by residents, organizations, businesses, and public officials living and/or working in Columbia Heights, the marketplace has succeeded in doing just that.

A few recent scenes at the marketplace: Local kids petting rabbits and chickens brought to the market by the children of a Mennonite farmer. Students from the Latin American Youth Center painting a mural on the wall of the La Casa Homeless Shelter. Older people and young mothers lining up to buy vegetables fresh from Virginia, Maryland, and Pennsylvania farms by using checks from the U.S. Department of Agriculture's Farmers Market Nutrition Program. The Malcolm X Drummers inspiring market goers to dance while the Coalition of Latino Merchants hosts a fiesta that brings kids out of the woodwork to take a blindfolded swing at a colorful, candy-filled piñata. Recent immigrants from Vietnam and El Salvador pushing their carts through the rubble of a formerly abandoned city lot early in the morning to find the best greens, tomatoes, and corn.

Not the sorts of things that happen too frequently in aisle 3 of your average national chain store—and the very reasons every community should have a market of its own! As Washington councilman Jim Graham said upon viewing the new scene in Columbia Heights at the beginning of the season, "This is the soul of the community in action." ■

Preserving the Harvest

The Art of Cheesemaking

By Heidi Eastham
Rucker Farm
(see page 197)

The art of cheese making is like the art of living: each day is an opportunity to use the materials you are given and make the very best you can from them. Cheese making is a traditional way of preserving and adding value to milk. Historically, cheese has provided families and local communities with a year-round source of dairy products, even serving as a form of barter among local farmers. Today farmstead cheese making serves a different purpose.

Tack House cheeses are a variety of goat's-milk cheeses made at Rucker Farm, located in the foothills of the Blue Ridge Mountains. In the past, farms in the Blue Ridge region produced cattle and apples; cheese making is a relatively new venture in the area. In an attempt to diversify our farm, we added dairy goats in 1997. This helped us make better use of our farmland and take advantage of our proximity to the Washington area market.

Our dairy consists of 30 milking does, freshening in the early spring of each year. We milk them for nine months to coincide with the availability of pasture, and then we let them rest for the remaining three months. The morning milk is made exclusively into cheese, while the evening milk is used for the rearing of the kids and the occasional monkey calf (a calf that has lost its mother). Our farm-made cheeses are unique because the milk is not held for any length of time; it goes directly from the goat to the cheese-making process, which ensures freshness. Seasonal changes and the availability of forages give each batch a distinct personality.

The vast majority of Rucker Farm cheese is sold daily on the farm. People come from the region and from out of town because they're willing to support this farmstead delicacy and experience the reality of how their food is made. When they go home, they take not only the cheese but also part of us with them. ■

Pawpaws

by R. Neal Peterson
Peterson Pawpaws
(see page 225)

Among the most delicate, perishable, and delectable of fruits, the pawpaw possesses a unique flavor resembling a tropical blend of bananas, pineapples, and mangoes. Indigenous to 26 states in the United States, the pawpaw is a true American native. In fact, fossil records indicate that its forebears established themselves in North America millions of years before the arrival of humans. Native Americans introduced pawpaws to European explorers, and European settlers from the East Coast westward to Michigan, Oklahoma, and Louisiana named towns, creeks, and islands after the pawpaw. And while John James Audubon painted the yellow-billed cuckoo on the branches of a pawpaw tree, the only way most Americans know of this unusual fruit is from the traditional folk song *Way Down Yonder in the Paw Paw Patch.*

Pawpaw trees are found most commonly near creek banks and river bottoms in the understory of rich broadleaf forests in the eastern United States. It is a small deciduous tree whose droopy leaves and slender branches give it a decidedly tropical appearance.

You can judge the ripeness of a pawpaw by feel and smell. Although some pawpaw varieties are firm at ripeness, most yield softly to the touch—like a ripe peach. Pawpaws are perfect for fresh eating. Simply cut one crosswise and scoop the flesh into your mouth, including the seeds. You can suck on the seeds until they're smooth and then spit them out. For such a delicate fruit, a pawpaw is surprisingly filling, and you'll find a little goes a long way. In cooking, pawpaws substitute well for bananas, but too much heat may drive off the most distinctive components of the fruit's delicate flavor.

Fresh pawpaws are available in the Mid-Atlantic from late August until early October. For more information, see www.pawpaw.kysu.edu. ◼

Pawpaw Zabaglione

serves 6

6 egg yolks
¼ cup sugar
¼ cup passion fruit liqueur
1 cup pureed pawpaw pulp
1 cup whipping cream

YELLOW BRICK
BANK RESTAURANT
Chef Michael Luksa
Shepherdstown,
  West Virginia

1. Place egg yolks and sugar in the top of a double boiler over simmering water. Combine and stir constantly with a whisk.

2. Meanwhile, carefully heat the liqueur over medium-low heat until warm (too much heat causes it to ignite). Add the warmed liqueur to the egg yolk and sugar mixture. Continue to cook, stirring constantly, until thickened. Remove from heat and allow to cool. Fold in the pawpaw puree.

3. Whip cream into stiff peaks, and fold into the pawpaw mixture. Serve chilled.

THE TROJAN HEN

A cynic knows the cost of everything but the value of nothing. An idealist knows about value but not about cost. To achieve sustainable agriculture, we have to consider both cost and value, and this essay does so in relation to a topic of increasing concern: farm animal welfare. But just as breaching the citadel of Troy took many years, so will progress against the citadel of conventional farming. And just as the siege of Troy finally succeeded through stratagem, so will that of conventional agricultural thinking. In this context, we shall develop the theory of the Trojan hen.

Cost of animal welfare

For many years, the conventional thinking in agriculture has been that it is vital to cut costs. Sometimes cuts can actually benefit farm animal welfare—for example, by reducing disease and mortality. Unfortunately, more of the effects on welfare are negative, such as giving animals less space. Profits from cutting costs are short-term because they're constantly pared away by competition on selling prices. Yet reductions in welfare are long-term.

Pressure for cheap food is therefore a major cause of problems in the area of farm animal welfare. That pressure is often attributed to consumers, but in recent years it results mainly from competition between producers. Most people could readily pay more for food. Indeed, most already pay more than necessary—some by buying specialist products (free range, organic) and more by buying convenience foods. The proportion of income that people spend on food has declined for many years. That decline is generally regarded as beneficial, but it has been a major factor in many negative developments: unreliable farm incomes, pressures on small-scale producers, reduced food security, concerns over food safety, loss of competitiveness for Third World producers, and environmental damage. Cheap food—or rather, apparently cheap food—incurs other external costs that are not reflected in the market cost. It is sometimes said that we pay for our food three times: through our wallets, through our taxes, and through our health.

Price of Animal Welfare

Some farmers can make a profit selling specialist products, such as high-quality or locally produced foods. They offset increased costs by increased income. Consumers who buy free-range eggs demonstrate that they're willing to pay for improved welfare. However, it is inappropriate to put the responsibility for animal welfare on consumers at the point of sale. Society does not burden shoppers with day-by-day responsibility for the welfare of human food producers, and neither should it do so with the welfare of the

by Michael C. Appleby
Humane Society

animals. The only case in which this choice has been properly put to the public occurred in Switzerland. In 1978 the Swiss public voted in a referendum to ban cages for laying hens, even though that public had been fully informed that the ban would increase the price of eggs.

Value of Animal Welfare

Standard of living is affected not only by the cost of our food. It is affected also by our being assured that food is good for us and that its production does not damage other people, animals, or the environment. Some animal protection organizations—such as the Royal Society for the Prevention of Cruelty to Animals in the U.K. and the American Humane Association in the U.S.—promote labeling programs for high-welfare farm products that cost a little more. Similarly, McDonald's and other fast-food chains have started requiring their egg suppliers to provide laying hens with more space and to make other improvements in animal welfare. None of those developments, though, is likely to encompass more than a small part of the market, thereby leaving many animals unaffected. To improve conditions for all animals, either legislation or a radically changed approach from the agricultural industry or both are necessary. The question is, How can we achieve such restructuring of agriculture?

Part of the answer must be in clear presentation of the costs and benefits involved. For example, the capital costs of animal production (housing and so on) typically account for about 10 percent of production costs. Suppose we double the space and facilities provided for the animals, increasing production costs by 10 percent. When a consumer buys a meal in a supermarket or restaurant, the cost of animal products in that meal accounts for only, say, 5 percent of its selling price. So a considerable improvement in animal welfare may add only 0.5 percent to the price of the meal. Most consumers wouldn't even notice such a change and would support it if asked. Competition should no longer be the main determinant of food prices.

Individual Actions Matter

The restructuring of agriculture will be a long struggle. Meanwhile, the actions of individual farmers who produce free-range eggs and other specialist products, in addition to the actions of consumers who buy them, are important in themselves. They are also important in leading the way. In Europe such small-scale developments have led to larger-scale changes, including legislation on farm animal welfare. We can regard such developments as a Trojan horse sent inside the citadel of conventional farming. Or perhaps, because free-range eggs have been our main illustration, a Trojan hen. ▪

The Cantaloupes of Halifax County

by Aileen C. Martin &
Wendy Rickard

Back in the 1940s and 1950s, it wasn't possible to walk into a grocery store in Virginia in January and buy a cantaloupe; they simply weren't available year-round. But come July, cantaloupe lovers were rewarded with a juicy sweetness they waited all year to enjoy.

The story of Turbeville cantaloupes is the story of a perfect blend of climate, soil, and skillful farming. Back in the '40s, a small group of farmers from Turbeville in Virginia's Halifax County took advantage of the region's unique climate and loamy soil and began growing cantaloupes. According to local historians, one of the growers returned from South America with seeds that produced an extraordinarily sweet and juicy cantaloupe. With this treasure of a melon thriving in their region, the growers joined together to form the Turbeville Cantaloupe Growers Association, through which they marketed the melons under the name Turbeville cantaloupes. You're likely to still see the name Turbeville cantaloupes on farm stands and in produce aisles, but since they're grown throughout the county, they're more commonly referred to today as Halifax lopes.

Prized for their flavor, Halifax lopes are the delicious payoff of an alluvial soil (the result of sediment deposited by a flowing river—in this case, the Dan River, which once flowed through the area), a mild climate, and skillfully handled irrigation. If irrigated too much or if too much rain falls on top of irrigated fields, the sugars in the cantaloupe get diluted. So sensitive are the melons to soil and climate that good ones don't grow to the north or south of the area.

Today in Halifax County eight producers grow cantaloupes on a commercial basis on 230 acres. And field trials are conducted every year to test new varieties for disease resistance, yield, and sugar content. For those more familiar with the tightly netted western cantaloupes most commonly found in supermarkets, Halifax lopes are distinctly different in both look and flavor. The Halifax growers' eastern cantaloupe has a netted skin that is divided into sections by longitudinal fissures. Locals know to look for the fissures to be sure they're buying local cantaloupes.

Halifax County's pride in its cantaloupes takes center stage every year at the Virginia Cantaloupe Festival, which until recently was hosted by John Wade on his Turbeville farm. Started in 1981 as a way to showcase the succulent goodness of cantaloupes grown locally in Halifax County, the festival draws thousands of people every July to the Halifax County Fairgrounds.

For cantaloupe lovers, Halifax lopes are the quintessence of sweet, juicy flavor. And they're loaded with vitamin A and calcium. So if you find yourself in Halifax County anytime from July to early October, pick up a Halifax lope and enjoy. ▪

The Community Canneries of Southside Virginia

*by Aileen C. Martin &
Fran McManus*

Take a walk through a typical supermarket, and no doubt you'll encounter a few thousand cans of fruits, vegetables, and prepared foods. So it's hard to imagine that canning was once a community activity, far afield and far more flavorful than the generic, homogeneous rows of canned goods that line supermarket shelves today. The good news is that community canning is still alive and an important part of community life in one small corner of Virginia.

Established in the 1930s, '40s, and '50s, community canneries grew up within the Virginia school system and were supervised by vocational agriculture and home economics teachers. In those days, tending a home garden was part of the vocational agriculture curriculum; canning and preserving were part of the home economics program.

Today gardeners and farmers still use county-run facilities to preserve fruits, vegetables, and meats for personal use. A walk through a typical community cannery reveals prep tables and sinks, jacketed steam kettles for cooking large batches of food, large pressure cookers, food mills for removing seeds and skins from tomatoes, and steamers to quick cook beans and remove skins from whole tomatoes. Ready to assist is a staff member who can operate the equipment and ensure that proper canning methods are being used. Cannery customers pay a small fee for each can or jar of food preserved.

At the height of their popularity, more than a hundred community canneries operated in the commonwealth of Virginia, and most of them were housed in buildings constructed or refurbished by the local community. The cost of construction was paid for by a variety of financing schemes, such as the sale of shares that were repaid with interest as funds accumulated from the cannery's use. Much of the canning equipment was donated by—and later purchased from—the U.S. armed forces.

During World War II, while men were away at war, women and children assumed responsibility for tending gardens, and they relied on community canneries for quick and efficient food preservation. In the late 1950s and '60s, cannery use declined because people began purchasing freezers to store food. In the early 1970s, canneries came back into vogue as food prices rose. Although there are very few canneries in operation today, various community canneries are regaining popularity among individuals and families concerned about the food additives found in commercially canned food.

In Southside Virginia, canneries can be found in Brosville, Callands, Wylliesburg, and Riverdale. They can also be found in nearby Henry County (Axton), Bedford County (New London), and Hanover County. ▣

Canning Season at a Community Cannery

Community canneries are full of laughter, conversation, and, most of all, community. People help each other peel, chop, and stir while carrying on conversations about local news, the quality of homegrown food, and recipes they like best. They're a great way to take advantage of the full bounty of a home garden and the low cost of in-season produce from local farms.

Community canneries are typically open from early July through mid-December. Beginning with beans and ending with ham, canners follow the seasons while preserving the best of the local harvest. The column on the right lists some of the foods that get preserved at a community cannery.

Recipes from the Cannery

Annie Lynskey Lovell's Lime Pickles

makes 16 to 20 quarts

At Home
Wash and slice thinly: 28 pounds (1 peck) burpless cucumbers

Put in nonmetal containers and fill with water. Add 2 cups of pickling lime, stir it in the water, and leave overnight.

The next morning, rinse the cucumber slices well 2 or 3 times. Put back into clean water. Add 2 tablespoons alum and stir. Add ice cubes and 2 cups of salt. Let sit for 2 hours. Drain.

At the Cannery
In a steam kettle, combine:
10 pounds of sugar
Pickling spice
14 cups apple cider vinegar
4 cups water

Bring to a boil, and cook until you can smell the spices. Turn down the heat and add the cucumber slices. Bring to a rolling boil, and boil for 10 minutes.

Put the hot cucumbers and juice into jars and seal tight. Put the jars in a cold-pack canner with a rack underneath. Add hot water up to the necks of the jars. Bring water to a boil. Cook for 10 minutes. Take the cucumbers out of the canner and set aside to cool. Listen for the pop to be sure they're sealed.

The longer the cucumbers sit, the better they taste. Refrigerate before eating and serve them ice cold.

What's Being Canned

July & August
Black-eyed peas
Butter beans
Corn
Green beans
June apples
October beans
Peaches
Summer squash
Tomatoes
Tomato sauce, soup
   & juice

September & October
Apples, apple butter
   & applesauce
Chili
Kale
Pears
Pinto beans
Sweet potatoes
Turnip greens
Vegetable soup

November & December
Beef
Cake in a can
Collards
Creecy greens
Deer
Ham
Pork sausage,
   tenderloin &
   barbecue

Throughout the cannery season
Soups
Stews

Ruth Burnette's Tomato Soup

At Home
Wash, core, and quarter: 1 bushel of ripe tomatoes*

Chop into small pieces:
2 to 3 pounds of onions
1 bunch of celery
1 or 2 fresh hot red peppers with the seeds removed

Combine the tomatoes, onions, and celery in a large container, and add 2 tablespoons of dried parsley.

At the Cannery
Pour the tomato mixture into a large kettle. Add a pint of water to start the tomatoes cooking. Heat the mixture and cook until the onions and celery are soft.

Put the tomato mixture through a food mill to remove the skins and seeds.

Return the juice to the kettle. Add:
2 cups of sugar
$\frac{1}{2}$ cup of salt
1 cup of cornstarch
1 cup of butter

Bring to a boil. Ladle into cans. Seal and process.

* During the summer, freeze whole ripe tomatoes from your garden and use them to make this soup. When using frozen tomatoes, don't add the pint of water to the kettle, because the frozen tomatoes will give off water as they thaw.

"It follows that there would be an effort to grow a tomato

THAT WAS SMALL ENOUGH AND SOLID ENOUGH TO BE HARVESTED BY MACHINERY YET WOULD BE EASIER TO PROCESS THROUGH THE CAUSTIC SODA BATH. THE LATTER CALLED FOR A TOMATO WITH LITTLE OR NO CORE. SUCH A TOMATO WAS DEVELOPED. THE CANNERS ON THE EASTERN SHORE DIDN'T PARTICULARLY CARE FOR THIS NEW BREED, BUT TO COMPETE, MOST OF THEM EVENTUALLY CHANGED TO THE SYSTEMS WHICH REDUCED COSTS. AS A RESULT, THE CANNING OF THOSE WONDERFUL, LUSH, TASTY FIELD TOMATOES BECAME A THING OF THE PAST. INCIDENTALLY, A CASE COULD BE MADE FOR GROWING GARDEN TOMATOES AND CANNING THEM AT HOME. MANY HOMES DID JUST THAT. GOOD OLD NAMES FOR FIELD TOMATOES LIKE MARGLOW, INDIANA BALTIMORE, RED ROCK, MATCHLESS, STOKESDALE, AND NEW STONE BECAME NO. 6203, OHIO 7870, V.F. 134-J-2, ETC. FOR THE OLD-TIMER IT WAS LIKE SUBSTITUTING SOCIAL SECURITY NUMBERS FOR PROPER NAMES."

—FROM *CANNERIES OF THE EASTERN SHORE* BY R. LEE BURTON JR.

Eating is a primal act. Everyone must eat, and we *are* what we eat. But our choices of what we eat also reflect our character: our temperament, values, ethics, and integrity. Eating makes a social statement; we eat with family and friends. Eating makes a political statement; what we eat affects what others will and won't have to eat. Eating makes a moral statement; what we eat reflects our code of ethics. Whether we think about it or not, eating is a reflection of our character.

As a society, we allow economics to dominate our choices—including our choices of what we eat. For the most part, we want our food to be quick, convenient, and cheap regardless of whether we buy it at a supermarket or a local fast-food franchise. Our eating choices reflect a society that wants things fast, easy, and without sacrifice. Sometimes we purposely choose an expensive restaurant. We like to *flaunt it*, even if we don't *have it*, so we *charge it*. But most people still want their food to be quick, convenient, and cheap.

Few stop to think that our demands for cheap food have forced our farmers to adopt industrial farming methods, to farm more efficiently by producing more food at lower dollar-and-cent cost. People don't understand that industrialization—with its specialization, standardization, and centralization of control—is in direct conflict with a diverse and dynamic society. As farms become industrial, they inherently threaten the environment. And with industrialization, farms have become fewer and larger, forcing thousands of farm families off the land and leaving scores of rural communities to wither and die. Few seem to understand that our quest for cheap food is destroying our natural environment and ripping apart the social fabric of our society.

Our demand for quick and convenient food has resulted in 80 cents of each food dollar's going to those who process, package, and distribute it. The food processing, marketing, and retailing sectors are controlled by giant multinational corporations whose decisions determine who will and will not have food to eat. Few seem to realize that our quest for quick, convenient food is putting the fate of humanity in the hands of a few giant corporations driven solely by profit and growth.

Fortunately, we still have choices. We don't have to allow the reflection of our individual character to be projected by a cheap, easy, fast-food culture. We can choose, instead, a culture that recognizes the value of positive relationships with other people and concern for the natural environment. Our actions can reflect the ultimate truth that caring is a source of joy, not sacrifice, and that stewardship gives our lives purpose and meaning. But to do so, we must take every opportunity to reflect our true

BEYOND ECONOMICS: EATING IS A REFLECTION OF CHARACTER

by John Ikerd
Professor Emeritus
of Agricultural
Economics,
University
of Missouri

social and moral character in our food choices.

We need to start choosing food that is worth the time, the effort, and the money rather than simply buying whatever is quick, convenient, and cheap. Ideally, we need to buy from local farmers who have defied industrialization and who choose instead to produce by means that are ecologically sound and socially responsible. We need to help those farmers to remain economically viable. Their products may be certified organic or called natural, ecological, or sustainable, but when you buy direct from farmers, you can ask them how they produce your food. If you can't buy direct, learn as much about your food as you can—not just about its physical attributes but also about the implications of how it was grown.

Buying food with character and from local farmers of good character is a reflection of your character. Eating may be primal, but eating also is social and moral. ▪

Regional Family Farms

The **Virginia Association for Biological Farming** (VABF) is an organization of farmers, gardeners, and supporters interested in biological agriculture, including organic farming, low-input sustainable agriculture, and biodynamics. The association views farms as living systems, recognizes that each farm must be treated individually and holistically, and promotes local and regional food systems that reduce energy use and maximize on-farm nutrient cycling.

As part of its mission, the VABF promotes a sustainable food system that is ecologically sound, economically viable, and socially just. It also works (1) to facilitate an increase in the number of farmers and gardeners using biological practices and an increase in the number of consumers demanding ecologically grown food and (2) to increase awareness about agriculture, its relationship to the environment, and its links to urban and rural lifestyles.

The association's Ecological Production Pledge (EPP) program offers educational programs including on-farm field days and workshops in sustainable and organic production practices. EPP also has an ecolabel through which growers can communicate to consumers their commitment to ecologically sound practices.

SUMMER RECIPES

Delicious Pasta with Cucumbers & Almond Sauce

SERVES 4

Toss together:

*1 pound buck-
wheat soba
noodles, cooked
and rinsed under
cold water*

*1 large cucumber,
peeled and diced
very small*

*5 scallions sliced
thin*

*1 cup Almond
Butter Sauce (see
recipe this page)*

*Big dash any
kind of hot sauce*

*Chopped fresh
cilantro*

*Season to taste
and serve at room
temperature.*

QUICK & BASIC RECIPES FOR SUMMER PRODUCE

Green Beans with Almond Butter Sauce

SERVES 4

1 cup almond butter (check the label to be sure the almonds have been roasted)

$^1/_2$ cup hot water

4 tablespoons Braggs liquid aminos, tamari, or low-sodium soy sauce

3 tablespoons brown rice vinegar or Japanese rice vinegar

Freshly ground black pepper

1 pound green beans, trimmed and either blanched or steamed

1. Combine the almond butter and hot water. Stir until well blended. Add the Braggs, vinegar, and pepper. Mix well and taste.

2. Trim each end of the beans, and cut or break them into 1$^1/_2$-inch pieces. Blanch (boil) them in salted water until tender—about 3 to 4 minutes—or steam them over boiling water.

3. Drain the beans well. Toss the warm beans with $^1/_4$ cup of the almond sauce.

Editor's note: Use the almond sauce as a dip with raw vegetables or with almost any steamed vegetable. It's also delicious over pasta.

Other ideas with green beans:

• Green bean salad with fresh corn, tomato, sliced scallions, extra virgin olive oil, basil, and salt and pepper.

• Green beans with roasted red peppers, garlic, olive oil, and basil, seasoned to taste with salt and pepper

• Green beans with chopped raw onion, sliced cherry tomatoes, basil, red wine vinegar, olive oil, and salt and pepper. (When you use an acid like lemon or vinegar to dress green beans, the beans will turn a little yellow after a while but their flavor will not change.)

**COOKING FOR
YOUR HEALTH
AND WELL-BEING**
Charlottesville, Virginia
Martha Hester Stafford
Chef/Owner

Cucumber & Peach Salsa

Combine and serve at room temperature with grilled chicken or fish:

1 medium cucumber, peeled (if waxed) and diced

2 very ripe, large peaches, diced

2 tablespoons minced onion or scallion

2 to 3 tablespoons rice vinegar

5 or 6 basil leaves, minced

1/2 teaspoon minced jalapeño pepper or a dash or two of pepper sauce

Sea salt

Good Basic Salsa

Combine & serve at room temperature: 1 large tomato, diced • 1 small onion, diced • 1/4 cup minced cilantro • 2 to 3 tablespoons fresh lime juice • 1/4 to 1/2 small jalapeño pepper, minced • Sea salt, to taste

Optional additions: Fresh raw corn • Diced cucumber • Diced yellow pepper

Broccoli with Horseradish

SERVES 4

Blanch in salted, boiling water until tender:

2 pounds broccoli, trimmed into bite-size pieces of florets (if you chose to use the stems, peel and cut into bite-size pieces)

In a large bowl, combine:

2 tablespoons prepared horseradish

4 tablespoons extra virgin olive oil

1/2 teaspoon sea salt

Freshly ground black pepper

Add broccoli. Toss well, adjust seasonings, and serve.

Great Greek Salad

Combine the following in proportions that suit your taste: Chopped tomatoes • Chopped cucumber • Kalamata olives, pitted and halved • Feta cheese, crumbled • Chopped fresh mint

Dress with a vinaigrette of: Red wine vinegar • Extra virgin olive oil

Season to taste with: Sea salt • Freshly ground pepper

Hot Pasta with Cold Tomato Sauce

1 to 2 pounds diced fresh tomatoes

1 cup fresh basil leaves chopped or torn

1 pound dried pasta such as fusilli, gemelli, rotelle, radiatore, or orecchiette

1/2 cup extra virgin olive oil

3/4 to 1 teaspoon sea salt

Freshly ground pepper

Put the diced tomatoes and basil in a large bowl. Cook the pasta according to the manufacturer's instructions. Drain and pour the pasta over the tomatoes and basil. Add the olive oil, salt, and pepper, and mix well. Taste and correct the seasoning to suit.

Quick
& Basic
Recipes
for
Summer
Produce
(continued)

Carrots:

*Grated Carrot
and Parsley
Salad dressed
with lemon juice
and olive oil,
seasoned to taste
with salt and
pepper*

*Steamed carrots
with fresh or dried
dill and butter
and seasoned with
salt and pepper*

*Steamed carrots
with olive oil and
fresh mint, chives,
or marjoram,
seasoned with salt
and pepper*

**COOKING FOR
YOUR HEALTH
AND WELL-BEING**
Charlottesville, Virginia
Martha Hester Stafford
Chef/Owner

Summer Squash Sauté

SERVES 2

2 tablespoons extra virgin olive oil

1 shallot, diced

4 small or 2 large yellow summer squash or zucchini sliced
in ¼-inch rounds

Large handful cherry tomatoes, cut in half or quarters

4 or 5 torn or roughly chopped basil leaves

Sea salt and freshly ground pepper

Options:

Add minced garlic or hot pepper flakes at the end of the cooking.

Top with a sprinkle of grated Parmesan.

1. Heat a medium sauté pan over medium-high heat for a minute or 2, and
   then add the oil. Add the shallot and cook for a few seconds until it is
   fragrant and translucent. Place the squash on the sizzling shallots, and
   sauté them together until the squash begins to brown.

2. Add the tomatoes to the pan, top with the basil leaves, and toss it all
   together until the tomatoes soften and their juice forms a bit of a sauce.

3. Season with salt and pepper, and taste to correct the seasoning. Serve
   as is as a side dish or over pasta.

Slow-Cooked Yellow Squash & Zucchini

Inspired by Deborah Madison

Slice the squash and zucchini into rounds. Sauté in a small amount of olive
oil over low heat in a single layer until the rounds are golden brown. Add
chopped garlic toward the end of the cooking. Season to taste with salt and
pepper, and garnish with basil, mint, cilantro, or chives.

Roasted Yellow Squash & Zucchini

Cut the squash and zucchini in half crosswise and slice each half lengthwise into 8 pieces. Toss with olive oil and thyme, and roast in a single layer
(if the squash is too crowded it will not brown) at 375°F for 40 minutes.
Season to taste with salt and pepper.

EASTERN SHORE CANTALOUPE & CHAMPAGNE SOUP

SERVES 6

2 large, ripe cantaloupes

½ bottle dry champagne

2 tablespoons finely chopped fresh peppermint

Mint sprigs for garnish

1. Cut the cantaloupes in half. Peel and seed 3 of the cantaloupe halves and cut into pieces. In a blender, puree the cantaloupe pieces in batches, adding champagne to each batch to thin to soup consistency.

2. Discard the seeds from the remaining melon half and scoop out the flesh with a melon baller. Add these balls to the soup. Stir in the mint.

3. Chill well and serve in chilled soup bowls. Garnish each serving with a sprig of fresh mint.

Chef's recommendation: A dry champagne, such as Veuve Clicquot Yellow Label

A magnificently vine-ripened cantaloupe grown in the sandy soil of the Chesapeake's Eastern Shore can actually bring tears to my eyes. The taste of the ripe, sweet flesh of the melon is almost a spiritual experience. If you're in the mood for a lovely Sunday brunch soup that is sure to please, this is it. This soup is so good, you'll want to be certain to have a designated driver at the table.

—CHEF JOHN SHIELDS

GERTRUDE'S
Baltimore
John Shields
Chef/Owner

SUMMER BERRY COMPOTE
with Ginger Ice Cream

SERVES 4 TO 6 DEPENDING ON PORTION SIZE

$^1/_2$ cup superfine granulated sugar

1$^1/_2$ teaspoons ground ginger

6 tablespoons (3 ounces) whole milk

$^1/_2$ teaspoon pure vanilla extract

1 pint heavy cream

$^1/_2$ pint fresh blueberries

$^1/_2$ pint fresh blackberries

$^1/_2$ pint fresh strawberries

$^1/_4$ cup turbinado (raw) sugar

1$^1/_2$ teaspoons dark rum

Pinch of freshly ground cinnamon

Crystallized ginger for garnish

Fresh mint for garnish

1. In a large bowl, combine the superfine sugar and ginger.

2. In a 1-quart saucepan, bring milk and vanilla extract just to a boil. Remove from heat and slowly add to sugar-ginger mixture, stirring all the while. Once sugar is completely dissolved, add heavy cream.

3. Follow directions for your ice cream machine.

4. Clean and rinse the berries, removing leaves and stems. Add turbinado sugar, rum, and cinnamon. Gently fold and stir until the berries are well coated with the sugar-rum mix. Refrigerate for at least 1 hour, stirring gently every 15 minutes.

5. To serve, place 1 or 2 scoops of ice cream in a chilled small bowl or compote dish, and spoon berries over top. Add another scoop of ice cream; garnish with crystallized ginger and a sprig of fresh mint.

Chef's recommendation: Smith-Woodhouse tawny port or other 10- or 20-year-old tawny port

**RESTAURANT
COLUMBIA**
Easton, Maryland
Stephen Mangasarian
Chef/Owner

ROASTED GREEN ONIONS

SERVES 4

8 medium green onions

1½ cups dry red or white wine

1 bay leaf

1 sprig fresh thyme

1 sprig fresh lavender

½ teaspoon salt

¼ teaspoon mixed peppercorns

1. Preheat oven to 325°F.

2. Wash the onions, slice the root end flat, and trim the green top, leaving an inch or 2. Place in a small roasting pan, and add the red or white wine (depending on what you're serving; for instance, white with chicken). Tie the bay leaf, thyme, and lavender into a bundle, and place in the pan with the salt and peppercorns. Cover the pan with parchment, and seal with foil. Roast until the onions are tender but holding their shape, about 1 to 1½ hours.

3. Remove the onions from the wine and set aside. Strain the pan juices; reduce to make the sauce. The mixture at this point can go in several directions: you can cook the jus down to a syrup, or reduce to half and add demiglace sauce or chicken or fish stock, or reduce by ⅔ and whisk in small chunks of unsalted, cold butter for a beurre blanc.

4. Cut the onions in half from top to root. Serve with a roasted fish, a grilled chicken, or any grilled meat. Center the onion on a dinner plate, place the meat over the base of the onion, and cover all with the sauce.

Chef's recommendation: 1999 Almedia Garret, Chardonnay, or another light, nonoaky yet fruity Chardonnay. A white Burgundy also would match.

Green onions are not scallions, but onions that are not cured to the brown skin we normally see in the market. They are sharp and have a sweetness under the bite that lends itself to wonderful flavors. And they make a great plate presentation. At the club in the month of July, our farmers bring us an onion called the Alicia Craig: it's an heirloom that is wonderful when cooked this way.

—CHEF JIM SWENSON

NATIONAL PRESS CLUB
Washington
Jim Swenson
Executive Chef

Vinaigrette

$^1/_2$ teaspoon Dijon mustard

$1^1/_2$ teaspoons balsamic vinegar

2 tablespoons sherry wine vinegar

6 tablespoons olive oil

$^1/_4$ teaspoon salt

Whisk all ingredients together in a blender.

ROASTED BEET SALAD

SERVES 4

4 medium beets

1 teaspoon kosher salt

1 teaspoon cumin seed

4 tablespoons extra virgin olive oil, divided use

3 tablespoons balsamic vinegar

1 tablespoon finely diced shallots

$^1/_2$ teaspoon salt

4 ounces mixed salad greens

Vinaigrette (see sidebar)

4 ounces fresh goat cheese

1. Preheat oven to 400°F.

2. Wash beets and cut off tops and bottoms. In a large bowl, combine kosher salt, cumin seed, and 1 tablespoon of the olive oil. Add beets and toss until well coated.

3. Wrap each beet in aluminum foil and place on a baking sheet. Roast in oven until soft, about $1^1/_4$ hours. Beets are done when a sharp knife slides through easily. When beets are cool enough to handle, peel and slice each into 8 wedges.

4. Combine balsamic vinegar, the remaining 3 tablespoons of the olive oil, shallots, and salt. Add beet wedges and toss gently until well coated.

5. In a large bowl, toss mixed greens with a small amount of Vinaigrette until well coated.

6. Set out 4 plates. Arrange 8 beet wedges in a circle near the outer edge of each plate, leaving enough room for the mixed lettuces in the center. Place greens in the center of each plate. Garnish with crumbled goat cheese, and dribble extra Vinaigrette around the outside circle of beets.

Chef's recommendation: Oakencroft Countryside White or other medium-bodied, dry white wine

ACACIA
Richmond, Virginia
Dale Reitzer
Executive Chef

LINGUINE ALLE MOLECCHE

(LINGUINE WITH SOFT-SHELL-CRAB SAUCE)

SERVES 4

1 small (4- to 6-ounce), firm tomato, grated

¾ pound linguine

5 tablespoons olive oil

2 garlic cloves, slightly smashed

4 soft-shell crabs, cleaned and each cut into 6 pieces

5 fresh basil leaves, finely chopped

1 tablespoon finely chopped Italian parsley

1 pinch crushed dried red pepper

Salt to taste

1. In a small saucepan over medium heat, cook grated tomato to remove excess water. Stir frequently to prevent burning.

2. Bring a pot of salted water to a boil and add the linguine.

3. As the linguine cooks, put the olive oil in a large sauté pan over medium-high heat. Add the garlic cloves; remove when they turn a nice gold. Add the soft-shell crabs and sauté for 1 minute. Add the drained grated tomato, basil, parsley, and red pepper. Cook for 4 more minutes. Remove from the heat.

4. Drain the cooked linguine and place in the pan with the crab-tomato sauce. Mix gently but well, sautéing for 1 minute. Add salt to taste and serve very hot.

Note: If you wish, you can eliminate the drained tomato and add ½ cup of dry white wine before adding the herbs. Reduce it completely and then add the remaining ingredients.

Chef's recommendation: A rich Barbera from Bruno Giacosa

This dish comes from an idea I received in Urbanna, Virginia, while visiting my friend Jimmy. The soft-shell crabs, just picked out of the water, looked so fresh and juicy. I immediately thought that if you could cook crabmeat for linguine, why not try it with a beautiful, juicy soft-shell crab?

This dish is prepared very quickly, so have all ingredients prepped and accessible before starting to cook.

—CHEF ROBERTO
DONNA

GALILEO
Washington
Roberto Donna
Chef/Owner

CRAB CAKES
with Mashed Potatoes & Creamed Corn

SERVES 4

For the crab cakes:

1¼ pounds jumbo lump crabmeat

Garlic-Shallot-Chili Paste (see sidebar on next page)

1 egg

1½ teaspoons Dijon mustard

1 tablespoon mayonnaise

1 tablespoon fresh lemon juice

1 teaspoon Chesapeake Bay seasoning

Pinch ground ginger

2 tablespoons chopped fresh parsley

¼ to ⅜ cup ground oyster crackers

Salt and freshly cracked black pepper to taste

Olive oil or clarified butter for sautéing crab cakes

For the mashed potatoes:

1¼ pounds Yukon Gold potatoes

1 tablespoon unsalted butter

2 tablespoons heavy cream

Salt and freshly ground pepper to taste

For the creamed corn:

4 ears sweet corn

½ cup heavy cream

1 finely diced grilled or roasted jalapeño pepper

Sugar, if needed

Salt and freshly ground white pepper

Unsalted butter

1789
Restaurant

1789
Washington
Ris Lacoste
Executive Chef

For the pan sauce:

1 pint cherry tomatoes

3 tablespoons dry white wine

1 tablespoon unsalted butter

1 tablespoon finely chopped cilantro

Salt and freshly ground pepper to taste

For the garnish:

Lime

Scallions, finely chopped

1. For the crab cakes, gently and carefully pick shells from the crabmeat, taking care not to break up the clumps of meat. Drain in a colander to remove excess liquid. In a small bowl, combine the Garlic-Shallot-Chili Paste, egg, mustard, mayonnaise, lemon juice, Chesapeake Bay seasoning, ginger, and parsley. Add this mixture and the crackers to the crab and combine gently. Season to taste with salt and pepper. Shape into 8 loose, 3-ounce cakes and refrigerate to set a little before sautéing.

2. Cook potatoes in salted water until soft. Drain and rice. Mix with butter, heavy cream, and salt and pepper to taste.

3. Blanch fresh corn for 1 minute in boiling, salted water. Drain and when cool, cut kernels off ears (should yield about 2 cups of corn). Place kernels in a saucepan. Barely cover with heavy cream. Add jalapeño and a pinch of sugar if needed. Cook until cream reduces slightly. Finish with salt, white pepper, and a little butter.

4. Cut cherry tomatoes in half. In a small nonreactive skillet, cook tomatoes, wine, and butter until tomatoes have softened but still hold their shape. Add cilantro, and season to taste with salt and pepper.

5. In a sauté pan, heat the oil or clarified butter. Sauté the crab cakes until golden brown, about 4 minutes per side.

6. To serve, place 1/4 cup of mashed potatoes in the center of each plate. Surround potatoes with creamed corn. Top with 2 crab cakes and pour the tomato sauce over the crab cakes. Squeeze lime juice over all and garnish with finely chopped scallions.

Chef's recommendation: A full-bodied Chardonnay, such as Cambria Katherine's Vineyard

Garlic-Shallot-Chili Paste

1 large shallot, coarsely chopped

3 garlic cloves, coarsely chopped

Olive oil for sautéing

1/8 teaspoon chili powder

Olive oil

Sauté the shallot and garlic in olive oil until soft; do not brown; puree in an electric coffee or spice grinder (this can be made ahead and stored, covered, in the refrigerator). Combine with the chili powder and add a generous amount of olive oil, stirring constantly. The mixture should have a burnt-orange color and should be very pasty. If needed, add more olive oil to make a thicker paste.

CHILLED VANILLA BLACKBERRY SOUP

SERVES 8

Fruit Puree:

1 cup champagne

Zest and juice of 1 lemon

2 pints blackberries

$^1/_2$ cup superfine sugar

Combine all in a nonreactive saucepan, and over low heat, bring to a simmer, stirring well until sugar is dissolved. Reduce heat. Cook 5 minutes, stirring occasionally. Cool mixture slightly, run through a blender, and strain through a fine sieve. Chill completely.

Vanilla Anglaise:

2 cups heavy cream

2 vanilla beans, split and scraped into cream

$^2/_3$ cup sugar

4 egg yolks

Lemon sorbet or crème fraîche

Over low heat, bring heavy cream and vanilla beans to a simmer. Whisk sugar and egg yolks together in an aluminum bowl. Slowly pour in the cream mixture, whisking the entire time. Return to the saucepan and cook over low heat, stirring slowly with a wooden spoon until slightly thickened (160°F). Chill in a bowl over ice. When completely chilled, mix together with the fruit puree, strain, and serve with lemon sorbet or crème fraîche.

Chef's recommendation: Barboursville NV Phileo Lot 98 or another sweet, white dessert wine

TABARD INN
Washington
Huw Griffiths
Pastry Chef

HEIRLOOM BEET & VIDALIA ONION SALAD
with Pink Peppercorn Vinaigrette

SERVES 4

10 to 12 baby golden beets, washed and greens trimmed

10 to 12 baby Chioggia beets, washed and greens trimmed

Pink Peppercorn Vinaigrette (see sidebar)

1 Vidalia onion (see note on page 89), cut in half and sliced very thinly

4 crostini (thin slices of baguette, toasted)

4 tablespoons of herbed goat cheese

4 cups of lettuce, washed, spun dry, and cut into thin, shredded strips

1. Put the beets into two separate saucepans. Cover with water and bring to a boil. Reduce the heat and simmer the beets until tender or until they can be pierced easily with the tip of a paring knife. Rinse the beets separately under cold running water for 3 minutes to cool them down. Remove from the heat; rub off the skin with an old kitchen towel or paper towels.

2. While the beets are cooking, prepare the Pink Peppercorn Vinaigrette (see sidebar).

3. Cut the beets into quarters while still warm, and combine with ¹/₄ cup of vinaigrette. Let cool. Add the Vidalia onion slices and more vinaigrette, if needed, to just lightly coat the beets and onion. Adjust seasoning with salt and pepper.

4. Smear each crostini with 1 tablespoon of the goat cheese, and broil until brown on the top. Arrange the shredded lettuce on 4 salad plates, divide the beets among the salads, and dress each salad with some of the remaining vinaigrette. Serve with the warm goat-cheese crostini.

Chef's recommendation: Trevor Jones Boots White 2000 or other white wine with floral nose and flavors of kaffir lime and passion fruit

Pink Peppercorn Vinaigrette

¹/₄ cup clover honey

2¹/₂ tablespoons sherry or cider vinegar

2 tablespoons pink peppercorns, crushed

2 teaspoons fresh thyme leaves

¹/₄ cup olive oil

Salt and freshly ground pepper to taste

Whisk the honey and sherry or cider vinegar together in a small bowl, adding the peppercorns and thyme. Slowly whisk in the olive oil until the vinaigrette emulsifies. Season with salt and pepper.

VIDALIA
Washington
Peter Smith
Executive Chef

CRISPY SOFT-SHELL CRABS
with Corn & Green Tomato Butter

SERVES 4

4 ears Silver Queen corn, kernels cut off the cob

1 tablespoon unsalted butter

4 Red Bliss potatoes, quartered

½ cup Green Tomato Butter (see sidebar)

Vegetable oil

8 soft-shell crabs, cleaned

2 cups flour

Chive spikes for garnish

1. Sauté the corn kernels in butter until heated but still firm.

2. Blanch potatoes in boiling water until fork tender. Drain and set aside.

3. Melt the Green Tomato Butter in a small saucepan.

4. Fill a heavy saucepan 2 inches deep with oil; place pan over medium-high heat until oil reaches 350°F; coat crabs with flour, and fry in the hot oil until golden, about 3 to 5 minutes. Drain on paper towels.

To assemble:

5. Place 2 tablespoons of melted Green Tomato Butter on each plate. Top with sautéed corn, and arrange 4 potato quarters on top of the corn in a ring. Top with crabs, and garnish with chive spikes.

Chef's recommendation: Château Montelena Chardonnay or another full-bodied Chardonnay with not much oak

208 TALBOT
St. Michaels, Maryland
Paul Milne
Chef/Owner

SMOKED TROUT ON POTATO CRISPS
with Goat Cheese, Corn Relish
& Currant Tomatoes

SERVES 6

2 tablespoons unsalted butter (plus butter to coat baking sheet), divided use

3 medium red potatoes

Salt and freshly ground pepper to taste

2 sides smoked trout, boned

3 ounces chèvre

Corn Relish (see sidebar)

6 small bunches currant tomatoes or 12 cherry tomatoes, diced, for garnish

1. Preheat oven to 400°F.

2. Melt the butter.

3. Using a mandoline or very sharp knife, slice potatoes into paper-thin slices. Butter a baking sheet that has sides to contain melted butter.

4. To make 6 flower-shaped crisps, arrange 4 potato slices overlapping in a ring; brush with melted butter. Repeat until all of the potato slices get used and you have 6 rings that each form a spiraling, circular pattern — the "flower." Bake until edges are crisp and centers are cooked, about 25 minutes. Gently but firmly flatten each flower with a broad spatula. Season with salt and pepper. Let pan cool for several minutes before *very carefully* lifting the potatoes. When ready to serve, remove from the cookie sheet with a thin spatula.

To assemble:

5. Break the trout into large pieces. Arrange potato crisps on 6 plates, and top each with 1 piece of chèvre, about 1 tablespoon. Divide trout evenly and sprinkle over chèvre. Top with Corn Relish and currant tomatoes.

Chef's recommendation: A dry, medium-bodied red wine, such as Jefferson Vineyards Cabernet Franc

Corn Relish

1 tablespoon unsalted butter

2 ears white corn, cut from the cob

1 tablespoon chopped chives

1 tablespoon chopped cilantro

1 teaspoon minced garlic

1 teaspoon fresh lime juice

Salt and freshly ground pepper to taste

In a small skillet, melt the butter. Add corn, and sauté until just cooked. Season with chives, cilantro, garlic, lime juice, and salt and pepper.

C&O RESTAURANT
Charlottesville, Virginia
Thomas Bowles
Executive Chef

BARBECUED ROCKFISH
with Sweet Corn, Roasted Peppers & Backyard Basil

SERVES 6

6 six- to seven-ounce rockfish fillets, skinned and boned

Salt and freshly ground pepper to taste

2 cups Sweet Corn Sauce (see next page)

2 teaspoons grapeseed oil

2 cups fresh corn kernels

1 cup roasted red peppers, cut into 1/3-inch strips

1/2 cup fresh basil from your backyard, cut into chiffonade

1 cup Equinox Barbecue Sauce (see next page)

1. Season rockfish fillets with salt and pepper. Heat well-oiled grill to high temperature. Grill fillets until medium, just before the center turns opaque and the flesh begins to flake when tested with a fork. Set aside.

2. Heat the Sweet Corn Sauce, and keep it warm.

3. Heat a medium-size skillet. Add grapeseed oil and corn kernels. Sauté corn until lightly browned. Add peppers and basil. Season to taste with salt and pepper.

4. Preheat broiler. Brush fillets with Equinox Barbecue Sauce, and bake under broiler to glaze.

5. Heat 6 large plates. Spoon 1/4 cup of corn sauce onto each plate. Mound corn and pepper in center of corn sauce, and top with rockfish. Drizzle additional barbecue sauce around plate, if desired. Serve immediately.

Chef's recommendation: Viognier Jaffurs or other floral, light white wine

EQUINOX
Washington
Todd Gray
Chef/Owner

Equinox Barbecue Sauce

1 cup chopped applewood bacon

$^1\!/_2$ small Vidalia or other sweet onion (see note on page 89),
    diced into large cubes

$1^1\!/_2$ teaspoons ground sumac (available in Middle Eastern markets)

$1^1\!/_2$ teaspoons ground dried chipotle pepper

$^3\!/_4$ teaspoon dried red pepper flakes

$1^1\!/_2$ cups apple cider vinegar

1 cup cola

1 cup ketchup

Salt and freshly ground black pepper to taste

Heat a medium-size saucepan until slightly hot. Add bacon, and render
for a couple of minutes. Add onion, sumac, chipotle, and red pepper flakes.
After sweating down onion until limp, deglaze with apple cider vinegar
and reduce by $^2\!/_3$; add cola, and reduce by half. Add ketchup, simmer
a few minutes longer, and puree. Finish with salt and pepper to taste.

Sweet Corn Sauce

$1^1\!/_2$ teaspoons grapeseed oil

$^1\!/_2$ small onion, diced into large cubes

4 ears of corn, cleaned and kernels removed

1 corncob

$^1\!/_2$ cup vegetable stock

$1^1\!/_2$ cups heavy cream

$^3\!/_4$ teaspoon turmeric

Salt and freshly ground pepper to taste

Heat a large pot on medium-high heat and add oil. Add onion, and sweat
down until almost limp; add corn kernels, and sauté until almost completely cooked. Add cob and deglaze with vegetable stock. Add cream and
turmeric, lower heat, and let simmer for 30 minutes. Remove sauce from
heat, and extract cob. Puree the sauce very well. Push through a fine-mesh
strainer by using a wooden spoon. Add salt and pepper to taste.

* Ten kinds
of tomatoes:
Red beefsteak,
yellow
beefsteak,
red cherry,
yellow cherry,
red pear,
yellow pear,
red currant,
yellow currant,
orange or yellow
sunburst,
and green grape.

PASTA WITH 10 KINDS OF TOMATOES,

Fresh Mozzarella & Balsamic Vinaigrette

SERVES 4

For the salad:

2 tablespoons olive oil

1 tablespoon balsamic vinegar

1/2 teaspoon finely chopped garlic

Sea salt and freshly ground black pepper to taste

3 cups tomatoes, 10 kinds,* washed and sliced; slice the large tomatoes, quarter the medium ones, halve the small ones, and leave the currant tomatoes whole

4 ounces fresh mozzarella, diced into 1/4-inch cubes

1 cup finely sliced (chiffonade) basil leaves, loosely packed

In a large bowl, combine the olive oil, balsamic vinegar, garlic, salt, and pepper; whisk until completely blended. Add the tomatoes, mozzarella, and basil; gently toss until well coated with the vinaigrette. Cover the bowl with plastic wrap, and set aside at room temperature.

For the pasta:

1 pound dried fettuccine or 2 pounds fresh

1 tablespoon olive oil, divided use

Bring a 2-gallon pot of water to a boil, and just before cooking the pasta, add 1/2 tablespoon of the olive oil to the water. Add the pasta, and boil until al dente or according to the manufacturer's directions. Drain completely, and toss with the remaining 1/2 tablespoon olive oil to prevent the pasta from sticking.

To serve:

Whole basil leaves for garnish

Arrange the pasta on 4 large, warmed dinner plates, and top with equal portions of the tomato salad. Garnish with whole basil leaves, and serve while warm.

Chef's recommendation: Étude Pinot Gris, Carneros, or a similar dry white wine

Nora

RESTAURANT NORA
Washington
Nora Pouillon
Chef/Owner

GARDEN SORREL VICHYSSOISE

SERVES 2

1 cup half-and-half

2 cups tightly packed, chopped sorrel, which has been washed and
stripped from the stems

1 or 2 tablespoons mashed potatoes (leftovers are fine)

1 or 2 teaspoons dry white wine

Fine-grind salt

Chive blossoms for garnish

1. Pour half-and-half into a blender, and start on medium speed.

2. Add sorrel gradually until incorporated and mixture is smooth, about
   2 to 3 minutes.

3. If the soup is too thin, add a small amount of mashed potatoes and pulse
   briefly. If it is too thick, add a teaspoon or two of white wine. Season
   with a pinch of salt. Garnish with chive blossoms and serve cold.

*Chef's recommendation: Cakebread sauvignon blanc or a light white wine displaying
citrus notes and balanced acidity*

*We grow an old-
world variety of
mild sorrel that
is called dock or
spinach dock; any
medium- to large-
leaf sorrel will do.*

—CHEF ROBERT
RAMSEY

FOX HEAD INN
Manakin-Sabot,
Virginia
Robert Ramsey
Executive Chef

Green Tomato Carpaccio

3 firm, medium-size green tomatoes

Kosher salt and white pepper to taste

2 tablespoons virgin olive oil

2 tablespoons Banyuls or aged sherry vinegar

Slice tomatoes crosswise as thinly as possible using a tomato knife, mandoline, or slicer.

Sprinkle 4 dinner plates with salt and pepper. Starting at the middle and working outward, lay overlapping tomato slices until you have an evenly shaped circle 6 inches in diameter.

Drizzle with the olive oil and the vinegar. Season with salt and pepper.

TABARD INN
Washington
David Craig
Former Executive Chef

CHESAPEAKE SOFT-SHELL CRAB
with Succotash & Green Tomato Carpaccio

SERVES 4

Green Tomato Carpaccio (see sidebar)

1/4 pound (1 stick) unsalted butter

1 medium yellow onion, finely diced

3 cloves garlic, finely sliced

1 cup shucked baby lima beans

2 cups Silver Queen corn kernels (about 4 medium ears)

4 jumbo velvet soft-shell crabs

Salt and pepper to taste

Flour to coat crabs

Canola oil

1. Assemble Green Tomato Carpaccio (see sidebar). Refrigerate until ready to assemble the meal.

2. To make the succotash, melt the butter in a heavy saucepan. Sauté the onions and garlic together until translucent and tender. Add the beans and continue cooking gently over medium-low heat until just tender, about 5 to 10 minutes. Add the corn and mix thoroughly. Cover with a lid and turn off heat.

3. To clean the crabs, use scissors to cut off the crabs' anterior carapace (face). Cut off the tips of the upper shell; lift the shell and remove the lungs on each side. Remove the flap on the back (the apron), and remove the gills (dead men's fingers).

4. Pat the crabs dry, and season with salt and pepper. Flour the crabs liberally on both sides. Shake gently to remove excess flour.

5. Heat 1/2 inch of canola oil in a heavy-bottomed pan large enough to hold the crabs without crowding. Sauté the crabs until golden brown and crispy on each side (4 minutes and 1 minute, respectively).

6. To assemble, adjust seasoning and warm the succotash. Remove the carpaccio from the refrigerator. Divide the succotash into 4 equal portions, spoon into the center of each plate over the carpaccio, and top with a crab.

HARICOTS VERTS *&* FRISÉE SALAD

SERVES 4 TO 6

$^1/_2$ pound haricots verts

$^1/_4$ cup Rocca Parmesan, grated

1 tablespoon aged balsamic vinegar

3 tablespoons extra virgin olive oil

Salt and freshly ground pepper to taste

1 head frisée (about $^3/_4$ pound), trimmed and washed

$^1/_4$ cup julienned Parma ham or Virginia country ham
   (cooked but not smoked)

$^1/_4$ cup julienned Gruyère

1. Blanch haricots verts in boiling water for 1 minute. Plunge into an ice
   water bath to stop cooking, and drain.

2. Combine Parmesan, vinegar, and olive oil. Season with salt and pepper.

3. In a salad bowl, combine frisée, Parma ham, Gruyère, and haricots
   verts. Pour dressing over all. Toss, adjust seasoning, and serve.

Chef's recommendation: Baileyana sauvignon blanc or another crisp, white wine

MELROSE
Park Hyatt Washington
Washington
Brian McBride
Executive Chef

Watermelon Salsa

³/₄ cup diced honeydew melon

³/₄ cup diced watermelon

1¹/₂ teaspoons minced Serrano chile with seeds

1¹/₂ teaspoons minced fresh mint

1¹/₂ teaspoons honey

1 tablespoon fresh lime juice

Combine.

VIETNAMESE SQUID SALAD
over Watermelon Salsa

SERVES 4

1 teaspoon tamarind juice

2 teaspoons sugar

2 tablespoons fish sauce

1 teaspoon fresh lime juice

¹/₄ cup olive oil

1 large garlic clove, minced

1 fresh hot chili (Thai, Serrano), thinly sliced

1 medium tomato, cut into wedges

¹/₄ medium yellow onion, diced

1 pound squid, cleaned

1 pound shrimp, cleaned, shelled, deveined, and tails removed

¹/₂ cup basil

¹/₂ cup roughly chopped cilantro

Watermelon Salsa (see sidebar)

1. Combine tamarind juice, sugar, fish sauce, lime juice, olive oil, garlic, and chili in a bowl. Stir to mix, and add tomato and onion. Set marinade aside for 1 hour, and then set aside ¹/₂ cup of marinade.

2. Marinate the uncooked squid and shrimp in the remaining marinade for 2 hours.

3. Light the grill, and oil the rack. Cook squid and shrimp in batches until done, about 5 to 8 minutes.

4. Slice squid into bite-size pieces. Transfer squid and shrimp to serving dish, and toss with the remaining ¹/₂ cup of marinade. Add the basil and cilantro, and toss. Serve warm or chilled over Watermelon Salsa.

Chef's recommendation: Domaine Weinbach Riesling Schlossberg Grand Cru or another racy but ripe Alsatian white wine

BICYCLE
Baltimore
Barry Rumsey
Chef/Owner

PIPIRRANA

SERVES 6 AS AN APPETIZER

1 teaspoon whole-grain mustard

4 tablespoons sherry vinegar

$\frac{1}{2}$ cup extra virgin olive oil

3 cups diced ripe tomatoes

$1\frac{1}{2}$ cups peeled, seeded, and coarsely diced cucumbers

$\frac{3}{4}$ cup coarsely diced green pepper

$\frac{3}{4}$ cup coarsely diced red pepper

$\frac{1}{4}$ cup finely diced shallot

Kosher salt to taste

4 tablespoons finely chopped chives

1. Make vinaigrette by whisking together mustard, vinegar, and olive oil.

2. In a large bowl, combine tomatoes, cucumber, peppers, and shallot.
   Add the vinaigrette and mix gently with a spoon. Add the salt.

3. Add chives. Mix again and serve.

*Chef's recommendation: Belondrade y Lurton Verdejo or another medium-bodied
white wine with character*

JALEO
Washington
José Ramón Andrés
Executive Chef/
Partner

COLD CUCUMBER SOUP

SERVES 6

2 English cucumbers, peeled and coarsely diced

1 bunch watercress leaves, no stems, plus a few extra leaves for garnish

Juice of one lime

Juice of one lemon

1 teaspoon kosher salt

Freshly ground black pepper to taste

1 cup sour cream

Heavy cream, if needed

1. Purée all ingredients in a food processor. (If needed, process in 2 batches and combine.) Thin with a little heavy cream if the soup is too thick.

2. Keep ice-cold until ready to serve. Ladle into bowls that have been kept in the refrigerator or freezer.

3. Garnish with a few leaves of watercress.

Chef's recommendation: A Loire sauvignon blanc, such as Sancerre les Coutes Reverdy Frères

CHEF CINDY WOLF
CHARLESTON

CHARLESTON
Baltimore
Cindy Wolf
Chef/Owner

BASMATI RICE SALAD
with Fennel, Tomatoes & Capers

SERVES 4

1½ cups Basmati rice

2 quarts salted water

½ teaspoon salt

5 tablespoons extra virgin olive oil, divided use

¼ cup finely diced red onion

½ cup finely diced fennel

½ cup finely julienned carrots

2 tablespoons finely chopped Italian parsley

2 tablespoons nonpareil capers (or the smallest you can find)

Zest from ½ lemon, grated

2 tablespoons fresh lemon juice

Salt and freshly ground pepper to taste

1 vine-ripened tomato, coarsely diced, for garnish

1. Rinse rice in cold water. Pour off water and repeat until rinse water is clear. Cover rinsed, drained rice with cold water and soak 20 to 30 minutes.

2. Preheat oven to 350°F.

3. Bring 2 quarts salted water to a boil. Drain rice, add to boiling water, and cook for 5 minutes. Drain. Transfer to an ovenproof pot with a tight-fitting lid. Stir in the salt and 1 tablespoon of the olive oil. Place pot in oven, and steam for 20 minutes. Remove from oven and allow to rest, covered, for 15 minutes without disturbing.

4. Uncover rice and stir gently to separate grains. When cooled to room temperature, stir into the combined red onion, fennel, carrots, parsley, capers, and lemon zest.

5. In a small bowl, emulsify the lemon juice and 4 tablespoons of the extra virgin olive oil. Just before serving, dress salad with 3 tablespoons of the vinaigrette. Taste, season with salt and pepper, and add more vinaigrette if needed. Garnish each serving with the diced tomato.

Chef's recommendation: A full-bodied sauvignon blanc, such as Clos de la Crêle Sancerre

**CASHION'S
EAT PLACE**
Washington
Ann Cashion
Chef/Owner

SAUTÉED FRESH FISH
with Fresh Corn Relish

SERVES 6

For the relish:

3 cups water

1 cup sherry vinegar

1 cup sugar

3 teaspoons sea salt

1 tablespoon freshly ground black pepper

8 ears corn, shucked

$1/4$ cup extra virgin olive oil, divided use

$1/2$ medium onion, peeled and finely chopped

Sea salt and freshly ground black pepper to taste

1 large red pepper, seeded and finely chopped

For the fish:

6 eight-ounce fresh fish fillets, such as cobia or rockfish

Sea salt and freshly ground black pepper

Extra virgin olive oil

The day before serving:

1. Make a base for the relish by combining the water, vinegar, sugar, salt, and ground pepper in a saucepan. Bring to a boil, reduce heat, and simmer for 5 minutes. Set aside.

2. Cook the ears of corn for 4 minutes in rapidly boiling, well-salted water. Remove to an ice bath and cool for 5 minutes. Slice the kernels from the cobs, being careful not to slice too deeply into the cob. Puree about $1/4$ of the corn kernels in a blender, using just enough water to liquefy. Season the puree with salt and pepper, and refrigerate. Set the rest of the corn kernels aside in a large mixing bowl.

3. Heat a medium nonstick pan to high heat. Add $1/8$ cup of the olive oil and the onion. Season the onion with the salt and pepper, and sauté for approximately 2 minutes. Set aside to cool. Follow the same procedure for the chopped red pepper.

SOUTHERN GRILLE
Richmond, Virginia
Jimmy Sneed
Former Chef/Owner

4. Add the sautéed onion, sautéed red pepper, and vinegar-sugar base to the corn. Combine well. Place in the refrigerator to marinate for 12 to 15 hours.

On the day of serving:

5. Heat a large cast-iron pan. Season both sides of the fish fillets with salt and pepper. Pour a very thin layer of olive oil in the pan, and sear the fillets, skin side up, until golden. Turn the fillets over, and cook 1 minute on the other side. Finish the fish in a 350°F oven if needed.

6. Strain the liquid from the corn puree, and add the puree to the chilled corn mixture. Adjust the seasoning. Serve hot or cold with sautéed fresh fish.

Chef's recommendation: Sancerre Grand Cuvée Fournier or another full-bodied Loire sauvignon blanc

**Local Foods
Local Flavors**

Monastery Country Cheese—Steeped in a tradition of prayer and work in the foothills of the Blue Ridge Mountains, the Sisters at Our Lady of the Angels Monastery combine monastic craftsmanship, ancient wisdom, and modern technology to produce a genuine Dutch Gouda called Monastery Country Cheese. Made in small batches from grade A milk produced by cows in the nearby Shenandoah Valley, Monastery Country Cheese is a mild and mellow semisoft cheese that acquires a richer flavor and a deeper color as it ages in Gouda's traditional red wax coating.

CHILLED PEACH SOUP
with Coconut Cream

SERVES 6

6 cups sliced fresh ripe peaches, skin removed; divided use

3 tablespoons sugar, divided use

1 cup fruity white wine

1/2 cup fresh lime juice

1/2 cup unsweetened coconut milk

1/2 cup sour cream

1/2 cup fresh mint leaves

1/4 cup olive oil

1. Combine 1 cup of the sliced peaches with 1 tablespoon of the sugar. Set aside.

2. Cut the remaining 5 cups of peach slices into pieces and place in a blender. Add wine, lime juice, and remaining 2 tablespoons of the sugar. Blend until very smooth. Pour into a large bowl. Set aside.

3. Combine coconut milk and sour cream. Stir until smooth.

4. Using a blender, blend mint leaves and olive oil until smooth.

5. To serve, ladle soup into chilled bowls. Top with coconut cream, mint oil, and peach slices.

Chef's recommendation: A full-bodied champagne, such as Bollinger Special Cuvée Brut

BISTRO ST. MICHAELS
St. Michaels, Maryland
David Stein
Chef/Owner

CRÈME AUDALOUSE

(TOMATO BISQUE)

SERVES 6

2 tablespoons unsalted butter

1/2 cup diced leek, white parts only

1/2 cup coarsely diced onion

1/4 cup coarsely diced carrot

1 tablespoon coarsely diced celery

4 tablespoons all-purpose flour

1 quart water

10 medium tomatoes, stems removed and cut into quarters

1 cup diced potatoes

4 cloves

2 bay leaves

1 tablespoon kosher salt

1/4 teaspoon cracked black peppercorns

1 tablespoon sugar

1 tablespoon red wine vinegar

3/4 cup heavy cream

1 tablespoon finely chopped fresh basil

1. Melt butter in a heavy 3-quart saucepan. Add the leek, onion, carrot, and celery. Sweat the vegetables and let simmer, covered, about 10 minutes; do not brown. Mix in the flour, blending well.

2. Add the water, tomatoes, potatoes, cloves, bay leaves, salt, and peppercorns. Bring to a boil. Reduce the heat, cover, and simmer for 1 1/2 to 2 hours until tomatoes soften and melt into thickened sauce. Remove the bay leaves; set soup aside to cool.

3. Puree the cooled soup in a blender or food processor. Return to the saucepan; before serving, reboil and add the sugar, vinegar, cream, and basil. Adjust the seasonings.

Chef's recommendation: Pinot Gris from Alsace, such as Trimbach

Prepare this soup during the late summer and fall by using overripe tomatoes. It is excellent served hot or cold.

—CHEF JACQUES
HAERINGER

L'AUBERGE CHEZ FRANÇOIS
Great Falls, Virginia
Jacques Haeringer
Executive Chef

PISTACHIO-CRUSTED BLUEFISH
with Savory Tomato Butter & Arugula Salad

SERVES 6

Pistachio Crust (see sidebar on next page)

For the Savory Tomato Butter:

2 plum tomatoes

1 cup Chardonnay or sauvignon blanc

1 shallot, finely chopped

$1/4$ cup white wine or champagne vinegar

$1/2$ cup heavy cream

2 tablespoons tomato paste

$1/2$ pound unsalted butter, cut into cubes

1 teaspoon finely chopped fresh savory

1 tablespoon finely chopped fresh Italian parsley

Juice of 1 lemon

Salt and freshly cracked pepper, to taste

For the bluefish:

Buttermilk

$1^1/2$ pounds fresh bluefish fillets (the firmer the fillets, the fresher the fish)

Vegetable oil or clarified butter to coat sauté pan

Arugula Salad (see next page)

1. Prepare Pistachio Crust (see sidebar). This can be done the day before serving. If keeping overnight, seal in an airtight container.

2. Blanch the tomatoes in boiling water for 5 seconds, immediately plunge into ice water, and let cool. Peel, seed, and cut into approximately $1/4$-inch dice.

3. In a 2-quart stainless steel pot, reduce the white wine, shallot, and vinegar to a syrupy glaze. Add the cream and tomato paste, turn down the heat, and cook for about 3 minutes. Slowly whisk in the butter cubes, making sure you don't boil the butter. You want only to melt it; the sauce will thicken as you add the butter. Finish the sauce with 2 tablespoons of the cooled diced tomato and the savory, parsley, lemon juice, and salt and

KINKEAD'S
Washington
Bob Kinkead
Chef/Owner

pepper. You can prepare this about 30 minutes before you plan to cook the bluefish.

4. Using a very sharp knife, cut the fillets straight down, into 1/8-inch-thick slices.

5. Dip the slices first into buttermilk and then, on one side only, into the pistachio–bread-crumb mixture. Place them on a cookie sheet or plate, crumbed side down. You can do this at least 3 hours ahead and refrigerate.

6. Warm a nonstick or well-seasoned sauté pan over medium-low heat for 1 minute. Add a small amount of vegetable oil or clarified butter. Without crowding, add bluefish slices crumbed side down, and sauté for about 30 seconds. The pistachios burn very easily, so don't let the pan get too hot. Turn the bluefish slices over and continue cooking for about 1 to 2 minutes.

7. To assemble, spoon about 2 tablespoons of the tomato butter on each of 6 plates at the 6 o'clock position; place 2 bluefish slices on top of the sauce. Place the salad at 12 o'clock. Serve.

Chef's recommendation: Peter Michael Chardonnay or another California Chardonnay

Arugula Salad

3/4 pound arugula, coarser lower stems trimmed

1/2 lemon

1 bulb fennel, julienned

2 roasted red peppers, peeled and julienned

2 tablespoons pitted, halved Calamata olives

4 1/2 tablespoons balsamic vinegar

6 tablespoons extra virgin olive oil

1. Wash the arugula twice in cold water to remove all sand; dry overnight in the refrigerator in a colander covered with a cloth.

2. In a saucepan, add the half lemon to salted water, bring to a boil, and blanch the fennel for 30 seconds. Drain and set aside.

3. Toss the arugula, peppers, fennel, and olives.

4. Whisk together the balsamic vinegar and olive oil. Season to taste. Toss the salad with enough vinaigrette to lightly coat the leaves.

Pistachio Crust

2 cups shelled pistachios

1 cup dry bread crumbs

1 teaspoon chopped fresh savory

Salt and freshly ground pepper, to taste

Puree the pistachios in a food processor for about 15 seconds or until they're the size of small pebbles. Add the bread crumbs and mix well. Add the savory, salt, and pepper, and again mix well.

Pesto

2 cups packed fresh basil leaves

4 cloves garlic

³/4 cup extra virgin olive oil

³/4 cup grated Parmesan cheese

³/4 cup pine nuts

Salt and pepper to taste

To make pesto, place all ingredients in a food processor, and puree.

CHILLED CORN SOUP
with Pesto & Heirloom Tomatoes

SERVES 6

6 ears corn, husks on

6 cups water

1 teaspoon salt, divided use

Freshly ground pepper to taste

2 tablespoons unsalted butter

1 cup chopped sweet onions

¹/2 cup peeled, diced yellow potatoes (Yukon Gold, Yellow Finn, or German Butterball)

¹/2 cup chopped celery

1 teaspoon chopped fresh thyme

¹/2 teaspoon fresh sweet marjoram

1 cup buttermilk

Pesto (see sidebar)

3 small heirloom tomatoes, diced

1. Preheat oven to 400°F.

2. Soak ears of corn in cold water for 1 hour. Drain and place on baking sheet. Roast for 5 minutes, turn corn over, and roast for another 5 minutes. Remove from oven and let cool. Remove husks, cut kernels from cobs, and set aside.

3. Chop cobs into 2-inch pieces, place in a large pot with the water, ¹/2 teaspoon of the salt, and pepper to taste. Bring to a boil, lower the heat, and simmer 1 hour; strain, discard cobs, and save broth.

4. Melt butter in a large pot over medium heat. Add onions, potatoes, celery, remaining salt, and pepper. Cook until vegetables are wilted. Add corn, corn broth, and fresh herbs. Simmer until vegetables are tender. Puree, strain by pressing through a medium-coarse strainer, and chill. Stir in buttermilk and adjust seasonings before serving. Garnish soup with a dollop of pesto and diced tomatoes.

Chef's recommendation: Château Potelle sauvignon blanc or another dry, crisp white wine

FOUR & TWENTY BLACKBIRDS
Flint Hill, Virginia
Heidi Morf
Chef/Owner

GAZPACHO WITH CILANTRO

SERVES 6 TO 8

2 English cucumbers, finely chopped

¼ medium yellow onion, peeled and finely chopped

1 green bell pepper, seeded and finely chopped

3 celery stalks, finely chopped

½ teaspoon crushed garlic

3 large, ripe tomatoes, finely chopped

3 tablespoons red wine vinegar

¼ cup olive oil

1 bunch cilantro, chopped

Juice of 2 lemons

1 cup tomato juice

Salt and freshly ground pepper, to taste

1. In a food processor, mix cucumbers, onion, pepper, celery, and crushed garlic. Process until the vegetables are the size of lentils; transfer mixture into a medium-size mixing bowl.

2. In the same food processor, add tomatoes, vinegar, olive oil, cilantro, and lemon juice. (Process in batches if your processor is small.) Process for 2 minutes.

3. Add to mixture in mixing bowl. Add tomato juice and stir well. Add salt and pepper to taste. Refrigerate for 20 minutes. Serve in chilled mugs or bowls.

Chef's recommendation: Vine Cliff Vineyards Chardonnay (Napa) or a full-bodied Chardonnay with a dry finish

BOAR'S HEAD INN
Charlottesville, Virginia
Alex Montiel
Executive Chef

FALL FARE

AMERICAN EEL
APPLE CIDER
APPLES
ARUGULA
ASIAN PEARS
BEEF
BEEF (FORAGE FED*)
BEETS
BISON
BLACK SEA BASS
BLUE CRAB
BLUEFISH
BOK CHOY
BROCCOLI
BROCCOLI RAAB
BRUSSELS SPROUTS
CABBAGE
CARROTS
CATFISH
CAULIFLOWER
CELERIAC
CELERY
CHANTERELLES
CHESTNUTS
CHICKEN
CLAMS
CLAMS (FARMED*)
COLLARDS
CONCH
COUNTRY CURED HAM
    (HANG TO EAT IN WINTER)
CRANBERRY BEAN
CROAKER
CUCUMBERS
DAIRY (PASTURED*)
DUCK (FARM RAISED*)
EGGPLANT
EGGS (CHICKEN)
EGGS (FORAGE FED*)
FARMSTEAD CHEESE (AGED)
FENNEL
FLOUNDER
GARLIC
GOOSE (FARM RAISED*)
GRAPES

GREEN BEANS
GREENS
GUINEA FOWL
HAYMAN POTATOES
HERBS
HONEY
HORSERADISH
KALE
KOHLRABI
LAMB (PASTURED*)
LEEKS
LETTUCES & SALAD GREENS
MONKFISH
MOZZARELLA (FRESH)
MUSCADINE GRAPES
MUSHROOMS
OKRA
ONIONS
OYSTER MUSHROOMS
OYSTERS
PARSNIPS
PEANUTS
PEARS
PEPPERS
PERCH (WHITE & YELLOW)
PORK
PORK (FORAGE FED*)
PORK (PASTURED*)
POTATOES
PUMPKINS
QUAIL
RABBIT (FARM RAISED*)
RABBIT (FORAGE FED*)
RADICCHIO
RADISHES
RAINBOW TROUT (FARMED*)
RASPBERRIES
RICOTTA (FRESH)
ROCKFISH (STRIPED BASS)
RUTABAGAS
SALSIFY
SCALLOPS
SEA TROUT (GRAY)
SHALLOTS
SHIITAKE MUSHROOMS
SHRIMP

FALL

EXPLORING THE
ENVIRONMENTAL
BENEFITS OF SMALL-SCALE,
LOCAL AGRICULTURE &
CELEBRATING THE FLAVORS
OF FALL IN THE
MID-ATLANTIC

SORREL
SPANISH MACKEREL
SPINACH
SPOT
SQUID
STRIPED BASS (FARMED* HYBRID)
SWEET POTATOES
SWISS CHARD
TATSOI
TILAPIA (FARMED*)
TOMATOES
TOMATOES (GREENHOUSE)
TURKEY
TURKEY (FORAGE FED*)
TURNIPS
VEAL
WALNUTS
WATERMELON
WINTER SQUASH

* SEE PAGE 233

FARMING IN THE FALL

I love the fall. Sixteen-hour days, no time off for months, the heartbreak of losing crops to weather or predators, equipment problems at the worst time. I love the fall. No meetings, no appointments, nothing but the purity of farming. The rest of the year has only been training for this season. We have done everything we can to prepare our vines and trees. They are healthy, and the crop is in balance. Now it is out of our hands. There used to be great stress in this, but now I know what I can control and what I cannot.

At Linden Vineyards we grow grapes, heirloom apples, and blueberries. I was attracted to the mountains of Virginia because of their all-but-vanished history of fruit growing. Abandoned orchards stretch hundreds of miles along the eastern slope of the Blue Ridge. Old varieties of apples with curious names and distinct flavor lost to the world of centralized distribution and Red Delicious. One of these abandoned orchards was named Monticello. Fortunately for us, Thomas Jefferson kept good records. He had a passion for wine and for horticulture that has been an inspiration to orchardists and winegrowers in Virginia. It has been exhilarating to learn from him. In the 1980s we planted about a dozen heirloom apple varieties. Over the years, it became apparent that the ones Jefferson had success with worked best on our farm too. Esopus Spitzenberg, Calville Blanc, and Newton Pippin adapted wonderfully to our site. Our customers, too, are intrigued by the history of these apples, but even more so, they love the personality of the flavor of each variety. We often describe the apples as if they were wine: strawberry aromas, firm texture, good acidity. In fact, we have learned that the wine-growing concept of farming for flavor makes just as much sense in the orchard.

After 20 years I have a certain intimacy with my corner of the world. I know when to pick based on taste, health of the plant, and weather conditions. Measurements of sugar content, acid, or pH become insignificant. Flavor and texture are everything. Every growing season gives us different flavors of both apples and grapes because of the variability of fall weather. This is something our customers and we used to fear. Now we marvel and celebrate the personality of each vintage year. ■

Linden

Linden Vineyards grows grapes at four different sites on the Blue Ridge. The combination of a cool, mountain microclimate and well-drained mineral soils helps create complex wines with fresh, assertive aromas and concentrated flavors. Constantly fine-tuning the vines—pruning, thinning, leaf pulling, tying, hedging, and yield reduction, all of which enhance wine flavor, aroma, and concentration—Linden makes wines that are unique in character and specific to the personality of each of its vineyard sites. Linden specializes in small lots of single-vineyard Chardonnay, Sauvignon Blanc, and red Bordeaux blends.

by Jim Law
Linden Vineyards
Linden, Virginia

THE IMPACT OF FARMING ON THE CHESAPEAKE BAY

The Chesapeake Bay area is well-known for recipes using blue crab, rockfish (striped bass), oysters, and waterfowl. But the bay is only a small part of Chesapeake country. The Chesapeake Bay watershed (that area in which every drop of rainwater eventually drains into the bay) covers 64,000 square miles in part or all of six states and Washington, D.C. It begins at the headwaters of the Susquehanna River near the Baseball Hall of Fame in Cooperstown, New York, and stretches south through Pennsylvania, Maryland, and Virginia. It also includes parts of West Virginia and Delaware.

From this watershed view, Chesapeake cuisine is far more than crab cakes and oyster stew. Consider the Amish and Mennonite farms in Lancaster County, Pennsylvania, that produce organic milk and chickens; massive farms of corn, soybeans, and wheat on Maryland's Eastern Shore and along big tidal rivers in Virginia like the Rappahannock; large poultry operations and fruit orchards in Virginia's Shenandoah Valley and the Eastern Shore; and small growers of fresh vegetables throughout the area. At every season, there is much to enjoy from this bountiful region.

The health of Chesapeake Bay depends on the quality of the water that feeds it through more than a thousand rivers, creeks, and streams. The bay relies on an intricate system of natural water filters for balancing its need for essential nutrients like nitrogen and phosphorus with keeping it free of pollutants that destroy habitat and marine life, including an excess of those nutrients. It's a tough balancing act in which millions of acres of farmland play an important role.

The Chesapeake Bay Foundation (CBF), the largest U.S. regional environmental organization, has long considered farming one of the best ways to use the land to benefit both people and the bay. In stark contrast to land covered with pavement and rooftops, well-husbanded farmland absorbs rainwater and slowly releases it to the bay. Crops, trees, and shrubs filter pollution and hold soil in place.

Even so, farms in the region are sold every day for development. Stemming that loss of farmland is vital if the region is to keep its farm economy healthy and to preserve both the family farm way of life and Chesapeake Bay.

When farmland is cultivated intensively without regard to soil conservation or pollution management, the effects can be devastating. The Chesapeake is now unbalanced, severely overenriched with nitrogen and phosphorus pollution (largely from excess fertilizer and animal waste). Agriculture is the leading source of those pollutants. When dairy cattle are allowed free access to streams, for example, they trample the banks,

by Geoff Oxnam
& John Page
Williams
Chesapeake Bay
Foundation

destroying the grasses, trees, and shrubs that are natural filters. Urine and manure increase the pollution load. Streams suffer eroded banks and run muddy and warm, while the tidal waters of the bay suffer from a continual buildup of sediment and algae.

On large grain farms, failure to apply winter cover crops means loss of topsoil through runoff. Heavy applications of nitrogen- and phosphorus-rich fertilizers intended to maximize yields create excessive polluted runoff. In the attempt to maximize cost-effectiveness with greater acreage and larger equipment, grain farmers sometimes remove hedgerows and cultivate land right up to stream banks, thereby eliminating the benefits of having trees and shrubs. In poultry-growing areas, chicken manure causes problems when farmers spread it onto already oversaturated fields.

Fortunately, many progressive farmers help minimize those negative effects by composting cow and poultry manure or implementing pollution management strategies. Government cost-share initiatives like the federal Conservation Reserve Enhancement Program (CREP) make it economically advantageous for many farmers to take marginal land out of production and improve its value for both water quality and habitat. State natural resources agencies and private organizations like CBF and Ducks Unlimited help farmers take advantage of CREP and other conservation programs with both technical assistance and additional cost-share funds.

Leaders in the farm community set superb examples of conservation and nutrient management for their colleagues. The trick here is persuading enough other farmers to participate in making a significant difference in restoring the bay's health.

Ultimately, the quality of what lands on our table depends on the quality of what grows on the land and in the water. Whether goose or oyster, duck or crab, all depend on healthy habitats. Farmland often holds many of the key terrestrial habitats—such as wetlands favored by waterfowl—and runoff affects the health of others: underwater grasses that are essential for blue crabs, rockfish, and speckled trout.

In the end, the greatest challenge lies in helping farmers keep good land working while reducing pollution and protecting pollution filters. That land best serves the Chesapeake—and the people of the region—when it grows crops, not new houses. ■

THE GROWING CONTRIBUTION OF FARMING

Farmland occupies roughly half the land in the contiguous United States, so how farmers use their land is critical to the country's environment, public health, and rural communities. Because farmland occupies so much area, farming is a major part of both the problem and the solution to almost all of the country's major environmental challenges:

(CONTINUED NEXT PAGE)

by Peter D. Bloome
Oregon State University Extension Service

I have a dream. In my dream, farmers stand before the rest of society and ask, What do you want? We can provide corn, wheat, soybeans, cotton, rice, and other commodity crops. We can provide cattle, hogs, chickens, sheep, turkeys, and other meat animals. We can provide milk, eggs, honey, wool, and other animal-derived products. We can provide fruits, vegetables, and nuts of many kinds. We can grow and raise foods that reflect different cultures and ethnic groups. We can provide trees for lumber and paper pulp.

We can replace fossil-energy use by capturing the energy of the sun—either directly, as solar energy, or indirectly, as windpower, hydropower, or geothermal power—or by growing crops. We can replace production systems that are reliant on high inputs of fossil energy with those that require lesser fossil energy sources.

We can provide wildlife habitat, including critical habitat for endangered species. We can provide wetlands, riparian areas, grasslands, woodlots, and stands of timber. We can provide aesthetics to enhance quality of life and local tourism, including landscapes of diverse crops, patches of native wildflowers, herds of pastured animals, and natural areas.

We can capture rainfall in soil rich in organic matter to replenish groundwater, and we can maintain in-stream flows during dry periods. We can provide water and air free of contaminants and pollutants. We can capture and hold carbon in soil organic matter and in growing plants to counter both the greenhouse effect and global warming. We can rotate crops to provide for much of our nitrogen needs and to control insect, weed, and disease pests. We can minimize pesticide use by taking advantage of natural control mechanisms.

We can provide immediate, compelling examples of the many ways in which we are connected to—and reliant on—the natural world by means of farm visits and tours, farmers markets, and other means. We can provide meaningful connections to the uniqueness of place and of each place as a natural home. We can connect the human spirit to the ecosystems on which that spirit is reliant. We can provide recreational experiences in which people re-create themselves in relation to the natural world.

We can provide all of those things—a full portfolio of ecosystem benefits—and all of the things we desire from our natural resource base.

So, what do you want and what will you pay? What will you pay in the private market and what will you pay in the public market? We can provide all of those things, but only if we receive an income that enables us to live on the land and manage it to produce its full portfolio of products and benefits.

My dream requires two paradigm shifts. The first requires that farmers—who have traditionally built their identity around their primary products—identify with the larger portfolio of products and benefits provided by our natural resource base. The second shift requires that society—which has come to expect low-cost food and fiber products while demanding that farmers also provide environmental benefits—pay living wages to farmers for all of the ecosystem benefits farmers provide.

The current trajectory in U.S. agriculture is one of radical capitalism; it is one wherein the last person standing gets everything. Huge social and environmental externalities are ignored. It seems clear to me that if society created markets through which farmers could offer products and benefits from the base of natural resources—including conservational, environmental, and social benefits—then a much more diverse, community-based system of land management would evolve. Simply redirecting federal dollars that currently target commodity program support would create the public market for social and environmental benefits. I believe the total costs of the system would be less, because all costs would be included. And the system would be much more diverse, much more resilient, and much more sustainable. ■

Regional Family Farms

Heifer International provides assistance for small-scale farmers in 49 countries on five continents throughout the world. Along with gifts of livestock, Heifer helps communities develop culturally appropriate and environmentally sustainable agricultural practices and build local organizational and leadership capacity. Heifer's work focuses on community building and promotes self-reliance, which builds self-esteem and helps families lift themselves out of poverty.

In the United States, Heifer program offices are located in rural and urban areas of endemic poverty throughout the eastern, central, and southwestern regions of the country. The mountainous counties in Maryland and West Virginia are sparsely populated and provide limited employment opportunities. Heifer's Family Agricultural Project focuses on developing successful meat goat enterprises in those regions, thereby helping small farmers find niche marketing opportunities for their agricultural products as an alternative to competing with large-scale farmers through conventional marketing channels.

ensuring clean water, saving endangered species and other wildlife, curbing sprawling development, and even combating climate change. Improved farm practices can also address major health concerns, including diseases from improper control of animal waste and the growing threat of dangerous bacteria that are resistant to antibiotics. In addition, farm programs help preserve and enhance the wildlife value of private forests. Such forests occupy another 20 percent of the land in the contiguous United States, so they too must play a vital role in the solving of major environmental problems.

—FROM THE
ENVIRONMENTAL
DEFENSE
WEB SITE

Country Hams

Loved by those who swear it is the only true choice, country ham has a flavor, texture, and quality all its own. Unlike city ham—which is processed in a wet cure (brine), sometimes smoked, and never aged—country ham is processed using a time-honored method whereby hams are packed in salt and slowly cured, sometimes smoked, and always aged. The salt draws out the meat's moisture, creating a firmer and more flavorful product.

The country ham tradition dates back to the early 1600s, when the Powhatan Indians taught the first settlers at Jamestown their techniques for smoking venison. In those days, settlers turned pigs loose on nearby Hog Island, where the pigs foraged for food in the woods and marshes. Settlers applied the venison-curing methods to pork, and the country ham was born.

Creating country hams was once a distinctly seasonal process: hogs were butchered in the fall when the weather turned cold, and the hams were rubbed with a mixture of salt and saltpeter, which gives the hams their mahogany color. They were then hung in the smokehouse for a year to cure, the flavor and texture benefiting from the rise in temperature as spring turned to summer.

Today, processing houses mimic the seasons when curing hams. Fresh hams are rubbed with a dry cure of salt, sodium nitrate, and pepper and kept at 40 degrees for a month or more, which allows the salt to penetrate the meat and draw out the excess moisture. The excess salt is then washed out, and the hams are hung in stocking nets in rooms kept at 50 degrees—spring-season temperature—for two weeks. Next, the hams are placed in a smokehouse, where slow-burning hickory fires allow the temperature to rise gradually from 50 to 85 to 95 degrees over the course of a week. The summer aging room is where the temperature is kept at 85 degrees, and the hams hang for four months to a year. According to Sam Edwards, president of S. Wallace Edwards & Sons in Surry, Virginia, "Time, temperature, and humidity are crucial factors in curing hams. Seasonal changes are essential in making a quality ham."

While country hams from Surry County once came from hogs raised on a diet of acorns, hickory nuts, and peanuts, most commercially cured hams are now made from grain-fed hogs raised in large-scale, confinement operations. You may not be able to find hams made from hogs raised on small-scale, local farms, but you can still find country hams made through traditional curing methods. Among the best are those by S. Wallace Edwards & Sons in Surry, Kite's Hams in Wolftown, and Calhoun's Ham House in Culpeper. ■

Curing Country Meat

by George Swingler
Charlottesville, Virginia

- Start with a wooden box lined with 1 to 2 inches of salt.

- Meat to be cured can be hams, side meats, shoulders, ribs, hog jowls, backbones, and pig feet.

- Rub or pat meat with black pepper, brown sugar, and salt. On top of the meat, add 1 inch of salt.

- Place meat in the box for 6 weeks. Remove and wash meat in warm water and borax. Hang to dry, uncovered, in a smokehouse for a couple of weeks. Reapply pepper, and hang in a paper sack until ready to use. Mold may appear; this is natural. Scrubbing before cooking removes the mold.

- Smoked ham requires the same process as described except that after washing in warm water and borax, burn green hickory wood in an open pit in the smokehouse floor. Build a fire twice a week for 3 weeks to create smoke, not fire. Smokehouse floors are dirt floors and can be used for smoking hams.

Slavka Kovarick stood crying amid the crowds and bustle in front of our stand at the farmers market. I had given her a sample of one of the large black mulberries we were selling. When I took her aside to find out what was wrong, she told me that the taste of the fruit had transported her to her childhood in Czechoslovakia—to a mulberry tree and a village she had not seen in 22 years.

I've witnessed that intimate connection between food and the human experience before: an old man's passionate reminiscence of the farm he grew up on after he ate one of our tree-ripe peaches, the wonder and innocence of tough urban teens as they sat in the field eating the heart out of a watermelon, parents' amazement after becoming involved with the farm and seeing their children eating vegetables for the first time in their lives.

I'm never surprised. Walking the anonymous aisles of the local supermarket with its 24-hour-a-day, seven-day-a-week, day-glow perfect piles of fruits and vegetables or visiting the vast, silent industrial fields that produce much of the food that Americans eat reminds me that food without a face can never satisfy or truly nourish.

There was a time when my little postage stamp farm seemed insignificant, when 12½ acres felt more like garden than farm, when the fresh food that we produce and sell at our produce stand and at the farmers market felt fractional compared with the hundreds of semi truckloads hauled away each day from the nation's huge industrial fields.

As the organic movement grew and demand for our food increased, I too slipped into thinking that bigger might be better. We quadrupled our acreage for a time and in the process discovered that while increasing acreage produces more food, it also produces more stress, higher management costs, lower quality, and less net income. My short-term desire to get bigger proved for me what has now been well documented: that small farms are 15 to 20 times more productive than their large-scale counterparts. But more important, I discovered that with every increase in scale came a decrease in connection to the land and to those who are eating the food from that land. That has been the story of America's farms ever since the late '60s, when then secretary of agriculture Earl Butz proclaimed that farmers had to "Get big or get out." Most were forced to choose the latter.

But while large-scale industrial agriculture seemed to fulfill its promise of producing volumes of cheap food, we were in fact paying for it many times after leaving the checkout counter: in terms of our health, the health and well-being of those doing the work, the depletion of topsoil, and the pollution of air and water. The food we were feeding our families was no longer safe to eat, and we were quickly losing the pleasure that only

SIZE MATTERS

by Michael Ableman
Fairview Gardens

Virginia ranks nationally in the top 10 in production of peanuts, apples, fresh-market tomatoes, summer potatoes, fresh-market strawberries, fresh-market cucumbers, fresh-market snap beans, cantaloupes, sweet potatoes, and fresh-market lima beans.

—VIRGINIA
AGRICULTURAL
STATISTICS SERVICE

fresh and local could provide. People wanted corn that tasted like corn and potatoes that were more than just a tasteless medium to convey ketchup and salt to their mouths.

As a result, farmers markets have exploded in numbers across the United States, chefs have rediscovered that the quality of fresh ingredients is critical to the outcome of the final dish, and small farms have found a new level of recognition and success. With that success, though, has come some loss. In the past 15 years, the organic movement—once a local, community-based alternative that focused on the importance of building and sustaining living soils—has been seduced by the very food production and distribution system it sought to change. Its roots as a movement are about more than substituting organic materials for chemicals. The movement wanted to redefine the food system as a whole and offer an alternative in which individual, social, and environmental health did not have to be a casualty of eating. Organic companies are now traded on Wall Street, the products of organic farms can be found on supermarket shelves—shrink-wrapped and next to the Cheetos—and a host of organocrats beholden to those with the most acres have created a vast bureaucracy to keep it all under control.

At the same time, many of us are scaling back and growing for our neighborhoods and local communities. We are returning to the values that brought us to farming in the first place: love of land and good food and the simple desire to share that with others.

This is why I farm. My back gets sore, or it's hot or it's cold or it's wet, or I'm tired, and my brain starts to add up how many of the same boxes I've filled and lifted and put away and filled and lifted year after year, how many trucks I've loaded and unloaded, how many rows I've cultivated, how many peach trees I've thinned, and how many carrots I've bunched. But an impulse far more powerful than my rational mind keeps me going cycle after cycle, worn out and exhausted by the time winter arrives and thoroughly excited to begin anew each spring: It feels good to look out and see fields full of food that will feed my neighborhood. I am proud that our strawberries are so sweet that local kids beg their moms for more. I like knowing that our carrots find their way into classrooms and school lunches and that they nourish young bodies. It's important that those who eat our food know where it was grown, whose hands hoed and harvested it, and what materials were used in its production. I want them to know that the land is well cared for and protected from development, that our food has been neither assaulted with an array of chemistry nor irradiated, and that its genetic makeup hasn't been messed with.

On this human scale, grower and eater can meet face-to-face. As a grower, I can explain why the melons are late, how we keep our asparagus white, and the best way to prepare green garlic. Eaters can tell me how they liked last week's potatoes, what's growing in their own gardens at home, and their favorite recipe for butternut squash. Knowing something about each other's lives makes for a real exchange and brings humanity and responsibility back into the system.

Waving flags and singing anthems may carry some shallow sense of belonging, but the real patriots, I believe, can be found quietly making compost, growing food for their neighbors, and selling at the local farmers market. This is the way we support true civic life, uphold the original goals of our democracy, and provide for the health and the pleasure of our communities. ■

Scuppernongs

Eating a muscadine or a scuppernong isn't like eating just any grape. These come with their own set of instructions. First, hold the grape with the stem scar up. Second, put the grape with the stem scar facing upward in your mouth and squeeze or bite the grape. Third, let the pulp and juice burst through the skin into your mouth. Finally, savor the fruity flavor.

If you're from North Carolina or Virginia, you know about these thick-skinned grapes, which go by the names scuppernongs and muscadines. Most southerners still refer to any bronze muscadines as scuppernongs. The purple or black varieties are commonly called muscadines.

The muscadine is actually a native American grape. When the early settlers arrived in America, they were familiar with the muscat grape, which is a French grape used in making muscatel wine. The early settlers called the sweet, musk-scented wild grapes they found here by the same name as the sweet grapes they had known in Europe, and that eventually became muscadine.

The scuppernong—the greenish or bronze variety of muscadine—was first called simply the big white grape. During the 17th and 18th centuries, cuttings of the mother vine were placed into production around Scuppernong, a small town in North Carolina. Specimans were transplanted or seeds or cuttings sown on neighboring farms and gardens, and with time, the scuppernong's reputation spread throughout the botanical world.

Through the years, these wonderful-tasting grapes have developed numerous nicknames, such as bullis, bullets, southern grapes, and swamp grapes. Though they still grow wild, most of today's muscadines and scuppernongs are grown in commercial vineyards. Harvest season is typically August through September. ■

WHEN HAS SHOPPING MEANT MORE?

by Ruth
Sullivan
Future Harvest—
Chesapeake
Alliance for
Sustainable
Agriculture

Small, family-run farms are a vital, functioning part of our landscape in the Chesapeake Bay region. As communities rapidly change, grow, and sprawl, however, we lose farms at an alarming rate. Cottage Farm Estates and Orchard View Acres, Wal-Marts, and Wawas are replacing farms, orchards, pastures, and woods. But farms don't have to slip into oblivion. They can remain vital, beautiful, and environmentally beneficial parts of our communities. We just have to take a few actions to support them.

The first way to support farms is to buy their products. Become a member of a Community Supported Agriculture farm. Shop at a local farmers market or farm stand. Ask for local, seasonal ingredients at your favorite restaurants. Demand local produce, meat, and eggs at your grocery stores. Buy directly from farmers. There are a surprising variety of products available directly from small farms in this region, including hot sauce, beef jerky, pastured poultry and beef, eggs, heirloom vegetables, farmstead cheese, medicinal herbs, cut flowers, soaps, native plants, Christmas trees, and wool. Your choices about the food you buy can have a big impact on the landscape around you.

The second way to keep small farms strong is to make sure there are voluntary farmland protection tools available for farmers. A combination of a strong customer base and financial incentives to keep the land from being developed can help ensure small farms stay part of your community. One tool, a conservation easement, helps farmers voluntarily protect their land from development. A conservation easement is a legal agreement: The landowner agrees to limit development of a property in perpetuity in exchange for cash or tax benefits. The landowner retains ownership of the property and can continue farming. As a result of the agreement, the landowner and the surrounding farms gain a confidence that comes from knowing at least one more farmer intends to stay in farming for the long haul. This certainty has important, far-reaching consequences in an area in which farms are being developed.

By supporting local, organic farms, consumers are supporting cleaner water, increased biodiversity, and the unique character of the place where they live. Organic agriculture is a management system that promotes biodiversity and uses natural cycles to their best advantage. Organic production aims to sustain the balance of natural systems and integrate the parts of the farming system into an ecological whole. Organic farmers rely both on healthy plants that are better able to resist disease and insect problems and on a diverse population of soil organisms, insects, and birds to keep pest problems in check.

I witness the benefits of diversity in my organic garden at home.

I count one of our biggest victories to have been over the tomato horn-worm. Tomato hornworms can do quite a bit of damage to tomato plants by shearing off the ends of branches and stripping the leaves off the stems, yet we never find one of these ugly creatures that isn't covered by white, oblong cocoons from a parasitic wasp. Emerging adult wasps derive nourishment from their caterpillar host and thereby weaken and eventually kill it. Wasps aren't the only natural predators we've attracted with our abstinence from pesticides, with our native flower and shrub plantings, with our cover crops, and with our composting: Bluebirds perch on cucumber trellises and eat from our insect smorgasbord. Organic farming creates a positive feedback loop; thanks to wasps and hungry birds, we didn't need to spray with pesticides. Thankfully, I know my husband and I won't be drinking these chemicals in our well water or finding them in the West River near our house.

In addition to their environmental advantages, small-scale, sustainably managed farms play a vital role in community landscapes, offering scenic beauty, rural character, and a sense of place. As landscapes become more generic with chain stores and cookie-cutter housing develop-ments, individual and community connections to a place become harder to develop and maintain. Strong, sustainably managed local farms, however, can help create an identity for a region. When we support local small farms, we become connected to the landscape that surrounds us: connected to the place our food comes from, to what our neighbors are doing, to the state of the land, and to the health of the water. Those connections are becoming harder and harder to find in our busy lives, yet we can renew them, with a bit of research, for the price of a bag of groceries. When was the last time shopping did that? ■

Resources for Living Local

Future Harvest–Chesapeake Alliance for Sustainable Agriculture (Future Harvest–CASA) is a nonprofit organization dedicated to supporting profitable and sustainable food and farming systems in the Chesapeake Bay region. Founded in 1998, the organization has a variety of resources available to help customers support local farms. Future Harvest–CASA's *Directory of Community Supported Agriculture in the Chesapeake Region* lists farms in Maryland, Virginia, and West Virginia that offer customers a variety of seasonal fruits, vegetables, herbs, and even eggs on a weekly basis. The organization's *Directory of Grass Farms in Maryland, Virginia and West Virginia* lists farms that sell pasture-raised and often organic beef, pork, poultry, and eggs to customers directly. Last, the new and compre-hensive *Landowner Survival Guide* discusses farmland protection strategies, lists publications, and identifies local organizations and agencies that can help.

SAVING SEEDS: THE GROWING THREAT TO OUR AGRICULTURAL BIODIVERSITY

To buy or not to buy organic? It's a question that can prompt the same anxiety-producing, am-I-dooming-the-planet panic as the cashier's inevitable "Paper or plastic?"

For many Americans, buying organic is a vote against big business and in favor of small farmers who tend the land the natural way—a referendum for a kinder, gentler world, in which ladybugs do the work of DDT and fields lie fallow instead of being zapped with petroleum-based fertilizers.

But the focus on organic versus conventional may have blinded us to a far more serious concern: a dangerous lack of genetic diversity among our nation's crops that threatens our abundant supply of fruits, vegetables, and grains. The past half century has brought about an unprecedented loss of agricultural biodiversity that has left us dangerously dependent on only a precious few seed types, experts say. "It's a very scary time we're going into," says New York University nutritionist Joan Gussow. "We're just on the edge of doing permanent, irreparable damage. And most people are totally unaware of the danger."

Loss of Biodiversity down on the Farm

Before the rise of corporate farming, small farmers typically used seed varieties they had developed over time—varieties ideally suited to the particular soil and climate of the area. For example, hundreds of different varieties of tomatoes or corn existed around the United States. Those unique varieties, called landraces, created a rich genetic diversity in agricultural plants that helped prevent widespread epidemics of plant diseases. Landraces also preserved an extraordinary variety of fruits and vegetables, many of them associated with specific regions or locations. "In some places, there might be a hundred varieties grown in a single region, each with its own special characteristics," says Michael Sligh, who directs research in sustainable agriculture at the Rural Advancement Foundation International. Thousands of landraces existed, from Harrison family beans and Ansault pears to Bonum apples and Jimmy Nardello's sweet Italian frying peppers.

The rise of modern agribusiness changed all that. Using advanced breeding techniques, researchers have created high-yielding hybrid seeds that were selected to ripen at the same time and store well over long periods—traits that make harvesting and delivery more efficient. (Unfortunately, as the tough, flavorless hothouse tomato testifies, taste and texture weren't necessarily high on the list of qualities.)

In the rush to plant these new and supposedly improved seeds, the landrace strains that had been passed down from generation to generation have been steadily abandoned. At the turn of the 20th century, 287 differ-

by Peter Jaret
Peter Jaret
Associates

ent varieties of carrots were being grown in the U.S.; today there are only 21. More than 300 varieties of sweet corn were being planted a hundred years ago; now there are 12. Peanuts? Incredibly, the 31 varieties once cultivated have shrunk to a mere 2.

It's the same for virtually every food crop in the United States. Hundreds of unique varieties once nurtured in farmers' fields have all but disappeared. Six thousand different kinds of apples were being grown on American farms in 1900; today 86 percent are gone. And an estimated 2,300 varieties of pears have vanished.

The consequences are far more serious than the loss of unique fruits, vegetables, and grains that few of us have ever seen or savored—from pink eggplants and white carrots to multicolored beets. Indeed, scientists are beginning to warn that the apparent abundance of produce we enjoy at the market is illusory—built on an increasingly small genetic base. That could be catastrophic if a plant disease suddenly spreads through these crops.

"Together landraces and wild relatives are the richest repositories of crop genetic diversity," say Jane Rissler and Margaret Mellon of the Union of Concerned Scientists. "They are the natural reservoir of the traits needed to maintain the vitality of modern crops. The genes for important traits like disease resistance are the natural capital on which both traditional crop breeders and genetic engineers depend." Yet today only two varieties of dry beans make up 60 percent of the nation's crop. Two kinds of peas account for 96 percent of the market. There may be dozens of different kinds of potato chips on store shelves, but only four varieties of potatoes make up the vast majority of the nation's crop. That makes them increasingly vulnerable to epidemics.

The hazards are just as serious in other parts of the world. In 1959 farmers in Sri Lanka grew 2,000 traditional rice varieties; today they grow just 5. In India 30,000 varieties of rice once grown have been replaced by 10 modern varieties that supply 75 percent of India's rice crop.

Fortunately, not all of the seeds that have been abandoned are lost. In the U.S. and other countries, many seeds are being saved in large, federally funded seed banks. So, when diseases begin to spread, plant breeders can turn to these living repositories to search for resistant varieties. But experts like Garrison Wilkes worry that many of the seeds that have been collected aren't being grown out often enough to ensure that they remain alive and viable.

And there are shocking gaps in the collection. A few years ago, Wilkes discovered that only two specimens of cranberries existed—one of the few fruits native to the U.S. "We could have been in real trouble if there'd been a problem," he says. "Right now, seed banks are an exit strategy for disaster, a life buoy. But if they aren't grown out, we could end up with a large collection of dead seeds. And once a seed dies, its genes become extinct."

Who Owns an Apple?

How have we come to such a pass? The rise of giant multinational agribusinesses is partly to blame. Local farmers were once the repositories of the world's agricultural biodiversity, gathering and exchanging seeds. But large companies have increasingly come to dominate. From 1984 to 1987 alone, almost one-quarter of the U.S. mail-order seed companies either went out of business or were taken over by other companies. By 1994 just 35 companies controlled more than half of the world's commercial seed market.

Over time, the huge multinational companies have gradually tightened their stranglehold not only on the market for seeds but also on the genetic information each seed contains. Incredibly, the United States has even given seed producers the right to patent their seeds—in effect, to own all rights to the genetic information the seeds contain. In 1992 one U.S. biotech company received a patent on all genetically engineered cotton varieties. In 1994 the same company was awarded a European patent on all genetically engineered soybeans.

These days it's not unusual for farmers who buy hybrid seeds to be required to sign agreements not to share the seeds, save them, or replant seeds from next season's crop.

The latest genetic techniques are even being used to engineer herbicide resistance into crops through the introduction of transgenes. At first glance, that seems to make sense; chemicals used for killing weeds won't affect cultivated plants. But instead of moving toward sustainable farming, the newly engineered seeds simply promote the continuing use of herbicides. Worse yet, the agreements that farmers must sign in order to plant these seeds may require them to use a particular herbicide.

The implications are deeply troubling. Farmers who were once the breeders and producers of their own seeds now must buy seeds from multinational companies that control not only the genetic information within the seed but in some cases also the farming methods that are used to grow them.

Worse still, experts worry that these newly engineered resistance genes, if they find their way into wild plants, could create superweeds that will be harder than ever to control. As the Union of Concerned Scientists warned in 1993: "Like the crops themselves that become weeds, these plants could require expensive control programs. In addition, the novel transgenes may affect wild ecosystems in ways that are difficult to evaluate."

The rise of immense multinational agribusinesses has also begun to destroy the economic basis of traditional farming, whereby local farmers were able to control the means of production. "In the name of profits, transnational business firms have rapidly gained commercial control over the earth's seeds and animal breeds," says Jeremy Rifkin, president of the Foundation for Economic Trends, "guaranteeing them a virtual monopoly over the world's food supply."

Bringing It Home

Against such sweeping forces, it's easy to think there's little we as consumers can do. The truth is, there's plenty. Consumers exert tremendous power simply by deciding what—and what not—to buy.

One way to ensure biodiversity is to plant a seed. In the past few years, amateur growers concerned about vanishing landraces have been collecting and exchanging so-called heirloom varieties, much as farmers a century ago did. Available through a half dozen seed exchanges around the country, heirloom seeds are now showing up on the shelves of many nurseries—including bicolored beets, Bonum apples, and Jimmy Nardello's sweet Italian frying peppers. By nurturing these and other long-abandoned varieties, gardeners are joining a grassroots effort to restore at least some of the extraordinary biodiversity that once existed in the fields of the U.S.

At the forefront of that effort are local farmers. Many of them have also begun to return to landraces. Check out a farmers market, and you're likely to find a growing variety of heirloom tomatoes, unusual varieties of pears, or exotic-looking beans. They may not be as perfectly round or packageable as hybrid varieties, but chances are they're much more flavorful.

Because local farmers are intimately tied to the community in which they work, they have a vested interest in the health of the environment. And because these are family farms, sometimes passed from generation to generation, local farmers are committed to keeping the soil fertile and the water plentiful. Small farmers typically have a closer relationship with the people who work for them. That, in turn, may make them more sensitive to the health threat posed by the use of chemical fertilizers and pesticides. While many of us worry about pesticides in the foods we eat, the people most at risk are farmworkers, who are continuously exposed to those chemicals. The U.S. Environmental Protection Agency estimates that nearly 4 million workers and their families are at risk because they handle pesticides. Exposure to these toxic chemicals results in more than 10,000 poisonings a year that require medical treatment.

Small farmers are also more likely to raise a variety of crops rather than single, vast monocultures, thereby creating built-in protection against pests and disease. Moreover, by supporting your local farmers, you'll be supporting the economic vitality of your own community. ▪

FOOD-MILES

Most of us are accustomed to walking into a Safeway, Kroger, or Giant Foods and expecting the same products no matter what the time of year. Grapes in the middle of winter, peppers in June, and bananas all the time. That wealth of food choices is made possible through a combination of things that allows farmers in regions thousands of miles away to view the Mid-Atlantic region as a prime customer base. The 3.5 million miles of interstate highways paid for and maintained by our tax dollars, a trucking industry with more than 1.7 million combination trucks on those roads, and the ultimate conclusion of a century-old trend of regional specialization in agriculture have led us to a supply of fruits and vegetables that travels more than the typical business executive. How else can we explain the shift from 19.5 percent of northeastern suppliers to the Jessup, Maryland, terminal market in 1980 to 8.3 percent in 1997?

The modern food system is now structured around long-distance supply chains that spread across the globe. Next time you're on the highway, keep an eye out for U.S. Foodservice trucks. U.S. Foodservice is the number one wholesale food service supplier in the United States, with $19 billion in sales, and is owned by Netherlands-based Ahold Inc. That's how your local restaurants, hotels, and hospitals receive most of their products. From fresh produce to poultry and from lumber to diapers, the North American trucking industry forms the backbone of the commonly lauded and critiqued modern food system. "If truckers stopped driving, then the whole U.S. would shut down in days, and you wouldn't be able to eat," said a truck driver at the Jessup terminal market. Indeed, people who transport our bread and butter have become so invisible to the American public that this entire sector of the food system escapes our attention.

It is that unseen by-product of our modern food system that demands more attention. Our collective addiction to nonregional foods has led to an increase in food-miles across the United States. A food-mile is the distance food travels from where it is grown or raised to where it is purchased by the consumer, and in studies conducted in Chicago, Boston, and Jessup, it has been documented that food-miles are steadily increasing. In analyzing U.S. Department of Agriculture data from the major terminal markets in those cities, a weighted average distance was created from arrival data for major fruit and vegetable crops. In Chicago the food-mile for the average pound of fresh produce increased 22 percent from 1981 to 1998; in Boston the food-mile increased from 2,002 miles in 1980 to 2,374 miles in 1995. Those figures are for raw fresh produce; other food products that are processed, packaged, or manufactured in some form would have substantially higher shipping distances.

In the Jessup analysis, it was clear that even if a crop were grown

Mid-Atlantic Farm Facts

Maryland ranks 16th in the U.S. in snap bean production, 14th in cucumbers and pickles, 10th in green peas, 13th in sweet corn, 13th in tomatoes, 13th in watermelons, and 18th in apples.

—MARYLAND
DEPARTMENT OF
AGRICULTURE

by Matthew Hora
Capital Area Food Bank

in the immediate region, it didn't necessarily translate into shorter shipping distances. This can be explained in part by the evolving structure of the farm and food industries, as some large, nationally based buyers and their distribution networks established contracts and favored grower-shippers across the U.S. From 1980 to 1997 the Northeast's share of apple distribution at the Jessup market plunged from 36.7 percent to 13.2 percent, potatoes dropped from 52.7 percent to 19.9 percent, and peaches declined from 52 percent to 7.9 percent. In each of those cases, a northeastern state lost a significant share of a traditional crop (New York apples, Maine potatoes, Pennsylvania peaches) to a western state.

A study by the Leopold Center for Sustainable Agriculture further documented the connections between those food-miles and the environmental effects of our modern food distribution system. In an analysis of carbon dioxide emissions in a local food system compared with the conventional system, it was found that the conventional system used 4 to 10 times more fuel than the Iowa-based regional and local systems. Considering that tractor trailers average 5.9 miles per gallon and that fuel usage for such vehicles increased from 6.7 billion gallons in 1965 to 20.2 billion gallons in 1997, the national trucking system is responsible for a significant amount of the massive national fossil fuel consumption and resulting carbon dioxide emissions that make the U.S. the world's largest emitter of greenhouse gases. With more than 485,000 truckloads of fresh produce leaving California annually, our dependence upon out-of-season fresh produce constitutes an especially significant sector of the trucking industry. This doesn't even address the added fuel costs of importing fresh produce from foreign countries through the use of jet planes or cargo ships to bring fresh produce into U.S. ports.

Once upon a time, products from another country or region were extravagant luxuries—like pineapples and spices in Colonial New England or even California tomatoes—when the first refrigerated railcars became operational in the early 1880s. Out of necessity, the food chain prior to World War I in the United States was still largely dependent on regional suppliers, which helped shape local foodways, or the cultural traditions based on acquiring, preparing, and consuming food. Buying locally was the only option for those who couldn't afford imported foods. With the development of high-speed, long-haul refrigerated trucks, the trend of regional specialization in agriculture steamrolled as the West Coast capitalized on its temperate climate irrigated by federally subsidized water projects; its huge expanses of flat, fertile fields; and a ready supply of cheap labor to become the world's leading producer of many fruits, nuts, and vegetables. That's one of the main reasons the Mid-Atlantic has become so reliant on nonregional sources for its foods. If something happened to disrupt that food distribution network, the agricultural infrastructure has become so specialized that the region would have to survive on eggs, broilers, seafood, field and sweet corn, soybeans, live-stock, and tobacco. While such a diet may sound repugnant to your ears, consider that the Mid-Atlantic region can and does grow a dazzling array of fresh produce, yet still we purchase Washington State apples in huge quantities, while the orchards of Pennsylvania and West Virginia decline and the food-miles that fuel our food system continue to grow every year. ■

Preserving the Harvest

The Heritage of Virginia Wine

by Jennifer McCloud
Chrysalis Vineyards
(see page 219)

Long before we started to write down what interests us and how we live our lives, saving the harvest by making wine was already an old and honored profession. The making and enjoying of wine has always been one of the more civilized human activities.

Those who settled in Virginia in the 1600s knew this when they asked their fellow colonists to plant grapevines. Thomas Jefferson knew this when he spent years experimenting with growing grapes for making wine.

What better way to save the fruit of the harvest? Transformed by the natural fermentation action of yeast, grape juice becomes wine. And when done just right, under the careful guidance of a skilled winemaker, a sublime beverage emerges that can live on for decades.

About the time that Jefferson was spending his last days at Monticello, not 65 miles away in Richmond, Dr. Daniel Norton, a hobby hybridist, was experimenting with American grape varieties in his backyard. When I daydream about these men who believed that America could produce great wines, I hope that Mr. Jefferson knew of Dr. Norton's pastime. For out of Norton's hobby came Norton's Virginia Seedling, an American grape variety. Later known simply as Norton, it was acclaimed "the best red wine of all nations" at the 1873 Vienna Universal Exhibition in Austria. That would have pleased Mr. Jefferson, I'm sure.

Virginia again is making wines worthy of world acclaim. Its climate is very much like some of the great wine-growing regions of Europe, and we're excited to participate in this renaissance of eastern American wine making that produces wines with elegance, balance, and style. We're making wines that reflect our *terroir,* as the French would say.

The Norton grape excites us too because it offers Virginia and other Mid-Atlantic farmers a profitable crop, capable of producing world-class wines. Norton is disease resistant, healthy, and hardy in our fields. And it's one we don't have to cajole to grow; it just *wants* to grow here. Norton is ours—the *real* American grape.

Mr. Jefferson, I think you would be proud. ■

Virginia Apples

Nothing is more distinctly American—or more telling of a region—than apples. As Michael Pollan describes in his book *The Botany of Desire,* apples are sweetness. They are both mutable and original. They are a model of nature's capacity for variety and diversity. And while they thrive throughout the world, apples, like people, reflect where they were born and raised.

Virginia is famous for its apples, a heritage that exemplifies the perfect blending of seed, soil, and climate. Many of the older varieties form a direct link to Virginia's history. And like the immigrants who planted them, apple seeds and scions—twigs that contain buds—brought over by early settlers were transformed by the soil, the climate, and natural selection to become something uniquely Virginian.

In the past, Virginians had access to an impressive variety of apples, and they matched their choice of apple to a particular use: they had their favorite sauce apples, eating apples, baking apples, drying apples, and cider apples. And they could choose from a wide range of apples available from early spring through late fall as well as ones that held up well in storage.

Because they take so long to bear fruit, orchards were usually the first thing settlers put into place on a farm—even before buildings were erected. According to Roger Yepsen in his wonderful little book *Apples,* "A family that wanted a tract of Virginia land was required to plant an orchard before claiming ownership."

In those seedling orchards, farmers would search for a tree that produced apples with desirable qualities, such as aroma, picking time, storability, resistance to disease, and superior flavor. In those days, the flavor of an apple was measured not so much in sweetness but in complexity and nuance—much like how we measure wine. Like people, apples grown from seed bear only some resemblance to their parents. Each apple tree grown from seed represents a distinct and unique variety. When a desirable tree was found, scions were cut from the tree and grafted onto other root stock. This is how all named varieties have been propagated. Every Golden Delicious apple in the world is a grafted clone of the one original Golden Delicious tree that began as a chance seedling on a West Virginia hillside.

Virginia's apple orchards were not an instant success. In the early 18th century, many of the grafted English varieties wilted from heat and humidity. But from the seedling orchards sprang new varieties that thrived in the summer heat, proving once again that apples are one of nature's more flexible gifts. By the middle of the century, European varieties were transformed into Virginia varieties, which ultimately dominated the nursery lists.

Since that time, growers have been learning how to use to their best advantage the mountainous terrain formed by the Blue Ridge and Appalachian ranges, where many of the region's best orchards are planted. Virginia's annual apple production ranges from 6 million to 10 million bushels, mainly in the Shenandoah Valley, the Piedmont, Roanoke, and the Southwest. The top variety is Red Delicious, but other varieties include Golden Delicious,

**Local Foods
Local Flavors**

Some of the apple varieties planted at Vintage Virginia Apples:

Albemarle Pippin
Arkansas Black
Arlet
Ashmead's Kernel
Black Twig
Bramley's Seedling
Calville Blanc d'Hiver
Carolina Red June
Chenango
  Strawberry
Court Pendu Plat
Cox's Orange Pippin
Crispin
Detroit Red
Dutchess of
  Oldenburg
Early Harvest
Esopus Spitzenburg
Golden Pearmain
Golden Russet
GoldRush
Grimes Golden
Haralson
Harrison
Hyslop Crab
Jonagold
King David
Lady Apple
Lodi

*(continued on
  next page)*

Maiden Blush
Margil
MonArk
Mother
Northern Spy
Pitmaston
   Pineapple
Pomme Gris
Pristine
Ralls
Razor Russett
Red Astrachan
Ribston Pippin
Rome Beauty
Roxbury Russett
Smokehouse
Spartan
Spigold
Summer Rambo
Turley Winesap
Virginia Beauty
Virginia Crab
Virginia Gold
Western Beauty
Wolf River
Yellow Bellflower
Yellow Transparent
York

*(For more
information
on Vintage
Virginia Apples,
see page 207.)*

Rome, Stayman, and York. A recent addition is Virginia's own Ginger Gold, which was discovered growing among the twisted uprooted trees in a Virginia orchard in the foothills of the Blue Ridge Mountains and which is a descendent of Golden Delicious and Albermarle Pippin apples.

While apples have learned to thrive in Virginia's humid climate, the conditions are ripe for disease, which is why many of Virginia's orchards are planted at elevations higher than 800 feet above sea level in the western part of the state. Still, Virginians say that even the apples grown in the eastern part of the state are of higher quality than anything found in the supermarket.

"I could put Virginia apples up for a blind taste test, and you could tell real quick which apple is from Virginia and which one isn't," says Nelson County orchardist Bill Flippin. Monticello, the home of Thomas Jefferson, prominently features a garden, orchards, and a vineyard. Jefferson's favorites were the Esopus Spitzenberg and the Newtown Pippin, says Peter Hatch, director of gardens and grounds at Monticello. Today the orchard has been restored to its 1812 original appearance.

Aside from disease, the modern practice of growing a dwindling handful of cloned varieties in vast orchards is believed to have rendered the apple less fit as a plant. That may explain why modern apples require more pesticides than almost any other food crop. According to Yepsen, "a supermarket apple is sprayed an average of 12 times on the tree; then it may be subjected to further treatment in storage; then it is likely to be embalmed under a protective layer of wax or shellac." Shipping is a huge part of the apple trade, and competition from China, Argentina, and New Zealand, which have flooded the American market with cheaply produced apples, is threatening Virginia's apple industry. With global trade making it easier and cheaper to ship apples across the world and into our supermarkets, it is more important than ever that Virginians, together with apple lovers throughout the Mid-Atlantic, support Virginia apple growers. ▪

THE NEXT STEP BEYOND ORGANIC

It was around a table at a meal—where everything that matters happens—that the topic was raised: organic food. We were a few friends and family members celebrating a birthday in a New Jersey restaurant when a discussion about organic food itself became the main course. Opinions were passed around like entrée samplings, and most of us dove in for a taste. Fueled by good food and great company, the discussion started playfully, turned animated, raised some ire, and eventually, some voices. Comments and concerns about the organic industry and its practices turned into questions about price and quality and whether organic fruits and vegetables really do taste better. As the conversation reached its pitch, a dinner guest who had not yet spoken broke through with a comment: "I don't buy organic only because it tastes better. I buy organic because it's better for the planet."

Yes. While organic farming has grown from a movement into an industry and more recently into a marketing strategy, its fundamental benefits have not changed. Organic farming works with natural processes to build healthy soils, conserve resources, and minimize waste and environmental damage. Pests are not viewed as problems but as indications of imbalance, and organic farmers respond with crop rotation and soil enrichment. When practiced as intended, organic farming is without question better for the earth, better for farms, and better for farmworkers.

So should we feel better about buying organic food—much of it shipped from thousands of miles away—simply because it's labeled organic?

No. As the great conservationist, farmer, essayist, and author Wendell Berry wrote, "Food is a cultural, not a technological, product." It is more than something we eat: it is a connection to our families, our regions, our culture, and our identities. Buying organic may be the point at which we start thinking about how our food is grown and raised, but it is by no means the last word. For that, we need to go beyond organic.

Among the farmers and others who embrace the philosophy—and not just the techniques—of organic, the word itself bears little resemblance to its original meaning. When, for example, organic farmers give in to pressures to get big, they lose their connection to the land they once worked. Skilled farmers have a kinesthetic relationship to the land; they know its characteristics, and they know how to respond to fluctuations.

When organic produce is shipped thousands of miles from its source, refrigeration and fuel consumption quickly outweigh whatever environmental benefits are gained by farming organically. Without the values that inspired organic agriculture for more than a hundred years, it becomes—like its conventional counterpart—a needy, resource-intensive, spiritless endeavor.

by Wendy Rickard
Eating Fresh Publications

Before organic went industrial, organic farming had been guided by experience, common sense, and respect for the land. Today the U.S. government has designed and approved a set of standards for organic — a useful step in a society that has become disconnected from the sources of its food and from the people who grow and raise it. Organic standards may help us know whether our foods are being genetically modified, irradiated, treated with pesticides, or injected with hormones, but that's not enough. They don't tell us who grew the food or how far it had to travel to get to our table. They don't tell us whether the farmworkers were treated fairly, whether the farmer was paid a fair price, or whether a small-scale local farm growing varieties of fruits and vegetables that are quickly disappearing went out of business because it couldn't compete.

When farming becomes standardized, industrialized, and reduced to a one-size-fits-all model, it becomes ineffective and unproductive in every respect, including economically. As organic farmer and author Michael Ableman says: "We quadrupled our acreage for a time and in the process discovered that while increasing acreage produces more food, it also produces more stress, higher management costs, lower quality, and less net income. My short-term desire to get bigger proved for me what has now been well documented: that small farms are 15 to 20 times more productive than their large-scale counterparts."

What is beyond organic is sustainability. A sustainable system embraces relationships, creates vibrant local economies, and works in harmony with the natural world. Like the fundamental nature of organic farming itself, a truly sustainable system succeeds because it recognizes that economic viability, environmental responsibility, and social justice are necessary in equal parts. When one or more are compromised for short-term profits, the system eventually breaks down.

In a sustainable agriculture system, farmers own the land they work and they work the land they own. Families know who grows their food, and the farmers know the families they feed. Most of what we eat is from our regions, and some of what we eat is shipped from great distances — instead of the other way around. Farmers are given a greater share of the food dollar, and they are recognized and rewarded for their expertise, hard work, and ability to grow and raise food that nourishes us.

Like organic farming, sustainable agriculture involves more than getting food on the table. It involves relationships that make life meaningful. It is the ultimate form of self-interest because when we take care of our farmers, their workers, our local businesses, and the environment, we *are* taking care of ourselves. What is beyond organic is the farm we can see and visit, taste and touch. It is as much a part of our lives as the meals we take with friends and family, the table where it all happens, and the food we eat. ■

FALL RECIPES

QUICK & BASIC RECIPES FOR FALL PRODUCE

Roasted Beets

Preheat oven to 375°F. Trim off the greens, leaving about an inch of stem attached. Wash the beets, wrap them in foil, and roast them until a sharp knife slides easily into the center. The time will vary according to the size of the beet. Medium to large beets will take from an hour to an hour and a half.

Cool, peel, slice, and dress with any of the following:

- Crumbled blue cheese, chopped toasted walnuts, olive oil, balsamic vinegar, sea salt, and pepper *or*
- Sliced onions, red wine vinegar, olive oil, dill, sea salt, and pepper *or*
- Chopped fresh rosemary, olive oil, white wine vinegar, sea salt, and pepper

Sautéed Beet Greens

Beet greens

Extra virgin olive oil

Sea salt

Freshly ground pepper

Garlic, chopped

Chopped fresh mint, basil, or dill (dried basil or dried dill is also fine)

Vinegar

1. Wash the greens in a bowl or sink full of water. Strip the leaves from the stem. Slice the stem into small pieces and tear the leaves into strips.

2. The amount of oil you use will be determined by the amount of beet greens you are cooking and the size of the pan you are cooking with. Heat enough olive oil to cover the bottom of the sauté pan you are using. You can add more oil later to season the greens. Once the oil is hot, add the stems and sauté for 3 to 4 minutes. Add the leaves and a small amount of water, sprinkle with salt and pepper, and sauté until tender. Add just a small amount of chopped garlic at the end of the cooking, and cook until it is soft but not brown.

3. Finish by stirring in the chopped fresh mint, basil, or dill; a splash of vinegar; more olive oil if you like; and salt and pepper.

COOKING FOR YOUR HEALTH AND WELL-BEING
Charlottesville, Virginia
Martha Hester Stafford
Chef/Owner

Swiss Chard Sautéed with Mushrooms & Onions

SERVES 2

1 tablespoon extra virgin olive oil

1 medium onion, sliced

8 ounces button mushrooms, sliced

Sea salt

2 bunches Swiss chard, washed, stemmed, and chopped; do not dry it

½ teaspoon dried rosemary

Dash of brown rice vinegar or rice wine vinegar

Freshly ground black pepper

1. Heat the oil in a 10- to 12-inch sauté pan. Add the onion and sauté on medium heat until translucent. Add mushrooms and sprinkle with salt. Continue to sauté until the mushrooms release their liquid, and then turn up the heat to cook away the liquid and brown the mushrooms.

2. Turn down the heat. Add the Swiss chard and rosemary. Cover and cook until the chard is barely tender, about 3 to 7 minutes. If the pan seems too dry, add a little water to it.

3. Remove lid, turn up the heat, and cook off any excess liquid. Finish the dish with a dash of vinegar, salt, and freshly ground pepper.

Roasted Carrots, Turnips & Parsnips

4 medium carrots, peeled and cut into 1-inch pieces

4 medium turnips, peeled and cut into 1-inch cubes

4 small parsnips, peeled and cut into 1-inch cubes

1 tablespoon minced fresh thyme or rosemary or 1 teaspoon dried

1 to 2 tablespoons extra virgin olive oil

Sea salt

Freshly ground pepper

Preheat oven to 350°F. Toss the vegetables, herbs, and olive oil together until the vegetables are well coated. Spread the vegetables on a sheet pan, and roast for 40 minutes or until they are golden brown and tender. Season with sea salt and pepper.

Quick
& Basic
Recipes
for Fall
Produce
(continued)

Easy Butternut Squash Soup

Original recipe by Katherine Alford

SERVES 8

1 tablespoon extra virgin olive oil

1 to 2 medium onions, diced

3 to 4 cloves of garlic, minced

2 to 3 teaspoons ground cumin

1 two-pound butternut squash, peeled and diced

3 to 4 cups water or stock

1 teaspoon salt

Freshly ground pepper

Chopped fresh parsley

1. Heat the oil in a pot large enough to hold all of the ingredients. Add the onions, and sauté over medium heat until they are translucent (it's fine if they brown a little). Add the garlic, and sauté it until it is soft but not brown.

2. Stir in the cumin, and cook for 2 or 3 minutes. Add the squash, and stir to coat each piece with the onion-garlic-cumin mixture.

3. Pour in the water or stock, making sure there is enough to cover the squash. Bring the mixture to a boil, turn down the heat, and let it simmer for 30 to 40 minutes or until the squash is very soft.

4. Cool the mixture slightly and puree using a blender or a food processor. Thin the soup, if desired, with more water or stock.

5. Add salt and pepper. Taste to be sure it is seasoned correctly, and serve with chopped parsley.

Note: For a sweeter soup, add orange juice or apple cider.

**COOKING FOR
YOUR HEALTH
AND WELL-BEING**
Charlottesville, Virginia
Martha Hester Stafford
Chef/Owner

SWEET POTATO FLAN

SERVES 12

1½ cups white sugar

6 tablespoons water

1 quart cream

7 whole eggs

3 egg yolks

1 cup dark brown sugar

1 teaspoon cinnamon

¼ cup Gosling's Black Seal rum (or another dark, spicy rum)

1 cup peeled, boiled, and mashed sweet potato

1. To prepare cups, place white sugar and water in a very clean, heavy-bottomed saucepan. Cook over medium-high heat until the sugar begins to brown. Watch constantly, but do not stir. Remove from heat and divide among 12 oven-safe glass custard cups. Be very careful! Caramel is over 300°F and can cause severe burns if it splashes onto the skin. Set aside and let cool.

2. Preheat oven to 275°F.

3. In a large mixing bowl, lightly whisk together cream, whole eggs, egg yolks, brown sugar, cinnamon, rum, and mashed sweet potato. Press mixture through a sieve.

4. Equally divide the flan mix among the prepared custard cups. Place the custard cups in a large roasting pan. Fill the pan with hot water until it reaches the middle of the cups.

5. Bake for 1½ to 2 hours until the middle of each custard is just set. They will firm up as they cool. Remove from water bath, and chill until completely set. To serve, run a knife around the inside edge of each flan. Invert onto a dessert plate, and shake gently until flan releases from cup. Serve immediately.

Chef's recommendation: A rich and racy Riesling, such as SGN Rangen de Thann Clos St. Théobald Domaine Schoffit

I learned how to make the perfect flan from Marcello Vásquez, an Argentine chef I worked with in Charleston, South Carolina. Here I've added my own southern twist with sweet potatoes, spice, and dark rum. Use free-range, organic chicken eggs that are no more than 3 days old. We have a great supplier in Springfield Farms, owned by David and Lily Smith.

—CHEF CINDY WOLF

CHEF CINDY WOLF
CHARLESTON

CHARLESTON
Baltimore
Cindy Wolf
Chef/Owner

CEDAR PLANK BLUEFISH
with an Orange-Rosemary Glaze & Sautéed Spinach and Shiitakes

SERVES 4

1/4 cup honey

1/4 cup bitter orange marmalade

1 1/2 teaspoons chopped rosemary

4 eight-ounce bluefish fillets

1 1/2 pounds spinach, trimmed and washed

2 cloves garlic, minced

2 tablespoons butter

1 cup julienned shiitakes

Salt and pepper to taste

1 pomegranate, seeds carefully removed and saved for garnish

Parsnip Chips (see sidebar)

1. Wash cedar oven planks* with soapy water, dry, and rub with salad oil.

2. Preheat oven to 350°F. Heat planks for 15 minutes.

3. For the glaze, mix together honey, marmalade, and rosemary. Place bluefish fillets on the planks, skin side down, and brush with the glaze. Bake in oven until done, about 20 minutes.

4. If spinach leaves are large, blanch briefly in boiling water. Remove to ice-water bath to stop cooking. Drain well.

5. Sauté garlic in butter until soft. Add shiitakes, and sauté until soft. Add blanched spinach, and stir to heat through. Season with salt and pepper.

6. Place baked bluefish on spinach; garnish with the pomegranate seeds and Parsnip Chips.

* *Note:* You may also use cedar grilling planks, which are thinner and do not need preheating. Oil the top of each plank with olive oil. Place prepared planks on cookie sheet before putting into oven.

Chef's recommendation: A medium-bodied, aromatic red wine, such as Witness Tree Pinot Noir

BISTRO ST. MICHAELS
St. Michaels, Maryland
David Stein
Chef/Owner

PEANUT-CRUSTED TILAPIA

SERVES 4

2 eggs, blended

1 cup milk

1 small onion, chopped and pulverized to juice in a blender

1 cup matzo meal

1 cup crushed peanuts (use mortar and pestle, and crush to small pieces, not to a paste)

¼ pound rice flour (rice flour has no gluten and gets very crispy when fried)

8 tilapia fillets

Vegetable oil for frying

Salt and freshly ground pepper to taste

Salad greens

Sweet Chili Vinaigrette (see sidebar)

1. Blend together the eggs, milk, and onion juice. Chill the mixture.

2. Mix together the matzo meal and peanuts to form the breading mixture.

3. At this point, you are ready to bread the fillets, but you can change the recipe to add any combination of flavor you wish. *For Thai:* Blend in unsweetened coconut milk and curry, and add finely sliced scallion to the breading mixture. *For Chinese:* Replace the milk with soy sauce, dry sherry, and sesame oil. *For Southern:* Add hot pepper sauce to the liquid mixture, and use equal parts of matzo meal and fine cornmeal. As you can see, the recipe can go anywhere you wish to go. So have fun and enjoy.

To assemble:

4. Set out 3 plates: one with rice flour, one with flavored egg batter, and one with flavored breading mix. Dredge tilapia in the rice flour, and coat evenly. Move the fish to the egg, and then to the breading. Keep breaded fish cold and uncovered until ready to prepare.

5. Heat a cast-iron skillet over medium heat. Coat with vegetable oil. Fry the fish until light brown. If not cooked through, finish in a hot oven. Season with salt and pepper. I like to serve this over salad greens tossed with Sweet Chili Vinaigrette.

Chef's recommendation: A crisp, fresh and fruity Chardonnay, such as Cape Indaba

Sweet Chili Vinaigrette

½ cup sweet chili sauce (Mae Ploy brand is available at most Asian markets)

¼ cup rice wine vinegar

½ teaspoon soy sauce

¼ teaspoon toasted sesame oil

Blend together.

NATIONAL PRESS CLUB
Washington
Jim Swenson
Executive Chef

RED & YELLOW TOMATO SALAD
with Lentils & Warm Goat Cheese

SERVES 8

¼ cup each of finely diced celery, carrot, onion, and leek

6 tablespoons extra virgin olive oil, divided use

1½ cups red lentils, checked carefully for small stones and rinsed

1½ cups small, dark-green lentils, checked carefully for small stones and rinsed

2 cloves garlic, chopped, divided use

4 tablespoons red wine vinegar

Salt and freshly ground pepper, to taste

2 ripe red tomatoes

2 ripe yellow tomatoes

4 tablespoons balsamic vinegar, divided use

2 tablespoons basil, cut into thin ribbons (chiffonade)

Grilled Red Onion Slices (see sidebar on next page)

8 ounces goat cheese

½ cup finely chopped walnuts

15 large basil leaves

2 cloves garlic

1 cup mayonnaise

1. Prepare a brunoise by slowly sautéing the diced celery, carrot, onion, and leek in 2 tablespoons of the olive oil until soft.

2. Place 1 quart of water and the red lentils together in a saucepan. Bring to a boil over medium-high heat. Remove from heat, cover, and let sit until lentils are cooked through, about 10 to 12 minutes. Drain and reserve. Bring another quart of water to a boil in a saucepan, and add the green lentils. Cook for 10 minutes or until cooked through but not mushy or crunchy. Drain and combine with the red lentils. Add half of the chopped garlic, the brunoise, 2 tablespoons of the olive oil, the red wine vinegar, and salt and pepper to taste. Reserve.

KINKEAD'S
Washington
Bob Kinkead
Chef/Owner

3. Core and thinly slice the tomatoes. Add 2 tablespoons of the balsamic vinegar, the remaining 2 tablespoons of olive oil, the remaining half of the chopped garlic, and the basil chiffonade. Marinate for at least 20 minutes. Add salt and pepper and if too tart, a pinch of sugar.

4. Toss the Grilled Red Onion Slices in the remaining 2 tablespoons of balsamic vinegar.

5. Preheat oven to 400°F.

6. Slice the goat cheese into 8 equal rounds, and coat with the chopped walnuts. Warm the goat cheese in the oven for 5 minutes.

7. Puree the basil leaves and garlic cloves. Stir into the mayonnaise.

8. To serve, divide the lentil salad mixture among 8 chilled plates. Spread lentils over each plate and then top with 6 tomato slices that are layered—first red, then yellow—in an overlapping circle around the edge of the plate. Fill the center of the plate with the grilled marinated onions, and top with the warm goat cheese. Drizzle basil mayonnaise over all, and garnish each plate with a fresh basil sprig.

Grilled Red Onion Slices

2 red onions, sliced in ¼-inch slices

Olive oil

Brush onion slices with olive oil. Cook over hot coals until limp and lightly charred, about 3 to 4 minutes. Turn and cook until done.

**Local Foods
Local Flavors**

*Nestled in the foothills of the Blue Ridge Mountains, **Rucker Farm Tack House Kitchen and Creamery** is a boutique creamery located in Flint Hill, Virginia. With only 30 goats—all permitted to range free—Rucker Farm uses only morning milk to create dairy products of a rare, poetic purity. Believing that good goat cheese is defined by its lingering scent and aftertaste, the farm produces Tome de Chèvre Rappahannock, which is best in late summer and into the fall, and Jordan River Chèvre, named for the Jordan River, which runs along the edge of Rucker Farm.*

SPINACH WITH RAISINS, PINE NUTS, & APPLES

SERVES 4 AS A SIDE DISH

3 tablespoons olive oil

3 tablespoons finely chopped shallots

¼ cup raisins

¼ cup peeled, cored, diced Granny Smith apples (cut into ¼-inch cubes)

¼ cup pine nuts

12 ounces washed, stemmed spinach, dried in a salad spinner

Kosher salt to taste

1. Set large sauté pan on high heat. When hot, add olive oil and shallots. Sauté until shallots soften.

2. Add raisins, apples, and pine nuts. Sauté until raisins plump.

3. Add spinach and salt. Cook until spinach is wilted but not soggy.

Chef's recommendation: Les Terrasses, Alvaro Palacios, or other traditional red wine from Priorat

JALEO
Washington
José Ramón Andrés
Executive Chef/Partner

I-CAN'T-BELIEVE-IT'S-NOT-CRAB CRAB CAKES

SERVES 4

2 cups coarsely grated zucchini

Salt

1 cup soft bread crumbs

1 egg, beaten

1½ teaspoons Old Bay seasoning

1 teaspoon Dijon mustard

1 tablespoon mayonnaise

Juice of ½ lemon

¼ cup chopped parsley

Vegetable oil, for frying

Tartar sauce

Lemon wedges

1. Place the grated zucchini in a colander; sprinkle lightly with salt. Let zucchini sit for about 30 minutes in the colander, allowing excess moisture to drain. Squeeze to remove additional liquid. (Zucchini should be fairly dry.)

2. Place the zucchini and bread crumbs in a large bowl, and mix together well.

3. Place the egg, Old Bay seasoning, Dijon mustard, mayonnaise, lemon juice, and parsley in a small bowl. Mix well.

4. Pour the egg mixture into the zucchini–breadcrumb mixture, and mix gently and thoroughly. Form into 8 patties the size of crab cakes. Heat a small amount of oil in a sauté pan, and cook patties on both sides, browning well. If you like, serve with tartar sauce (I jazz mine up with some chopped capers and fresh basil) and lemon wedges. A platter of vine-ripened tomatoes and sweet corn on the cob as accompaniments are my favorites.

Chef's recommendation: A semisweet white wine, such as Peter Lehmann Sémillon

Zucchini is one of those vegetables that just will not stop growing in my little garden plot at the end of the summer. Every year, I find myself trying out as many versions of zucchini-something as possible. This is one of my favorite recipes. Besides using up those extra zucchini, it's a creative solution if you're trying to cut back a tad on crab consumption to give the crab population a chance to replenish—a delicious win-win for everyone.

—CHEF JOHN SHIELDS

GERTRUDE'S

GERTRUDE'S
Baltimore
John Shields
Chef/Owner

Editor's note:
Caul is the fatty membrane that surrounds the intestines of an animal—usually pigs or sheep. After it softens through soaking, caul fat is spread out into a thin, translucent, netlike sheet that is wrapped around meat in need of basting. It melts away during cooking or baking. Caul fat can be ordered from your local butcher. It should be used right away or frozen for later use.

PORCHETTA DI POLLO AVVOLTA NELLA PANCETTA CON CAVOLI

(CHICKEN BREAST STUFFED WITH PANCETTA HAM & SERVED WITH SAUTÉED CABBAGE)

SERVES 8

4 whole, boned breasts of chicken, same size, skin on

6 tablespoons olive oil, divided use

2 tablespoons chopped fresh rosemary

2 tablespoons chopped fresh sage

2 tablespoons chopped fresh thyme

2 tablespoons finely crumbled dried bay leaves

Salt and freshly ground pepper to taste

8 thin slices pancetta

1/4 pound caul fat, rinsed and soaked in warm water until soft (see sidebar)

3 rosemary stalks, each with a garlic clove skewered on the end

1 cup dry white wine

Sautéed Cabbage (see sidebar on next page)

1. Cut chicken breasts down the center to divide into 2 lobes. Lay chicken, skin side up, in a single layer in a large glass pan. Sprinkle with 3 tablespoons of the olive oil and 1 tablespoon each of the rosemary, sage, thyme, and bay leaves. Marinate the chicken in the refrigerator for 6 hours.

2. When ready to cook, sprinkle the skinless side of the chicken pieces with salt and pepper and the remaining 1 tablespoon each of rosemary, sage, thyme, and bay leaves. Place one lobe of each chicken breast on top of the matching lobe, skin side out. Drape 2 pieces of pancetta on each stack, and then wrap the entire bundle with a piece of caul fat, securing the ends together with a small metal lacing pin.

3. Preheat oven to 375°F.

4. Heat the remaining 3 tablespoons of olive oil in a large sauté pan. Sauté the chicken bundles, along with the rosemary-and-garlic stalk, carefully turning the chicken once so that each bundle is golden on both sides. Place the chicken bundles on a rack in a roasting pan, and pour the

GALILEO
Washington
Roberto Donna
Chef/Owner

juices from the sauté pan into the roaster. Roast until the chicken is cooked through, about 30 minutes depending on the size of the breasts. Remove roaster from the oven, remove rack and chicken from pan, and set aside. Place pan on burner over medium heat. Add white wine and stir to loosen the brown bits on the bottom. Transfer this pan juice to a saucepan, reduce by half, and keep warm.

5. Slice each chicken bundle in half widthwise. Place a few teaspoons of the reserved pan juice on top of each bundle and serve with Sautéed Cabbage on the side.

Chef's recommendation: Dolcetto, Prunotto, or some other lively, fruity Piedmontese red wine

**Local Foods
Local Flavors**

EcoFriendly Foods — Under the tutelage of Joel Salatin of Polyface Inc., Beverley and Janelle Eggleston of Emerald Family Farms learned early on how to go beyond organic when it comes to raising beef, pork, chicken, rabbit, and squab. In addition to refraining from the use of hormones, steroids, and antibiotics, the Egglestons have stayed true to their belief that small farms produce better-quality farm products. So when demand for high-quality meat products began to rise, rather than getting bigger, the Egglestons pooled the resources of small family growers like themselves and Polyface farm. In 1999, they launched EcoFriendly Foods as a distribution system to help minimize the cost of distribution and maximize the amount farmers can keep. In 2002, EcoFriendly Foods began renovations on a building in Moneta, Virginia, outside Roanoke. Today the federally inspected processing facility not only enables EcoFriendly Foods to centralize processing, packaging, and distribution systems to the benefit of all of the farmers in its network, but with the addition of a commercial kitchen, the organization is developing a line of value-added products, such as vacuum-packed dry-aged and smoked meats and a complementary line of sauces, marinades, and stocks.

Sautéed Cabbage

1 head cabbage

6 ounces coarsely diced pancetta

1 cup olive oil

Wash the cabbage and slice it into thin strips. Blanch in boiling water for 3 minutes. Drain and immerse immediately in an ice-water bath to stop cooking. Set aside to drain.

Sauté the pancetta in the olive oil over medium heat. When crispy, drain all but 3 tablespoons of the oil. Add the cabbage, and cook for 5 more minutes.

BUTTERNUT SQUASH SOUP
with Cabbage & Surry Sausage

SERVES 6

6 tablespoons grapeseed oil, divided use

1 yellow onion, peeled and sliced

2 medium butternut squashes, peeled and diced

1 cup amaretto liqueur

2 cups rich vegetable or chicken stock

2 cups heavy cream

1 sachet of 1 cinnamon stick, 8 whole cloves, and 8 black peppercorns tied in cheesecloth

Salt and freshly ground pepper to taste

2 cups green cabbage, sliced

½ cup Surry sausage or other fresh, mild sausage, casing removed and coarsely chopped

¼ cup chives, minced, for garnish

1. In a large saucepan or casserole, heat 5 tablespoons of the grapeseed oil to medium temperature. Add onion and butternut squash, and sauté for 5 minutes. Add amaretto, stock, cream, spice sachet, and salt and pepper. Cook soup over low heat until squash is tender, approximately 30 minutes.

2. Meanwhile, in a small casserole, sauté cabbage and sausage in the remaining tablespoon of the grapeseed oil until sausage is rendered and cabbage is cooked through.

3. Cool the soup slightly and puree in a blender or food processor. Pass soup through a fine-mesh strainer. Keep warm.

4. Heat 6 large soup dishes. Ladle soup into each dish, place cabbage and sausage in center, and sprinkle with chives. Serve immediately.

Chef's recommendation: Chardonnay Clos Pegase or other full-bodied Chardonnay with great balance

Equinox

EQUINOX
Washington
Todd Gray
Chef/Owner

PEAR & GORGONZOLA DOLCE TART

SERVES 4

1 cup heavy cream

1 egg yolk

1 egg

6 ounces Gorgonzola cheese, diced

Salt and freshly ground pepper

2 ripe Seckel pears or small, ripe Bartlett pears

1 nine-inch pie shell, baked

4 tablespoons apricot jelly

Cayenne pepper or dried chipotle chili, ground to powder

Spinach Salad (see sidebar)

1. Preheat oven to 350°F.

2. Mix cream, egg yolk, and egg. Beat until combined, and add Gorgonzola. Season with salt and pepper.

3. Peel, halve, and core pears; slice thinly. Pour Gorgonzola mixture into pie shell. Top with fanned-out pears.

4. Bake on lower rack of oven until set and lightly browned—about 35 minutes—turning pan around if necessary. Let custard cool slightly.

5. In a small saucepan, heat apricot jelly until liquefied. Strain and mix with cayenne or chipotle powder to taste. Spread over the tart.

6. Serve warm with Spinach Salad.

Chef's recommendation: Louis Latour Aloxe-Corton or another big, complex Pinot Noir from Côte de Nuits, Oregon, or New Zealand

Spinach Salad

6 cups young, tender spinach

1/2 recipe Walnut Vinaigrette (see page 33)

1/4 cup unsweetened, dried cranberries

1/4 cup toasted walnuts, seasoned to taste with cayenne pepper and salt

1 1/2 ounces enoki mushrooms

Micro or baby greens

Toss spinach with enough vinaigrette to lightly coat leaves—about 3 to 4 tablespoons. Garnish with cranberries, walnuts, mushrooms, and micro greens.

BICYCLE
Baltimore
Barry Rumsey
Chef/Owner

**Warm Bacon &
Yam Vinaigrette**

*4 strips applewood-
smoked bacon*

*1 medium orange
yam, finely diced*

Salt and pepper

*¹/₂ cup clear
chicken stock*

*4 tablespoons
sherry vinegar*

*Render the bacon
in a pan until
fully crisp. Remove
bacon and drain on
paper towels. Add
the yam dice to
the bacon fat in
the pan, coating
thoroughly, and
sauté over medium
heat, stirring once
or twice until dice
are just tender
crisp. Season with
salt and pepper to
taste; add the
chicken stock.*

*Cover the pan and
cook quickly until
the bacon fat
reemerges.*

*Add the vinegar.
Stir gently. Cover
and keep warm.*

TABARD INN
Washington
David Craig
Former Executive Chef

SEARED CHESAPEAKE ROCKFISH

with Black-Eyed Peas, White Sweet Potatoes, Curly Kale & Warm Bacon & Yam Vinaigrette

SERVES 4

1 small onion, finely diced

2 cloves garlic, finely sliced

¹/₄ pound (1 stick) unsalted butter

2 cups white sweet potatoes, diced to equal the size of the peas

2 cups fresh black-eyed peas

Kosher salt and freshly ground white pepper to taste

1 to 1¹/₂ cups clear chicken stock

Canola oil

4 six-ounce rockfish fillets, skin evenly scored

1¹/₂ cups firmly packed, small julienne of curly kale, blanched and shocked

1. Prepare the Warm Bacon & Yam Vinaigrette (see sidebar).

2. Sauté the onion and garlic in the butter until translucent. Add the white sweet potatoes, increase the heat, toss thoroughly, and sauté quickly. Add the peas, season with salt and pepper to taste, and add enough stock to cover. Cover pan with a lid and cook quickly until potatoes and peas are just tender. Remove from heat and keep warm.

3. Preheat oven to 425°F.

4. Pour canola oil, ¹/₈ inch deep, into a hot, heavy-bottomed, ovenproof skillet large enough to hold the fillets without crowding. Heat oil until hazy. Season both sides of the fish liberally with salt and pepper. Skin side down, quickly sear the fish in the oil until crisp and golden; turn and sear the other side.

5. Place the pan in the oven and roast the fish until no longer translucent.

6. To serve, spoon the vinaigrette evenly over 4 warmed dinner plates, reserving a little for dressing the fish. Fold the kale through the still-warm white-sweet-potato-and-black-eyed-pea ragout. Divide the mixture evenly into 4 portions, mound in the center of each plate, top with a fillet, and dress with a little of the remaining vinaigrette.

SMOKED CORN CHOWDER
with Crabmeat Garnish

SERVES 6

6 to 7 ounces hickory chips

1 pound fresh corn kernels

6 tablespoons olive oil

1 medium yellow onion, chopped

1 medium carrot, chopped

2 celery stalks, chopped

1 quart chicken stock

1 bunch fresh thyme, leaves stripped from stalks

1 quart heavy cream

Salt and pepper to taste

Crabmeat for garnish

1. Place hickory chips in a bowl, cover with water, and soak for 30 minutes.

2. In the meantime, set and light a charcoal grill using natural wood charcoal. Place the soaked hickory chips on the hot coals, and burn until they become charcoallike. Suffocate the flame, and place the corn kernels in a perforated pan over the smoking chips. (You can use a disposable aluminum baking pan by punching holes through the bottom with a skewer.) Place lid on the grill, and smoke the corn until the hickory chips burn out.

3. In a saucepan, heat olive oil just until smoking. Add onion, carrot, and celery, lightly sautéing until tender. Add the smoked corn. Stir for a minute, and add the chicken stock. Bring to a light boil, and add thyme leaves. Reduce the chicken stock by half, and then add the heavy cream. Bring to a light boil again.

4. Allow mixture to cool slightly. Using a blender or hand mixer, blend mixture until smooth; press through a fine strainer.

5. Slowly cook soup to creamy consistency. Add salt and pepper to taste. Garnish with fresh crabmeat.

Chef's recommendation: Rapidan River Semi-Dry Riesling (Virginia) or a fruity, semidry, well-balanced Riesling

BOAR'S HEAD INN
Charlottesville, Virginia
Alex Montiel
Executive Chef

SMOKED BLUEFISH SALAD

SERVES 4

For the mousseline sauce:

1 egg yolk

1 tablespoon Dijon mustard

2 lemons, divided use

1 cup canola or vegetable oil

1 cup whipped cream

Salt to taste

For the salad:

4 cups water

$^1/_2$ cup julienne celery

$^1/_2$ cup julienne celery root

$1^1/_2$ cups smoked bluefish or rainbow trout, boned and shredded with
a fork into small chunks

1 cup julienne Granny Smith apples (use peeled apple from coulis recipe)

1 tablespoon chopped chives

3 tablespoons diced tomatoes

Granny Smith Apple Coulis (see next page)

1. Create a mousseline by whisking together egg yolk, mustard, and the
   juice of one lemon. Slowly add oil, and whisk until mixture is the consistency of mayonnaise. Fold in whipped cream. Season with salt.
   (Use leftover mousseline in other dishes in place of mayonnaise.)

2. Bring the water to a boil. Blanch the celery for 20 seconds, immediately
   place in an ice bath, and set aside for a few moments. In the same pot of
   boiling water, blanch the celery root for 1 minute, and place in the ice
   bath with the celery. Drain both and set aside.

3. Combine celery, celery root, bluefish, apples, chives, tomatoes, 2 tablespoons of the mousseline, and juice of 1 lemon in a large bowl. Mix
   carefully until well coated. Add salt to taste.

*Chef's recommendation: A dry, medium-bodied white wine, such as Barboursville
Pinot Grigio*

ACACIA
Richmond, Virginia
Dale Reitzer
Executive Chef

Granny Smith Apple Coulis

$\frac{1}{2}$ cup sugar

$\frac{1}{4}$ cup water

$1\frac{1}{2}$ Granny Smith apples, divided use

$4\frac{1}{2}$ teaspoons lemon juice plus extra to brush on peeled apple

6 tablespoons very cold water

1 teaspoon salt

Make a simple syrup by combining sugar and water in a small saucepan over high heat. Stir constantly until mixture comes to a boil. Remove from heat and let cool. Peel 1 apple — saving peels — and brush lightly with lemon juice to prevent browning. Set peeled apple aside to use in salad. Cut the half apple into slices. Put apple peels and slices in the freezer for 15 minutes. Combine lemon juice, semifrozen apple slices and peels, 6 tablespoons of the simple syrup, and cold water in blender. Puree on high speed until apple and peel liquefy, adding more water if needed to help blend. Season with salt, and strain through a mesh strainer.

**Local Foods
Local Flavors**

Vintage Virginia Apples — *In a hillside orchard located only a few miles from Monticello, Charlotte Shelton and her family founded Vintage Virginia Apples for the purpose of bringing back the regional varieties prized by earlier generations of Virginians. With the help of regional heirloom apple experts, Shelton chooses uncommon varieties of apples that can thrive at her Albemarle County site. Her farm, Rural Ridge Orchard, now features about 200 varieties of apples — including several that were favored by Thomas Jefferson. Vintage Virginia Apples offers flavorful alternatives to the half dozen apple varieties currently available in grocery stores. Vintage Virginia Apples also holds workshops on growing and using different types of apples and has started a nursery of trees for those interested in attempting to grow their own favorites. A number of heirloom peach and plum varieties are also cultivated.*

Thyme Cream

½ cup cream

1 bunch thyme

Place cream in a small saucepan. Add thyme, and reduce by ⅓. Strain and keep warm until ready to serve.

BUTTERNUT SQUASH SOUP

SERVES 6

3 pounds butternut squash
   (about 2 medium or 3 small)

Olive oil

6 slices bacon, cut into ½-inch pieces

2 Granny Smith apples, divided use

1 onion, chopped

2 tablespoons white wine vinegar

1 cup apple juice plus some additional

6 cups chicken stock

2½ three-inch cinnamon sticks

1 cup heavy cream

1 ounce thyme leaves

Salt and freshly ground
   white pepper to taste

Thyme Cream (see sidebar)

Croutons for garnish

Chopped parsley for garnish

1. Preheat oven to 350°F.

2. Cut butternut squashes in half lengthwise, and brush the cut surfaces lightly with olive oil. Place, cut side down, on a baking sheet, and roast in oven until completely soft—about 45 minutes. Let cool, and peel off skin. Using a fork or the back of a large spoon, mash flesh to make pulp.

3. In a heavy-bottomed soup pot, sauté bacon over medium heat until crisp. Remove half the bacon and set aside to drain on paper towels. Core and chop one apple. Add chopped apple and onion to soup pot, and sauté until onion is translucent. Add vinegar and the cup of apple juice. Raise heat, bring to a boil, and reduce by half.

4. Add squash pulp, chicken stock, and cinnamon sticks. Simmer until cinnamon sticks expand and begin to unfurl, about 20 minutes.

5. Strain pulp from stock. Remove cinnamon sticks and discard. Puree pulp in a blender.

6. Combine pureed pulp and stock mixture. Add cream and thyme. Steep over low heat for 30 minutes.

7. Strain through a fine-mesh sieve. Adjust thickness with additional apple juice. Season with salt and white pepper.

8. Core and dice the remaining apple. Serve soup in warmed bowls. Top with Thyme Cream, diced apple, remaining bacon, croutons, and parsley.

Chef's recommendation: Duckhorn sauvignon blanc or another full-bodied, dry white wine

208 TALBOT
St. Michaels, Maryland
Paul Milne
Chef/Owner

MELROSE CRAB CAKES
& Rémoulade Sauce

SERVES 6

2 pounds premium jumbo lump crabmeat

4½ teaspoons Dijon mustard

2 whole eggs

3 tablespoons finely chopped parsley

2 drops pepper sauce such as Chile Man Louisiana Lightnin' (see page 55)

⅔ teaspoon Worcestershire sauce

Salt and freshly ground pepper to taste

½ cup fresh white-bread crumbs

2 teaspoons clarified, unsalted butter

1 cup fresh watercress, longer stems removed

3 zucchini, sliced lengthwise, brushed with oil, seasoned with salt and pepper, and grilled

4 tomatoes, cut in half, brushed with oil, seasoned with salt and pepper, and grilled

Rémoulade Sauce (see sidebar)

1. Preheat oven to 400°F.

2. Pick through crab carefully to remove small pieces of shell. Be careful not to break apart lumps.

3. Mix mustard, eggs, parsley, pepper sauce, Worcestershire, salt, and pepper in a bowl. Add crabmeat and toss gently. Fold in bread crumbs gently to barely hold mix together. Form into 12 three-ounce patties.

4. Heat butter in a skillet. Add crab cakes, and brown on both sides. Place in oven for 8 to 9 minutes to heat through.

5. For each serving, place 2 crab cakes on a bed of fresh watercress with grilled zucchini and grilled tomatoes on the side. Top crab cakes with Rémoulade Sauce.

Chef's recommendation: Fisher Coach Insignia Chardonnay or a well-rounded oak-aged Chardonnay

Rémoulade Sauce

1 cup mayonnaise

2 anchovies, drained and finely chopped

1 tablespoon finely chopped fresh parsley

1½ teaspoons finely chopped cornichons

½ teaspoon finely chopped capers

1 tablespoon fresh lemon juice

1 drop pepper sauce

1 small clove garlic, finely chopped

¼ teaspoon Worcestershire sauce

Salt and freshly ground pepper to taste

Combine all ingredients and mix well.

MELROSE
Park Hyatt Washington
Washington
Brian McBride
Executive Chef

Fried Pot Crusts

3 cups steamed rice

Canola oil

Press rice firmly into a 10-inch nonstick frying pan and cook over low heat about 15 minutes until rice begins to get crusty. Slide the rice cake carefully onto a plate, turn rice cake over, return to pan, and toast the other side. Cool, and cut into 8 wedges.

Pour oil into a medium-size frying pan to a depth of ³/₄ inch. Heat oil to 365°F, and fry wedges until crispy on both sides. Remove and drain on paper towels.

**FOUR & TWENTY
BLACKBIRDS**
Flint Hill, Virginia
Heidi Morf
Chef/Owner

THAI CURRY
with Local Shiitake Mushrooms
& Swiss Chard on Fried Pot Crusts

SERVES 4

6 tablespoons canola oil, divided use

³/₄ cup chopped shallots

1¹/₂ cups coconut milk

1¹/₂ teaspoons red curry paste

2 tablespoons nam pla (Thai fish sauce)

1¹/₂ tablespoons sugar

³/₄ pound shiitake mushrooms, thinly sliced

¹/₃ pound ruby Swiss chard, stems and leaves julienned

¹/₄ cup basil, julienned (Thai basil, if available)

Fried Pot Crusts (see sidebar)

1. Heat 3 tablespoons of the oil in a heavy saucepan over medium-high heat. Add shallots, stir, and fry until golden and crisp. Remove from heat. Add coconut milk.

2. Stir curry paste with a bit of water until smooth. Add to coconut milk mixture along with fish sauce and sugar.

3. Sauté shiitakes in 2 tablespoons of the oil until lightly browned, and add to curry. Bring curry mixture to a boil, reduce heat, and simmer for a few minutes.

4. Sauté chard in the remaining 1 tablespoon of oil until tender. Add chard and basil to the curry sauce. If the mixture seems too thick, add a little water to thin it. (You want enough liquid to soak into the Fried Pot Crusts.) Serve curry sauce over Fried Pot Crusts.

Chef's recommendation: Singha beer

CREAM OF FRESH TURNIP SOUP
with Turnip Greens & Fresh Virginia Scallops

SERVES 6

$^1/_4$ pound fresh turnip greens

5 medium turnips

2 to 3 cups chicken stock

1 pound Virginia bay scallops

2 cups Cream Base (see page 31)

Sea salt and fresh ground black pepper

1. Remove and discard the stems of the turnip greens. Halve the leaves lengthwise, and slice them into thin strips. Bring a large pot of salted water to a boil. Cook a small portion of the greens approximately 4 to 6 minutes. Remove with slotted spoon and put into an ice bath. Taste greens to see if the salt content of the cooking water is correct. Adjust, if necessary, and then cook and cool the remaining greens. Drain thoroughly and combine with first batch of cooked greens. Set aside.

2. Peel the turnips and cut into large cubes. Bring a pot of salted water to a boil. Add the turnip cubes and cook until soft. Cool in ice water.

3. Puree the turnips in a food processor or blender until smooth, adding stock as necessary. Push through a fine-mesh strainer.

4. Pour $^1/_4$ inch of water into a wide skillet; bring to a simmer. Add scallops, and simmer gently until barely done, about 30 seconds. Drain and set aside.

5. Return turnips to heat, and add the Cream Base. Once it's hot, add the greens and scallops. Season with salt and pepper to taste. Serve hot in hot bowls.

Chef's recommendation: Chenin Blanc or Viognier from Pine Ridge, Napa Valley

SOUTHERN GRILLE
Richmond, Virginia
Jimmy Sneed
Former Chef/Owner

Black Beans

1/2 cup black beans

3 cups water

Sort and rinse beans well. Bring water to a boil in a 1-quart saucepan. Add black beans. Lower heat to a simmer and cook until soft, approximately 45 minutes to 1 hour. Drain and reserve the beans.

SHELLFISH & CHICKEN STEW
with Black Beans & Smoked Surry Sausage

SERVES 4

Black beans, cooked (see sidebar)

3 tablespoons olive oil

1 medium onion, sliced lengthwise

2 chicken breasts (preferably free range), cut into strips approximately 1/2-inch wide

2 links smoked Surry sausage, cut into 1-inch pieces

1 teaspoon finely chopped fresh thyme

1 teaspoon finely chopped fresh oregano

1 tablespoon finely chopped parsley

1/2 to 1 teaspoon red pepper flakes depending on spiciness preference

1/4 teaspoon freshly ground black pepper

1/4 teaspoon salt

3 cloves garlic, minced

1 medium green pepper, sliced lengthwise

1 tomato, cut into wedges

4 large shrimp, peeled and deveined

8 littleneck clams, washed to remove grit

1 cup chicken stock

1 cup shrimp stock or clam juice

1. Cook the beans (see sidebar).

2. In a heavy-bottomed sauté pan, combine olive oil, onion, chicken, and sausage. Cook over medium heat until onions become transparent. Add thyme, oregano, parsley, red pepper, black pepper, salt, garlic, green pepper, tomato, shrimp, clams, stocks, and the black beans.

3. Bring to a boil, immediately lower heat, and simmer, covered, for 10 minutes or until clams just open and shrimp are firm to the touch. Don't overcook or the chicken will be tough.

Chef's recommendation: The flavors of this dish are brought out equally well when matched with red or white wine. Try a good Pinot Noir, such as those from Bethel Heights Winery, or find a sauvignon blanc that is not too grassy and has not too much citrus.

RESTAURANT COLUMBIA
Easton, Maryland
Stephen Mangasarian
Chef/Owner

SAUTÉ OF PARSNIPS, CHESTNUTS & BRUSSELS SPROUTS

SERVES 4 AS A SIDE DISH

16 chestnuts

1 cup chicken stock

1 celery rib, cut in half

1 medium carrot, peeled and cut in half

Salt and freshly ground pepper to taste

1 pound parsnips

2 cups Brussels sprouts

Olive oil

1 tablespoon chopped Italian parsley

1. To peel chestnuts, cut a deep *X* on the flat side of the outer shell. Place in cold water to cover, and bring to a boil. Remove chestnuts from the hot water, and while they're still hot, peel off the shells and inner husks. If the chestnuts are fresh, this should not pose a problem.

2. Over medium heat, in a sauté pan, cook the chestnuts in chicken stock with the celery, carrot, and salt and pepper until just tender, about 7 minutes. Remove chestnuts from stock and let cool.

3. Peel parsnips and cut in quarters lengthwise. Cut each piece in half, removing and discarding the tough inner cores.

4. Trim and halve the Brussels sprouts, or, if they are very small, leave them whole.

5. Film the sauté pan with olive oil, and heat over medium-high heat. Add the parsnips and Brussels sprouts, and sauté over medium heat, covered, turning vegetables from time to time until they begin to cook through and the parsnips begin to turn pale gold in spots. You may add a little water to the pan to facilitate the cooking process and to prevent overbrowning. After 5 minutes, add the chestnuts. Heat chestnuts through, about 5 more minutes.

6. Season with salt and pepper. Toss with the parsley and serve. This dish is excellent with roast chicken or pork.

Chef's recommendation: A fully extracted Rhône, such as Domaine du Pavillon–Mercurol Crozes–Hermitage

CASHION'S EAT PLACE
Washington
Ann Cashion
Chef/Owner

TARTE AUX POIRES
(PEAR TART)

SERVES 10

2 cups water

1²⁄₃ cups granulated sugar, divided use

6 medium Bartlett pears

1 stick (¹⁄₂ cup) plus ¹⁄₂ tablespoon unsalted butter to grease tart pan,
divided use

Pâté Sucrée (see page 216)

3 large eggs, divided use

1¹⁄₃ cups blanched, sliced almonds

2 tablespoons flour

For the pears:

1. Combine the water and 1 cup of the sugar in a wide saucepan, and bring
to a boil. Peel, core, and halve the pears, and add them to the sugar
syrup. Boil gently until the pears are tender but still slightly firm; the
cooking time will vary from 2 to 5 minutes depending on the ripeness of
the fruit. A sharp knife blade, when inserted into the pears, should meet
some resistance. Remove pears from the syrup, drain, and cool.

To prepare the Pâté Sucrée tart dough:

2. Grease an 11-inch tart pan with a removable bottom with ¹⁄₂ tablespoon
of the butter.

3. Roll out the Pâté Sucrée dough on a floured surface to 13¹⁄₂ inches in
diameter and ¹⁄₈ inch of thickness. Lightly roll the dough around the
rolling pin, lift it, and unroll it onto the tart pan. Gently form the dough
and press it down against the pan. Trim excess dough, leaving a ¹⁄₄-inch
border of dough above the rim. Patch any tears with the dough trimmings. Chill the prepared crust for 30 minutes before baking. (Wrap
and freeze extra dough for another use.)

4. Preheat oven to 375°F.

5. Prick the crust bottom and sides with a fork. Cut a piece of wax paper to fit into the tart pan. Fill with rice, dried beans, or dough weights. (In place of these, you may put a second tart-pan bottom over the wax paper, thereby sandwiching the dough.) Bake for 6 to 8 minutes. Remove from the oven, and carefully lift the wax paper with the dough weights from the crust. Beat one of the eggs, and brush over the entire crust. Bake for 10 more minutes until golden brown. While the crust is baking, prepare the custard.

For the custard:

6. Place the almonds and ⅓ cup of the sugar in a food processor fitted with a steel blade. Grind the almonds for approximately 1 minute to form a coarse meal. Set aside (overprocessing will result in an almond butter).

7. Soften the stick of butter, and combine with the remaining ⅓ cup of sugar. Cream with an electric mixer on medium speed for about 1 minute. Add the flour and blend well. With the mixer still running, add the 2 remaining eggs, one at a time, until each is incorporated into the mixture. Pour in the almond meal and blend thoroughly.

To assemble the tart:

8. Pour the mixture into the prebaked and slightly cooled tart crust (approximately ⅔ full). Place the pear halves—stem ends pointing in, toward the center—in overlapping concentric circles, filling the tart shell. Return the tart to the 375°F oven, and bake for 25 more minutes, until the custard is set and nicely browned. Trim any excessively dark crust edges. Serve at room temperature.

Chef's recommendation: A lightly sparkling Crémant d'Alsace, such as Earl Adam Pierre Ammerschwihr

Meadow Creek Dairy—*a family farm in the mountains of southwestern Virginia — produces cheeses that reflect the diverse pastures and soils of the region. Meadow Creek's full-flavored and ecologically friendly products are the result of sustainable farming methods and dedication to managing the land and cattle for health rather than mass production. Meadow Creek Dairy uses only fresh, unpasteurized milk from its own grade A dairy.*

Pâté Sucrée
FOR TARTE AUX POIRES

MAKES TWO 11-INCH TART CRUSTS

1½ sticks unsalted butter

1 teaspoon confectioners' sugar

1¾ cups all-purpose flour

½ cup almond flour (see below)

Pinch of salt

½ teaspoon vanilla extract

1 egg

Have all ingredients measured and ready.

If using an electric mixer: With the dough hook or flat whip, blend the butter (slightly softened and cut into pieces), sugar, flour, almond flour, and salt until crumbly. Add the vanilla extract and the egg, mixing only long enough to blend all of the ingredients.

If kneading by hand: Place the almond flour and pinch of salt in a mixing bowl. Sift the flour and confectioners' sugar into the same bowl. Thoroughly mix the contents. Turn out the dry ingredients, and mound in the center of your work surface. Make a well in the flour and place the butter, cut in pieces, in the center. Using your fingertips, blend the butter into the flour until the dough is crumbly. Add the vanilla extract and the egg, lightly beaten. Knead only long enough to completely mix the ingredients.

Form the dough into a ball, wrap in plastic, and refrigerate overnight. Take out 30 minutes before rolling.

Hint: Make almond flour by grinding whole, blanched almonds in a food mill or food processor to the texture of coarse meal.

Pâté Sucrée keeps for several days in the refrigerator if well wrapped. You may prepare the dough ahead and freeze it. Defrost in the refrigerator for 24 hours before using.

L'AUBERGE CHEZ FRANÇOIS
Great Falls, Virginia
Jacques Haeringer
Executive Chef

GINSENG MOUNTAIN GRILLED LAMB

SERVES 4

1 whole lamb rib section, split, frenched, chine bone removed, and cut into double-rib chops

1 cup olive oil

Juice of 1 lemon

1 tablespoon cracked pepper

Sea salt

8 to 10 woody rosemary branches, soaked in water for 30 minutes

1. Trim excess fat from chops. Combine oil, lemon juice, and pepper in a nonreactive pan, and marinate chops for 2 hours, turning once or twice.

2. Prepare and light grill.

3. Remove chops from marinade, shake off excess oil, and season chops lightly with sea salt.

4. Toss rosemary branches onto open charcoal fire. When flames calm, sear marinated chops over the smoke. Move to a slower part of the grill and continue grilling until medium rare.

Chef's recommendation: Domine Drouhin Pinot Noir or another American Pinot Noir with balanced spice and earthiness

Baby lamb comes from Ginseng Mountain farm in Blue Grass, Virginia, twice a year. We trim woody branches of our rosemary for this dish.

—CHEF ROBERT RAMSEY

**Local Foods
Local Flavors**

***Ginseng Mountain Farm** lambs are grown on their mother's milk and on grass from the mountains of Highland County, Virginia. The lambs are naturally raised and 100 percent free of growth hormones, stimulants, and antibiotics. Debora Ellington treats new customers to a jar of her homemade jelly and a few favorite recipes. And she welcomes new recipes or tips she can pass along to lamb lovers.*

FOX HEAD INN
Manakin-Sabot,
  Virginia
Robert Ramsey
Executive Chef

CRAB & SHIITAKE CAKES
with Tomato-Ginger Sauce

SERVES 4

For the tomato-ginger sauce:

1 tablespoon canola oil

2 tablespoons shallots, minced

1 tablespoon garlic, minced

1½ pounds tomatoes, coarsely chopped (about 2 cups)

2-inch piece of ginger, peeled and sliced thinly across the fibers

Sea salt and freshly ground black pepper to taste

1. Heat the oil in a medium saucepan. Add the shallots and garlic, and sauté until soft, stirring from time to time. Add the tomatoes and ginger, stir thoroughly, and bring to a boil. Reduce the heat, and simmer for about 5 minutes. Remove the pan from the heat and cool slightly. Transfer the sauce to a blender, and puree until smooth. Season to taste with salt and pepper.

For the crab and shiitake cakes:

4 tablespoons canola oil

2 tablespoons minced shallots

1 tablespoon minced garlic

3 ribs celery, washed and minced

1 small carrot, peeled and minced

1 small red or yellow pepper, seeded and minced

½ pound shiitake mushrooms, washed, stemmed, and sliced thinly

2 eggs or 4 egg whites, beaten

4 tablespoons minced cilantro

1 pound jumbo lump crabmeat, picked clean of shells and cartilage

Sea salt and freshly ground pepper to taste

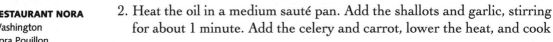

RESTAURANT NORA
Washington
Nora Pouillon
Chef/Owner

2. Heat the oil in a medium sauté pan. Add the shallots and garlic, stirring for about 1 minute. Add the celery and carrot, lower the heat, and cook

until softened, about 2 minutes. Add the pepper and mushrooms. Stir and sauté until the mushrooms are soft and fully cooked, about 3 minutes. Remove from the heat, and let cool for about 10 minutes.

3. Preheat broiler.

4. Combine the sautéed vegetables with the eggs, cilantro, and crabmeat, being careful not to break the lumps of crab. Season to taste with salt and pepper.

5. Shape mixture into 12 small crab cakes; they will be very soft and delicate. Put the crab cakes on a sheet pan and broil them, on one side only, for 3 to 4 minutes or until nicely browned. Do not turn over the crab cakes. They are too delicate.

6. To serve, pour a pool of the tomato-ginger sauce in the centers of 4 warm dinner plates, and arrange 3 crab cakes on each plate.

Chef's recommendation: A bone-dry, crisp white wine—such as Furmint Heidi Shrock from Austria—or a Sancerre or Pouilly Fumé

**Local Foods
Local Flavors**

CHRYSALIS
VINEYARDS

Chrysalis Vineyard*—At the foothills of the Northern Blue Ridge and Bull Run mountains is Chrysalis Vineyards, which features alternative, vinifera varieties of wines, such as the French Viognier, Petit Verdot, Tannat, Fer Servadou, and Petit Manseng and the Spanish Albariño, Tempranillo, and Graciano. Established in 1997 by Jennifer McCloud, Chrysalis is restoring the native American grape, the Norton, to its eminence among fine wines and currently has the largest planting of the grape in the eastern United States.*

PAN-ROASTED MONKFISH

& Mashed Acorn Squash with Tarragon-Walnut Vinaigrette

SERVES 4

For the acorn squash:

3 acorn squash, cut in half and seeds removed

3 tablespoons unsalted butter

$1/4$ cup heavy whipping cream

$1/4$ teaspoon freshly grated nutmeg

$1/8$ teaspoon cayenne pepper

Salt and freshly ground pepper to taste

For the fish:

1 cup dried cèpes

4 six-ounce monkfish tail fillets, skin removed

Salt and freshly ground pepper to taste

2 tablespoons olive oil (for cooking)

For the vinaigrette:

2 tablespoons chopped fresh tarragon

2 tablespoons toasted walnuts

$1/2$ cup olive oil

$1/2$ teaspoon fresh lime juice

Salt and freshly ground pepper to taste

For the garnish:

Grapeseed or peanut oil for frying

$2^1/2$ cups spinach chiffonade (washed, spun dry, and cut into thin strips)

$1/2$ cup julienned yellow squash

1. Preheat oven to 400°F.

2. Place squash halves, cut side down, in a baking pan. Add enough water to cover the bottom of the pan with $1/4$ inch of water. Bake until flesh is very soft, about 1 hour.

VIDALIA
Washington
Peter Smith
Executive Chef

3. Remove pulp from the squash and place in medium-size saucepan. Add the butter, cream, nutmeg, cayenne, salt, and pepper. Mash with a paddle until well incorporated. Do not overmix.

4. Grind dried cèpes to a fine powder in an electric coffee–spice grinder. Dredge the fish on both sides in the cepe flour, and season to taste. Heat a large frying pan over medium-high heat. Add olive oil, and sear fish on both sides. Reduce heat to medium, cover, and roast fish until desired doneness, about 10 to 12 minutes.

5. Puree all of the ingredients for the vinaigrette in a food processor at high speed until well blended. Season to taste.

6. Heat ½ inch of grapeseed or peanut oil to 380°F. Separately fry the spinach and squash until crisp. Drain on paper towels.

7. To assemble, place one scoop of squash on each of 4 warmed plates. Slice each of the monkfish tails into 3 slices. Arrange on top of the squash. Spoon vinaigrette around the puree, and garnish with fried vegetables.

Chef's recommendation: Testarosa Michaud Vineyard 1997 Chardonnay or other white wine with hints of pear, tangerine, and grapefruit and a long-lingering finish

**Local Foods
Local Flavors**

...
Summerfield

Summerfield Farm was started in 1983 with one cow, a calf, and three bales of alfalfa hay. Owners Jamie and Rachel Nicoll were determined to raise the finest milk-fed veal without confining or drugging the calves. Today the Nicolls produce some of the region's most flavorful free-range veal, spring lamb, farm-raised fallow venison, poultry and gamebirds, and stocks (veal, game, lamb, and chicken) made from the bones and trimmings of their meat. The animals are raised alongside their mothers and are free to roam, play, and chase their mothers for milk. When they begin to ruminate, grass, grain, and hay are made available.

Basil Dipping Sauce

¼ cup fish sauce

¼ cup fresh lime juice

1 tablespoon chili-garlic sauce

1 tablespoon sugar, preferably superfine and instant dissolving

2 large basil leaves, shredded

Combine all ingredients and mix well.

DUCK & ZUCCHINI FRITTERS
with Basil Dipping Sauce

SERVES 6 AS AN APPETIZER

1 tablespoon salt

1 small zucchini, julienned to 1-inch lengths

1 tablespoon soy sauce

2 tablespoons sliced scallions

1 tablespoon grated ginger

1 teaspoon finely chopped garlic

1 teaspoon Five Spice Powder

1 pound duck meat, trimmed of sinews, fat, and skin

1 egg

Salt and freshly ground pepper to taste

Clarified unsalted butter or peanut oil for pan frying

Basil Dipping Sauce (see sidebar)

1. Salt the zucchini and let rest in a bowl for 20 minutes. Rinse with cool water, and using your hands, squeeze out as much liquid as possible.

2. While zucchini is resting, combine soy sauce, scallions, ginger, garlic, and Five Spice Powder in a mixing bowl.

3. Pulse duck meat in a food processor until just pureed through (no big lumps). Pulse in the egg, add to the spice mixture, and combine well using your hands. Fold in zucchini, and season with salt and pepper. Form duck mixture into silver dollar–size cakes.

4. Heat a large iron skillet until drops of water sizzle on the surface. Fry cakes, in batches, in ⅛-inch of melted clarified butter or oil until crispy but still a little pink on the inside. Drain on paper towels and serve with Basil Dipping Sauce.

Chef's recommendation: Michal Shaps Viognier or another dry, aromatic white wine

C&O RESTAURANT
Charlottesville, Virginia
Thomas Bowles
Executive Chef

SMOKED TROUT MOUSSELINE

SERVES 4

½ cup crème fraîche

1 tablespoon smooth Dijon mustard

1 tablespoon chopped dill

8 ounces Mt. Walden smoked trout fillets

Salt and freshly ground pepper to taste

2 bunches arugula, trimmed, washed, and spun dry

Crusty bread

1. In a medium bowl, thoroughly mix together crème fraîche, mustard, and dill to make a mustard sauce.

2. Using your hands or 2 forks, gently break or shred the smoked trout into small pieces. Add to the sauce, blending well with a fork. Season with salt and pepper.

3. Serve chilled on fresh arugula with crusty bread.

Chef's recommendation: A full-bodied Chardonnay, such as Barboursville Reserve

Mid-Atlantic Farm Facts

*The Farm at Mt. Walden's Applewood smoked trout—
Walden Mountain is the maker of natural gourmet smoked
products, including Applewood smoked trout. The trout are
hatched and raised in mountain spring water and are free of
all chemical residues. They are trimmed, boned, and filleted
by hand—not by machine—and are then brined in a salt and
water mixture with no artificial ingredients. After the brining,
the trout are then placed by hand on smoking racks and loaded
into wood-burning rotisserie smokers with applewood log fires
burning from behind. The Farm at Mt. Walden uses applewood
because of its immediate availability in Virginia's Shenandoah
Valley and the delicate flavor it adds to the product.*

TABARD INN
Washington
Andrew Saba
Executive Chef

ENDIVE, WALNUT *&*
BLUE CHEESE SALAD
with Port Vinaigrette

SERVES 6

3 heads endive

1 head frisée, separated from the stem, cleaned, and spun dry

1 small head radicchio, cut into ½-inch bands

½ medium red onion, julienned

½ cup walnuts, roasted and finely chopped

¾ cup Port Vinaigrette (see next page)

Salt and freshly ground pepper to taste

3 Poached Pears (see next page)

9 ounces blue cheese of your choice

1. Arrange 4 or 5 leaves of endive across the top of each plate.

2. Toss together the frisée, radicchio, onion, walnuts, and some of the Port Vinaigrette. Season with salt and pepper, and add more dressing if necessary. Always be careful not to overdress.

3. Drizzle a bit of dressing on each endive leaf; place a fluffy cluster of the salad mix in the center of each plate—at the base of the endive leaves. Cut the Poached Pears into slices; arrange fanned slices of pear wherever you like. Sprinkle the salads with crumbled blue cheese to taste.

Chef's recommendation: Fess Parker Viognier or a crisp Chablis

1789
Restaurant

1789
Washington
Ris Lacoste
Executive Chef

Port Vinaigrette

makes 3¹/₂ cups

1 cup port

¹/₂ cup red wine vinegar

1¹/₂ teaspoon Dijon mustard

1 shallot, diced

1 cup peanut oil

¹/₄ cup walnut oil

Salt and freshly ground pepper to taste

Reduce 1 cup port to ¹/₄ cup. Combine the reduced port, red wine vinegar, Dijon mustard, and shallot in a nonreactive bowl. (A wet towel placed under the bowl helps keep it in place while whisking.) Whisk ingredients together and then emulsify with a steady drizzle of, first peanut oil, then walnut oil. Taste for balance before all of the oil is added. More or less oil may be needed depending on the acidity of the vinegar. Season with salt and pepper. The vinaigrette will last a long time in the refrigerator.

Poached Pears

2 cups port

1 cup water

¹/₂ cup sugar

1 vanilla bean

3 firm, ripe red Bartlett pears, peeled, stems left on

Combine the port, water, sugar, and scraped vanilla bean in a medium-size, nonreactive saucepan. Place the pears in the liquid that, ideally, should reach halfway up the pears (adjust with more port/wine/sugar if necessary). Bring to a boil and then gently simmer, turning the pears occasionally so that all sides are coated. Cook until the pears are soft but not mushy, about 45 minutes. Store pears in their poaching liquid to increase the depth of color and flavor. They can be prepared 2 to 3 days ahead and kept covered in the refrigerator. The poaching liquid can be saved and used again or reduced to make a syrup or sauce for other uses.

Peterson Pawpaws

In 1980, Neal Peterson undertook to create a new domesticated fruit crop from the wild pawpaw. With assistance from the University of Maryland, he raised 1,400 trees from seed from historical collections of pawpaw dating to the early 20th century. Twelve years later, 18 seedlings stood out as superior, and they are currently being tested at universities across the United States. Three of the types have been named and will soon be available to the public through Peterson Pawpaws.

WHERE TO FIND CHEFS
WHO ARE COOKING FRESH

JOSÉ RAMÓN ANDRÉS
Jaleo
480 7th Street NW
Washington, DC 20004
202-628-7949

Chef José Ramón Andrés's culinary
skills are deeply rooted in his
Mediterranean heritage, and it
shows. Jaleo's extensive menu of
more than 60 different tapas reflects
the rich, regional diversity of
classical and contemporary Spanish
cuisine.

THOMAS BOWLES
C&O Restaurant
515 East Water Street
Charlottesville, VA 22902
434-971-7044
www.candorestaurant.com

A Charlottesville institution, C&O
operates on three floors, each with
its own unique environment. Chef
Thomas Bowles's offerings are best
described as French Provincial
with influences by the American
Southwest and the Pacific Rim.

ANN CASHION
Cashion's Eat Place
1819 Columbia Road NW
Washington, DC 20009
202-797-1819

Chef Ann Cashion's seasonal cuisine
is grounded in traditional French,
Italian, and American cooking. The
handwritten menu changes daily,
allowing the kitchen to fully explore
the bounty of regional growers and
producers. The atmosphere is casual
yet sophisticated, making Cashion's
Eat Place a top choice among
Washington residents and visitors
to the capital alike.

DAVID CRAIG
formerly of Tabard Inn
Washington, DC
(see Tabard Inn contact information
under Andrew Saba, page 231)

ROBERTO DONNA
Galileo
1110 21st Street NW
Washington, DC 20036
202-293-7191
www.robertodonna.com

Chef Roberto Donna's award-
winning Galileo has been a
Washington institution for 17 years.
Winning a James Beard Best Chef
Mid-Atlantic Region award,
Donna's innovative northern Italian
cuisine features an ever-changing
menu focused on the freshest, most
seasonal, and most interesting
ingredients in the marketplace.

TODD GRAY
Equinox
818 Connecticut Avenue NW
Washington, DC 20006
202-331-8118
www.equinoxrestaurant.com

Sleek and modern, Equinox offers
a truly regional and seasonal
experience. Chef Todd Gray
remains true to his Mid-Atlantic
roots by showcasing local products
with a firm grip on traditional
culinary technique.

HUW GRIFFITHS
Pastry Chef, Tabard Inn
Washington, DC
(see information under Andrew
Saba, page 231)

JACQUES HAERINGER
L'Auberge Chez François
332 Springvale Road
Great Falls, VA 22066
703-759-3800
www.aubergefrancois.com

About 30 minutes from the center of
Washington in Great Falls, Virginia,
L'Auberge Chez François is a
French country inn specializing in
Alsatian cuisine. Under the skilled
direction of Chef Jacques
Haeringer, the restaurant combines
warm hospitality with good food. It
has been voted favorite restaurant
18 years in a row by readers of
Washington magazine.

BOB KINKEAD
Kinkead's
2000 Pennsylvania Avenue NW
Washington, DC 20006
202-296-7700
www.kinkead.com

This large, brasserie-style seafood
restaurant situated on two floors is
the work of Chef Bob Kinkead, four-
time winner of the James Beard
Best Mid-Atlantic Chef award. He
describes Kinkead's restaurant as
"an American brasserie with a heavy
emphasis on seafood," but he is
clearly not restricted by boundaries.

RIS LACOSTE
1789
1226 36th Street NW
Washington, DC 20007
202-965-1789
www.1789restaurant.com

Voted one of America's Top Tables
by *Gourmet* magazine readers, 1789
sits in a two-story Federal-style
town house on a quiet residential
street in Georgetown. Chef Ris
Lacoste is internationally recognized
for using indigenous American
ingredients like venison, American
lamb, Maryland rockfish and soft-

shell crab, Maine lobster, and Alaska halibut and salmon in simple yet classic recipes that bring out those ingredients' natural flavors.

STEPHEN MANGASARIAN
Restaurant Columbia
28 South Washington Street
Easton, MD 21601
410-770-5172

Located in a historic home that dates from 1795, Restaurant Columbia is an American restaurant with an American wine list. Changing the menu every three weeks to take advantage of market conditions, Chef Stephen Mangasarian offers his vision for American cuisine that is an amalgam of cooking styles brought to the New World by various ethnic groups.

BRIAN McBRIDE
Melrose
Park Hyatt Washington
1201 24th Street NW
Washington, DC 20037
202-419-6755
www.hyatt.com/usa/washington/hotels/restaurants_wasph.html

Melrose is an upscale, four-diamond restaurant in Washington's fashionable West End. It offers contemporary American cuisine that emphasizes seafood. After 11 years at Melrose, Chef Brian McBride remains committed to using only the finest and freshest ingredients.

PAUL MILNE
208 Talbot
208 North Talbot Street
St. Michaels, MD 21663
410-745-3838
www.208talbot.com

Located in Maryland's historic St. Michaels, 208 Talbot is a small, intimate restaurant serving innovative American cuisine.

Chef Paul Milne changes the menu frequently to take advantage of the area's abundance of fresh seafood and local produce.

ALEX MONTIEL
Boar's Head Inn
200 Ednam Drive
Charlottesville, VA 22903
434-296-2181
www.boarsheadinn.com

The four-star, four-diamond Old Mill Room at the Boar's Head Inn features American food with a French accent. Executive Chef Alex Montiel and his international staff are renowned for their imaginative cuisine and superb wine selection.

HEIDI MORF
Four & Twenty Blackbirds
650 Zachary Taylor Highway
   (Route 522)
Flint Hill, VA 22627
540-675-1111

Chef Heidi Morf's new American menu at Four & Twenty Blackbirds changes every three weeks and includes the flavors of many ethnic cuisines. A small fine-dining restaurant in the foothills of the Blue Ridge Mountains, it earned a three-star rating from *Washington* magazine and is one of the top 40 D.C. area restaurants rated by *Zagat Guide* readers.

NORA POUILLON
Restaurant Nora
2132 Florida Avenue NW
Washington, DC 20008
202-462-5143
www.noras.com

A longtime advocate of organic, seasonal, locally produced ingredients, Chef Nora Pouillon earned her restaurant organic certification—the first restaurant ever to receive that designation. Restaurant Nora in

Washington offers creative dishes that are balanced, flavorful, and delicious.

ROBERT RAMSEY
Fox Head Inn
1840 Manakin Road
Manakin-Sabot, VA 23103
804-784-5126

The cuisine at the Fox Head Inn is described as Virginia *terroir* without being gimmicky. It is also award winning, using many of the fresh herbs, fruits, and vegetables that come out of the Fox Head Inn's own garden and from its own fruit trees, which Chef Robert Ramsey tends to himself.

DALE REITZER
Acacia
3325 West Cary Street
Richmond, VA 23221
804-354-6060
www.acaciarestaurant.com

Since 1998, Acacia has served as Richmond's premier destination dining experience. Chef Dale Reitzer—named 1999's Best New American Chef by *Food & Wine* magazine—demonstrates his vast experience with local and regional ingredients by changing the menu daily.

BARRY RUMSEY
Bicycle
1444 Light Street
Baltimore, MD 21230
410-234-1900
www.bicyclebistro.com

Bicycle Bistro in Baltimore features American contemporary cuisine that incorporates local, regional, and seasonal produce, seafood, and meats. Described by the *Washington Post* as "the sort of place every eclectic, progressive neighborhood dreams of having," Chef Barry Rumsey's menu spotlights original dishes that allow the flavor and quality of local ingredients to shine.

ANDREW SABA
Tabard Inn
1739 N Street NW
Washington, DC 20036
202-785-1277
www.tabardinn.com

Dine on New American cuisine in one of Washington's oldest hotels. Chef Andrew Saba and Pastry Chef Huw Griffiths create ever-changing seasonal dishes and desserts that soar with culinary expression. Aromatic sauces, engaging appetizers, sublime desserts, and the pristine quality of the seafood, meat, and poultry entrées are testaments to the skill and creative spirits of Chef Andrew and Chef Huw.

JOHN SHIELDS
Gertrude's
Baltimore Museum of Art
10 Art Museum Drive
Baltimore, MD 21218
410-889-3399
www.johnshields.com

Located at the Baltimore Museum of Art, Gertrude's is the restaurant of public television chef John Shields. With its emphasis on the freshest and finest foods of the region, Gertrude's celebrates Chesapeake cuisine.

PETER SMITH
Vidalia
1990 M Street NW
Washington, DC 20036
202-659-1990
www.vidaliadc.com

Specializing in extraordinary cuisine that highlights the richness of Chesapeake Bay and Virginia farmlands as well as foods indigenous to America, Vidalia offers a distinctive and exciting restaurant experience that exudes Southern charm. Under the direction of Executive Chef Peter Smith, Vidalia's menu changes constantly.

JIMMY SNEED
Richmond, Virginia

Chef Jimmy Sneed treats southern cooking like religion. As the former chef/owner of the Southern Grille and the Frog and the Redneck, he offered Richmond diners traditional treats like meatloaf, short ribs, ham hocks, collards, and possibly the best fried chicken anywhere. He's also an avid promoter of Virginia's Hayman yams, which he proclaims are so sweet, your teeth will stick together. Ardent fans are eagerly awaiting Chef Jimmy's next culinary adventure.

MARTHA HESTER STAFFORD
Cooking for Your Health
  and Well-Being
Charlottesville, VA 22903
434-293-7178

Martha Hester Stafford is a cooking teacher and recipe writer and lives in Charlottesville, Virginia. She specializes in teaching people how to deliciously increase the amount of vegetables in their diet by focusing on organic, local, seasonal produce. She has taught for the Institute for Culinary Education in New York, Kings Cooking Studio in New Jersey, and the Seasonal Cook in Charlottesville. For classes and monthly recipes, check her Web site at www.unityresources.com.

DAVID STEIN
Bistro St. Michaels
403 South Talbot Street
St. Michaels, MD 21663
410-745-9111

This Parisian-style bistro on the main street of historic St. Michaels specializes in local produce and seafood. Chef David Stein master-

fully combines Maryland regional favorites, traditional American dishes, and French/Mediterranean influences.

JIM SWENSON
National Press Club
529 14th Street NW
Washington, DC 20045
202-662-7514

The Fourth Estate at the National Press Club features some of the finest cooking in the city. Chef Jim Swenson—who serves a thousand meals a day at this 4,200-member club for journalists, lobbyists, and government officials—buys seasonal produce from local specialty growers and fashions his menus on food items he considers new and interesting.

CINDY WOLF
Charleston
1000 Lancaster Street
Baltimore, MD 21202
410-332-7373
www.charlestonrestaurant.com

Chef Cindy Wolf's deluxe water-front restaurant evokes the warm, rich gentility of the Southern spirit. The lively menu—which incorporates the finest seasonal seafood, game, and fresh produce—is complemented by Charleston's award-winning wine cellar and exemplary service.

CONTACT INFORMATION

AUTHORS

MICHAEL ABLEMAN
Center for Urban Agriculture
   at Fairview Gardens
598 North Fairview Avenue
Goleta, CA 93117
805-967-7369
FairviewG@aol.com
www.fairviewgardens.org

MICHAEL APPLEBY
The Humane Society
   of the United States
2100 L Street, NW
Washington, DC 20037
301-258-3111

PETER D. BLOOME
Oregon State University
   Extension Service
101 Ballard Extension Hall
Corvallis, OR 97331-3606
541-737-2713

**WILLIAM DOHERTY,
LESLIE BAUTISTA, BARBARA
CARLSON, JANE GUFFY,
SUE KAKUK &
BUGS PETERSCHMIDT**
Putting Family First
5270 Yvette Street
Greenfield, MN 55357
763-745-5264
www.puttingfamilyfirst.info

HEIDI EASTHAM
Rucker Farm
Tack House Kitchen and Creamery
P.O. Box 423
Flint Hill, VA 22627
540-675-3444

GEORGE ELLISON
P.O. Box 1262
Bryson City, NC 28713
ELLISONGEORGE@cs.com

JOHN FRIEDRICH
Community Harvest
2437 15th Street, NW
Washington, DC 20009
202-667-8875
info@communityharvest.org
www.communityharvestdc.org

CHRIS FULLERTON
Tuscarora Organic Growers
   Cooperative
HCR 71 Box 168-B
Hustontown, PA 17229
814-448-2173

ALEXANDRA GREELEY
Vegetarian Times Magazine
11458 Links Drive
Reston, VA 20190
703-471-6454
cookasia@earthlink.net

BRIAN HALWEIL
Worldwatch Institute
1776 Massachusetts Avenue NW
Washington, DC 20036
202-452-1999
halweil@worldwatch.org
www.worldwatch.org

CHUCK HASSEBROOK
Center for Rural Affairs
P.O. Box 406
Walthill, NE 68067-0406
402-846-5428
www.cfra.org

ELIZABETH HENDERSON
Peacework Organic Farm
2218 Welcher Road
Newark, NY 14513
315-331-9029
ehendrsn@redsuspenders.com
www.gvocsa.org

PAIGE HOGGE
Buster's Seafood and Crab Farm
Urbanna, VA 23175
804-758-5924

MATTHEW HORA
Capital Area Food Bank
645 Taylor Street NE
Washington, DC 20017
202-526-5344
horam@cfoodbank.org
www.capitalareafoodbank.org

BARBARA B. HUYETT
Sunnyside Farm and Orchards
Route 2
Charles Town, WV 25414
304-725-7990

JOHN IKERD
5121 South Brock Rodgers Road
Columbia, MO 65201
573-874-0408
www.ssu.missouri.edu/faculty/jikerd

PETER JARET
Peter Jaret Associates
Petaluma, CA 94952
707-778-8256
pjaret@sonic.net

C. L. "CORY" KORAL
Jordan River Farm
6 Shiloh Lane
Huntly, VA 22640
888-267-7432
540-636-9388

JAMES HOWARD KUNSTLER
127 Circular
Saratoga Springs, NY 12866
518-581-1876
Kunstler@aol.com

JIM LAW
Linden Vineyards
3708 Harrels Corner Road
Linden, VA 22642
540-364-1997
www.lindenvineyards.com

JOY LOKEY
L'Esprit de Campagne
P.O. Box 3130
Winchester, VA 22604
540-955-1014

JEFF MANN
English Department
Virginia Polytechnic Institute
and State University
Blacksburg, VA 24061-0112

AILEEN C. MARTIN
2514 Martin Drive
Axton, VA 24054
434-685-7135

JENNIFER McCLOUD
Chrysalis Vineyards
23876 Champe Ford Road
Middleburg, VA 20117
540-687-8222 (local)
800-235-8804 (toll free)
www.chrysaliswine.com

PETER D. MITCHELL
Fauquier County Agricultural
    Development Office
35 Culpeper Street
Warrenton, VA 20186
540-349-5314
peter.mitchell@fauquiercounty.gov
www.fauquiercounty.gov/govern-
ment/departments/agdev/

GEOFF OXNAM
SASS Communications
201 Forbes Street
Annapolis MD 21401
410-263-8448

R. NEAL PETERSON
Peterson Pawpaws
P.O. Box 1011
Harpers Ferry, WV 25425
nealp@mountain.net
www.petersonpawpaws.com

NORA POUILLON
Restaurant Nora
2132 Florida Avenue NW
Washington, DC 20008
202-462-5143
nora@noras.com
www.noras.com

JOEL SALATIN
Polyface Farm
363 Shuey Road
Swoope, VA 24479
540-885-3590

MICHAEL SHUMAN
Community Ventures LLP
3713 Warren Street, NW
Washington, DC 20016
202-364-4051
shuman@igc.org
www.progressivepubs.com

RUTH SULLIVAN
Future Harvest–Chesapeake
    Alliance for Sustainable Agriculture
106 Market Court
Stevensville, MD 21666
410-604-2681
rsullivan@friendly.net
www.futureharvestcasa.org

GEORGE SWINGLER
Rose Hill Market
633½ Rose Hill Drive
Charlottesville, VA 22903

SUSAN TEDDER
Gentleman's Ridge Farm
589 Gentleman's Ridge Road
Blairs, VA 24527
434-791-2382
www.gentlemansridge.com

JOHN PAGE WILLIAMS
Chesapeake Bay Foundation
6 Herndon Avenue
Annapolis, MD 21403
410-268-8816
chesapeake@cbf.org
www.savethebay.cbf.org

LINDA WILSON
Butter Pot Farm
5314-2 Ross Neck Road
Cambridge, MD 21613
410-228-3818

ANN HARVEY YONKERS
FRESHFARM Markets
3802 Jocelyn Street NW
Washington, DC 20015
202-362-8889
annyonkers@aol.com
info@freshfarmmarket.org
www.freshfarmmarket.org

**FEATURED PRODUCTS
AND ORGANIZATIONS**

**AMERICAN FARMLAND
TRUST**
1200 18th Street NW, #800
Washington, DC 20036
202-331-7300
info@farmland.org
www.farmland.org
(see page 76)

APPALACHIAN HARVEST
Appalachian Sustainable
    Development
P.O. Box 791
Abingdon, VA 24212-0791
540-623-1121
asd@eva.org
www.appsusdev.org
(see page 64)

BAY FRIENDLY CHICKEN
3713 Warren Street NW
Washington, DC 20016
202-238-0010
shuman@igc.org
(see page 124)

BERGEY'S DAIRY
2221 Mt. Pleasant Road
Chesapeake, VA 23322
757-482-471
(see page 85)

BLUE RIDGE DAIRY
12745 Milltown Road
Lovettsville, VA 20180
540-822-4363
www.blueridgedairy.com
(see page 41)

BUSTER'S SEAFOOD AND CRAB FARM
Urbanna, VA 23175
804-758-5924
(see page 115)

BUTTER POT FARM
5314-2 Ross Neck Road
Cambridge, MD 21613
410-228-3818
(see page 61)

CHESAPEAKE BAY FOUNDATION
6 Herndon Avenue
Annapolis, MD 21403
410-268-8816
410-269-0481 (from Baltimore)
301-261-2350 (from D.C. metro)
chesapeake@cbf.org
www.savethebay.cbf.org
(see page 169)

CHILE MAN
35796 Milligan's Run Lane
Purcellville, VA 20132
540-668-7160
www.thechileman.com
(see page 55)

CHRYSALIS VINEYARDS
23876 Champe Ford Road
Middleburg, VA 20117
540-687-8222 (local)
800-235-8804 (toll free)
www.chrysaliswine.com
(see page 219)

ECOFRIENDLY FOODS
3397 Stonyfork Road
Moneta, VA 24121
540-297-9582
276-466 8689
bevegg@ecofriendly.com
www.ecofriendly.com
(see page 201)

EVERONA DAIRY
23246 Clarks Mountain Road
Rapidan, VA 22733
540-854-4159
(see page 37)

FOOD ROUTES NETWORK
P.O. Box 443
Millheim, PA 16854
814-349-6000
www.foodroutes.org
(see page 6)

FRESHFARM MARKETS
3802 Jocelyn Street NW
Washington, DC 20015
202-362-8889
info@freshfarmmarket.org
www.freshfarmmarket.org
(see page 8)

FROM THE GROUND UP
Clagett Farm
11904 Old Marlboro Pike
Upper Marlboro, MD 20772
301-627-4662
clagettfarm@cbf.org
www.clagettfarm.org
(see page 66)

FUTURE HARVEST–CHESAPEAKE ALLIANCE FOR SUSTAINABLE AGRICULTURE
106 Market Court
Stevensville, MD 21666
410-604-2681
Fhcasa@umail.umd.edu
www.futureharvestcasa.org
(see page 177)

GENTLEMAN'S RIDGE FARM
589 Gentleman's Ridge Road
Blairs, VA 24527
434-791-2382
www.gentlemansridge.com
(see page 91)

GEORGETOWN FARM
Rural Route 1, Box 14W
Madison, VA 22727
540-948-4209
888-328-5326
www.eatlean.com
(see page 47)

GINSENG MOUNTAIN FARM
Ginseng Mountain Farm & Store
Debora Ellington
U.S. Route 220 North
Blue Grass, VA 24413
540-474-3663
ginseng@cfw.com
(see page 217)

GOODNESS GROWS IN NORTH CAROLINA
North Carolina Department
   of Agriculture
P.O. Box 27647
Raleigh, NC 27611
919-733-7125
www.ncagr.com
www.goodnessgrowsinnc.org
(see page 180)

HEIFER PROJECT INTERNATIONAL
P.O. Box 8058
Little Rock, AR 72203
800-422-0474
info@heifer.org
www.heifer.org
(see page 171)

L'ESPRIT DE CAMPAGNE
P.O. Box 3130
Winchester, VA 22604
540-955-1014
(see page 109)

LINDEN VINEYARDS
3708 Harrels Corner Road
Linden, VA 22642
540-364-1997
www.lindenvineyards.com
(see page 167)

MICHAEL LUKSA
Yellow Brick Bank Restaurant
201 East German Street
Shepherdstown, WV 25443
304-876-2208
(see page 122)

MARYLAND CERTIFIED ORGANIC GROWERS COOPERATIVE
Jack & Beckie Gurley
16813 Yeoho Road
Sparks, MD 21152
410-472-6764
giftcal@aol.com
www.organiccoop.com
(see page 69)

MEADOW CREEK DAIRY
6724 Meadow Creek Road
Galax, VA 24333
276-236-2776
888-236-0622
www.meadowcreekdairy.com
(see page 215)

MONASTERY COUNTRY CHEESE
Our Lady of the Angels Monastery
3365 Monastery Drive
Crozet, VA 22932
434-823-1452
(see page 157)

NIMAN RANCH
1025 East 12th Street
Oakland, CA 94606
510-808-0330
www.nimanranch.com
(see page 51)

PETERSON PAWPAWS
P.O. Box 1011
Harpers Ferry, WV 25425
nealp@mountain.net
www.petersonpawpaws.com
(see page 225)

POLYFACE FARM
363 Shuey Road
Swoope, VA 24479
540-885-3590
(see page 17)

RUCKER FARM
P.O. Box 423
Flint Hill, VA 22627
540-675-3444
(see page 197)

SHAWNEE SPRINGS
Shawnee Canning Company
212 Cross Junction Road
Cross Junction, VA 22625
800-713-1414
www.shawneesprings.com
(see page 111)

SLOW FOOD USA
434 Broadway, 7th Floor
New York, NY 10013
212-965-5640
www.slowfood.com
(see page 12)

SPRINGFIELD FARM
16701 Yeoho Road
Sparks, MD 21152
410-472-0738
(see page 53)

SUMMERFIELD FARM
10044 James Monroe Highway
Culpeper, VA 22701
540-547-9600
jamienicoll@msn.com
www.summerfieldfarm.com
(see page 221)

SUNNYSIDE FARM AND ORCHARDS
Route 2
Charles Town, WV 25414
304-725-7990
(see page 3)

THE FARM AT MT. WALDEN
Walden Foods
150 Kelly Drive
Front Royal, VA 22630-6987
540-622-2800
800-64-TROUT
www.waldenfoods.com
(see page 223)

TUSCARORA ORGANIC GROWERS COOPERATIVE
HCR 71 Box 168-B
Hustontown, PA 17229
814-448-2173
(see page 5)

VINTAGE VIRGINIA APPLES
Rural Ridge Farm
P.O. Box 210
North Garden, VA 22959
434-297-2326
fruit@vintagevirginiaapples.com
www.vintagevirginiaapples.com
(see page 207)

VIRGINIA ASSOCIATION FOR BIOLOGICAL FARMING
P.O. Box 503
Buena Vista, VA 24116
540-633-0089
www.vabf.org
(see page 130)

VIRGINIA INDEPENDENT CONSUMERS AND FARMERS ASSOCIATION
1702 East Market Street
Charlottesville, VA 22902
(see page 118)

VIRGINIA SEAFOOD
Virginia Marine Products Board
554 Denbigh Boulevard, Suite B
Newport News, VA 23608
lltvasfd@infi.net
www.virginiaseafood.org/
757-874-3474
(see page 97)

VIRGINIA'S FINEST AND VIRGINIA GROWN
Virginia Department of Agriculture
  & Consumer Services
1100 Bank Street
Richmond, VA 23219
804-786-2373
www.vdacs.state.va.us/vagrown/
www.vdacs.state.va.us/vafinest/
(see pages 18 and 72)

WEST VIRGINIA GROWN
West Virginia Department
  of Agriculture
1900 Kanawha Boulevard East
State Capitol, Room E-28
Charleston, WV 25305
304-558-2210
(see page 181)

FOOD NOTES

CHEFS, RESTAURANTS & LOCALLY RAISED FOODS

A restaurant's use of locally raised foods is determined by the chef's commitment to the quality of farm-fresh local foods, by the chef's ability to access locally raised foods, and by the owner's willingness to allow foods to be purchased locally. A change in ownership or chef can cause a change in a restaurant's menu and its commitment to local growers. If a menu doesn't specify that many of the ingredients used come from local sources, be sure to ask. If the restaurant is not—or is no longer—buying from local farms, write the owner a note asking for inclusion of locally grown foods on the menu.

FOOD SAFETY

Raw Eggs

The consumption of raw eggs is the subject of much debate. Your chances of getting sick from eating raw eggs depends to a large extent on the quality of the eggs and your own susceptibility to illness. If you do use raw eggs, be sure they are very fresh. Raw eggs and sauces made with raw eggs should be kept refrigerated. Never serve raw eggs to young children, the elderly, or people with compromised immune systems.

Recommended Internal Temperatures for Roasted Meats

Poultry: 180°F
Beef, lamb & pork: 160°F

SEASONAL AVAILABILITY

The Seasonal and Seafood Availability charts on pages 226 and 228 are compiled from a variety of sources. These include interviews with farmers, FRESHFARM Market weekly e-mail newsletters, and availability charts from the Virginia Marine Products Board and from the Delaware, Maryland, North Carolina, and Virginia departments of agriculture. Additional assistance was provided by Chris Fullerton of Tuscarora Organic Growers Cooperative and by Rich Marini, Dr. Orson K. Miller Jr., and Dr. Herbert D. Stiles of Virginia Tech.

At any given time, the availability of local produce will vary depending on the weather. Retailers' supplies of local produce will also vary depending on the geographic and climatic range of the local farmers who supply those retailers.

For a full selection of locally grown produce, visit your local farmers market, join a Community Supported Agriculture project, or shop at stores that specialize in local produce.

For a list of what is currently available at the farmers market, visit the FRESHFARM Market site at www.freshfarmmarket.org.

RESOURCES FOR HANDLING, STORAGE & PRESERVATION

The Big Book of Preserving the Harvest
by Carol W. Costenbader

Eat Fresh, Stay Healthy
by Tony Tantillo & Sam Gugino

Fresh from the Farmers' Market
by Janet Fletcher

The Green Kitchen Handbook
by Annie Berthold-Bond

Keeping Food Fresh
by the Gardeners & Farmers of Terre Vivante

Parsley, Peppers, Potatoes & Peas
by Pat Katz

Putting Food By (4th Edition)
by Janet Greene, Ruth Hertzberg & Beatrice Vaughan

Rolling Prairie Cookbook
by Nancy O'Connor

Stocking Up (3rd Edition)
by Carol Hupping

TERMS

In the lists of seasonal foods included on the opening page of each season, we have included the following terms:

Farm raised is used to differentiate animals such as ducks and rabbits that are raised on farms as opposed to those hunted in the wild.

Farmed refers to fish and other seafood that are raised or managed in confined or open waters as opposed to those caught in the wild.

Forage fed is a term coined by Joel Salatin to refer to animals that for most of the year either are allowed to freely seek out their own food in pastures or are fed fresh grasses that are cut and carried from the field. During times of the year when it is ecologically or seasonally inappropriate to keep animals on pasture, the animals are fed stored grasses, locally raised corn, or freshly cut grasses under shelter.

Pastured refers to animals that are raised on seasonal grasses and are then dried off (dairy) or sent to slaughter (meat) when the pastures are no longer accessible or sufficient. Although pastured products are seasonal, some farmers provide frozen pastured meats out of season.

SEASONAL AVAILABILITY*

	JAN	FEB	MAR	APR	MAY	JUN	JUL	AUG	SEP	OCT	NOV	DEC
APPLES	■	■	■	■				■	■	■	■	■
APRICOTS							■	■				
ASPARAGUS				■	■							
BEANS, GREEN						■	■	■	■			
BEETS						■	■	■	■	■	■	■
BLACKBERRIES							■	■				
BROCCOLI				■	■	■	■	■	■	■		
CABBAGE						■	■	■	■	■	■	■
CANTALOUPE							■	■	■			
CARROTS							■	■	■	■		
CHERRIES						■						
CORN, SWEET							■	■	■			
CUCUMBERS					■	■	■	■	■			
EGGPLANT						■	■	■	■	■		
FENNEL					■				■			
FIGS								■	■			
GRAPES								■	■	■		
GREENS—Arugula, Chard, Collards, Kale & Mustard			■	■	■	■	■	■	■			
HAYMAN POTATOES	■	■	■	■							■	■
LEEKS						■	■	■	■	■		
LETTUCE & SALAD MIX				■	■	■	■	■	■	■	■	■
MUSHROOMS	■	■	■	■	■	■	■	■	■	■	■	■
ONIONS & GARLIC						■	■	■	■	■		
PEACHES						■	■	■	■	■		
PEARS & ASIAN PEARS								■	■	■	■	■
PEAS					■	■						
PEPPERS, SWEET & HOT						■	■	■	■	■	■	
PLUMS							■	■	■			
POTATOES						■	■	■	■	■	■	■
RADISHES						■	■	■	■	■	■	
RASPBERRIES							■			■		
SQUASH, SUMMER						■	■	■	■	■		
SQUASH, WINTER								■	■	■	■	■
STRAWBERRIES				■	■							
SWEET POTATOES									■	■	■	■
TOMATOES						■	■	■	■	■		
TURNIPS				■	■			■	■	■	■	■
WATERMELON						■	■	■	■			

*DATES ARE APPROXIMATE FOR FARM MARKET AVAILABILITY. SEE PAGE 233 FOR OTHER RESOURCES ON SEASONAL AVAILABILITY.

STORAGE/PRESERVATION*	STORAGE	PRESERVATION
APPLES	REFRIGERATE (VP) • ROOT CELLAR: 33°F, MOIST • DRY: 55°F, DARK	SAUCE • APPLE BUTTER • DRY • JUICE • CIDER
APRICOTS	ROOM TEMPERATURE • IF RIPE, REFRIGERATE IN PLASTIC	DRY • FREEZE • JAM • CAN • JUICE
ASPARAGUS	REFRIGERATE (SP): WRAP BASE IN DAMP TOWEL	DRY • FREEZE • CAN • PICKLE
BASIL	REFRIGERATE WITH ROOTS IN WATER	DRY • FREEZE (BLANCHED) • IN OIL • VINEGAR
BEANS, GREEN	REFRIGERATE (VP) UNWASHED 40°F–45°F	FREEZE • PICKLE • CAN
BEETS	REFRIGERATE (OP) • ROOT CELLAR: 33°F–40°F, MOIST	DRY • FREEZE • CAN • PICKLE • RELISH
BOK CHOI & TAT SOI	REFRIGERATE (VP) • ROOT CELLAR: 33°F, DAMP	DRY • FREEZE AS PART OF PREPARED DISH
BROCCOLI	REFRIGERATE (OP)	FREEZE • DRY • IN OIL
CABBAGE—Napa, Savoy	REFRIGERATE (VP)	DRY • FERMENT (SAUERKRAUT)
CARROTS	REFRIGERATE (SP) • ROOT CELLAR: 33°F–40°F, MOIST	DRY • FREEZE • CAN • PICKLE • RELISH
CHERRIES	REFRIGERATE (VP) UNWASHED IN PLASTIC	DRY • FREEZE • CAN • JAM • JUICE
CORN, SWEET	REFRIGERATE IN PLASTIC WITH HUSK ON	DRY • FREEZE • CAN
CUCUMBERS	REFRIGERATE UNWASHED IN PLASTIC AT 45°F–50°F	PICKLE
EGGPLANT	ROOM TEMPERATURE (SHORT TERM), REFRIGERATE (SP)	DRY • FREEZE AS PART OF PREPARED DISH
ESCAROLE & RADICCHIO	REFRIGERATE (VP) • ROOT CELLAR: 33°F, MOIST	—
FENNEL	REFRIGERATE IN PLASTIC	LEAVES: FREEZE, DRY • SEEDS: DRY
FIGS	REFRIGERATE IN PAPER BAG OR COVERED ON PLATE	FREEZE • DRY • CAN
GRAPES	REFRIGERATE (VP) • ROOT CELLAR: 33°F, MOIST	FREEZE • DRY • JUICE • PICKLE • JAM
GREENS—Arugula, Chard, Collards, Kale & Mustard	REMOVE BANDS OR TIES, REFRIGERATE (SP): UNWASHED	FREEZE • DRY • CAN
JERUSALEM ARTICHOKES	REFRIGERATE (LOW HUMIDITY) • IN GROUND	DRY • FREEZE • PICKLE
LEEKS	REMOVE BANDS, REFRIGERATE (OP) • ROOT CELLAR: 33°F, MOIST	FREEZE • DRY
LETTUCE & SALAD MIX	REMOVE BANDS, REFRIGERATE (VP) UNWASHED	FIRM LETTUCE CAN BE USED IN SAUERKRAUT
MELONS	ROOM TEMPERATURE (IF HARD) • REFRIGERATE 40°F–45°F	FREEZE
ONIONS & GARLIC	DRY STORE: COOL, DRY, WELL VENTILATED, DARK (GARLIC)	FREEZE (ONIONS) • DRY • PICKLED • IN OIL
PARSNIPS	REFRIGERATE (OP) • ROOT CELLAR: 33°F, MOIST • IN GROUND	FREEZE • CAN • DRY
PAWPAWS	ROOM TEMPERATURE (FEW DAYS) • REFRIGERATE: RIPE OR UNRIPE	FREEZE: PULP OR AS PART OF PREPARED DISH • JAM
PEACHES & NECTARINES	ROOM TEMPERATURE • IF RIPE, REFRIGERATE	FREEZE • DRY • CAN • JAM • JUICE
PEARS & ASIAN PEARS	ROOM TEMPERATURE • IF RIPE, REFRIGERATE	DRY • CAN • SAUCE • PICKLE • PEAR BUTTER • JUICE
PEPPERS, SWEET & HOT	ROOM TEMPERATURE (COOL) • REFRIGERATE (LONGER STORAGE)	FREEZE • DRY • CAN • PICKLED • SAUCE • IN OIL
POTATOES	DRY STORE: COOL, DARK, VENTILATED • ROOT CELLAR: 40°F, MOIST	DRY • CAN • FLOUR • STARCH
RADISHES	REMOVE GREENS, REFRIGERATE (OP) • ROOT CELLAR: 33°F, MOIST	PICKLE
RUTABAGAS & TURNIPS	REFRIGERATE IN PLASTIC • ROOT CELLAR: 33°F, MOIST	FREEZE • CAN (FERMENTED)
SCALLIONS	REMOVE BANDS, REFRIGERATE IN PLASTIC	PICKLE OR FREEZE AS PART OF PREPARED DISH
SQUASH, SUMMER	REFRIGERATE (VP): 41°F–50°F	FREEZE • DRY • CAN • PICKLE
SQUASH, WINTER	DRY STORE: 50°F–55°F, DARK, WELL VENTILATED	FREEZE • CAN
STRAWBERRIES	ROOM TEMPERATURE (EAT THAT DAY) • REFRIGERATE: DRY, AIRTIGHT	FREEZE • DRY • JAM
SWEET POTATOES	DRY STORE: 55°F–60°F, DARK, WELL VENTILATED	FREEZE • DRY • CAN
TOMATOES	ROOM TEMPERATURE (62°F–68°F), HUMID, OUT OF DIRECT SUN	DRY • CAN • IN OIL • IN SALT • JUICE • JELLY • SAUCE

*SEE PAGE 233 FOR OTHER RESOURCES ON STORAGE & PRESERVATION.
JAM IS USED TO INDICATE SOME FORM OF FRUIT PRESERVE: JAM, JELLY, PRESERVE, OR CONSERVE.
OP = OPEN PLASTIC BAG • SP = SEALED PLASTIC BAG • VP = VENTED PLASTIC BAG

MEAT & SEAFOOD CHART

	JAN	FEB	MAR	APR	MAY	JUN	JUL	AUG	SEP	OCT	NOV	DEC
AMERICAN EEL			X	X	X	X	X	X	X	X	X	
ATLANTIC MACKEREL	X	X	X	X	X							X
BEEF (forage fed*)	X	X	X	X	X	X	X	X	X	X	X	X
BLACK SEA BASS	X	X	X	X	X	X	X	X	X	X	X	X
BLUE CRAB	X	X	X	X	X	X	X	X	X	X	X	X
BLUEFISH			X	X	X	X	X	X	X	X	X	X
CATFISH			X	X	X	X	X	X	X	X	X	X
CATFISH (farmed*)				X	X	X	X	X	X	X		
CLAMS	X	X	X	X	X	X	X	X	X	X	X	X
CLAMS (farmed*)	X	X	X	X	X	X	X	X	X	X	X	X
CONCH	X	X	X	X	X	X	X	X	X	X	X	X
CROAKER			X	X	X	X	X	X	X	X	X	
DAIRY (pastured*)	X	X	X	X	X	X	X	X	X	X	X	X
DOGFISH				X	X	X	X					
EGGS (forage fed*)	X	X	X	X	X	X	X	X	X	X	X	X
FLOUNDER	X	X	X	X	X	X	X	X	X	X	X	X
LAMB (pastured*)									X	X	X	X
MONKFISH	X	X	X	X	X	X	X	X	X	X	X	X
OYSTERS	X	X	X	X	X	X	X	X	X	X	X	X
PERCH (WHITE)	X	X	X	X	X	X	X	X	X	X	X	X
PERCH (YELLOW)	X		X	X	X	X	X	X	X	X	X	X
PORK (forage fed*)	X	X	X	X	X	X	X	X	X	X	X	X
PORK (pastured*)									X	X	X	X
RABBIT (forage fed*)	X	X	X	X	X	X	X	X	X	X	X	X
RAINBOW TROUT (farmed*)	X	X	X	X	X	X	X	X	X	X	X	X
ROCKFISH (STRIPED BASS)	X	X	X	X	X	X	X	X	X	X	X	X
SCALLOPS	X	X	X	X	X	X	X	X	X	X	X	X
SCUP	X	X	X	X	X							
SEA TROUT (GRAY)	X	X	X	X	X	X	X	X	X	X	X	X
SHAD/SHAD ROE		X	X	X								
SHRIMP (North Carolina)				X	X	X	X	X	X	X	X	X
SOFT-SHELL CRAB				X	X	X	X	X	X	X		
SPANISH MACKEREL					X	X	X	X	X	X	X	X
SPOT				X	X	X	X	X	X	X	X	
SQUID	X	X	X	X	X	X	X	X	X	X	X	X
TILAPIA (farmed*)	X	X	X	X	X	X	X	X	X	X	X	X
TURKEY (forage fed*)							X	X	X	X	X	X

THIS CHART COMBINES DATA FROM MARYLAND, NORTH CAROLINA, AND VIRGINIA. DATES ARE APPROXIMATE.
SEE PAGE 233 FOR OTHER RESOURCES ON SEASONAL AVAILABILITY AND DEFINITIONS OF TERMS MARKED *.

INDEX TO INGREDIENTS & RECIPES